Dog Stories

Cathay Books

First published in Great Britain in 1981 by Octopus Books Ltd
This edition published in 1984 by Cathay Books
59 Grosvenor Street
London W1
Reprinted 1985

Illustrated by Caroline Holmes-Smith
ISBN 0 86178 241 0

Printed in Czechoslovakia
50551/3

Dog Stories

Contents

Contents

Dodo

GERALD DURRELL

The Magenpies liked the dogs, although they seized every opportunity to tease them. They were particularly fond of Roger, and he would frequently go and call on them, lying down close to the wire netting, ears pricked, while the Magenpies sat on the ground inside the cage, three inches away from his nose, and talked to him in soft, wheezy chucks, with an occasional raucous guffaw, as though they were telling him dirty jokes. They never teased Roger as much as they teased the other two, and they never attempted to lure him close to the wire with soft blandishment so that they could flap down and pull his tail, as they frequently did with both Widdle and Puke. On the whole the Magenpies approved of dogs, but they liked them to look *and* behave like dogs; so when Dodo made her appearance in our midst the Magenpies absolutely refused to believe that she was a dog, and treated her from the beginning with a sort of rowdy, jeering disdain.

Dodo was a breed known as a Dandy Dinmont. They look like long, fat, hair-covered balloons, with minute bow legs, enormous and protuberant eyes, and long flopping ears. Strangely enough it was due to Mother that this curious misshapen breed of dog made its appearance among us. A friend of ours had a pair of these beasts which had suddenly (after years of barrenness) produced a litter of six puppies. The poor man was at his wits' end trying to find good homes for all these offspring, and so Mother, good-naturedly and unthinkingly, said she would have one. She set off one afternoon to choose her puppy and, rather unwisely, selected a female. At the time it did not strike her as imprudent to introduce a bitch into a household exclusively populated by very masculine dogs. So, clasping the puppy (like a dimly conscious sausage) under one arm, Mother climbed into the car and drove home in triumph to show the new addition to the family. The puppy, determined to make the occasion a memorable one, was violently and persistently sick from the moment she got in the car to the moment she got out. The family, assembled on the veranda, viewed Mother's prize as it waddled up the path towards them, eyes bulging, minute legs working frantically to keep the long, drooping body in motion, ears flapping wildly, pausing now and then to vomit into a flower-bed.

'Oh, isn't he *sweet*?' cried Margo.

'Good God! It looks like a sea-slug,' said Leslie.

'Mother! Really!' said Larry, contemplating Dodo with loathing, 'where did you dig up that canine Frankenstein?'

'Oh, but he's *sweet*,' repeated Margo, 'What's wrong with him?'

'It's not a him, it's a her,' said Mother, regarding her acquisition proudly; 'she's called Dodo.'

'Well, that's two things wrong with it for a start,' said Larry. 'It's a ghastly name for an animal, and to introduce a bitch into the house with those three lechers about is asking for trouble. Apart from that, just look at it! How did it get like that? Did it have an accident, or was it born like that?'

'Don't be silly, dear; it's the breed. They're *meant* to be like that.'

'Nonsense, mother it's a monster. Who would want to deliberately produce a thing that shape?'

I pointed out that dachshunds were much the same shape, and they had been bred specially to enable them to get down holes after badgers. Probably the Dandy Dinmont had been bred for a similar reason.

'She looks as though she was bred to go down holes after sewage,' said Larry.

'Don't be disgusting, dear. They're very nice little dogs, and very faithful, apparently.'

'I should imagine they have to be faithful to anyone who shows interest in them: they can't possibly have many admirers in the world.'

'I think you're being very nasty about her, and, anyway, you're in no position to talk about beauty; it's only skin deep after all, and before you go throwing stones you should look for the beam in *your* eye,' said Margo triumphantly.

Larry looked puzzled.

'Is that a proverb, or a quotation from the *Builders' Gazette*?' he inquired.

'I think she means that it's an ill-wind that gathers no moss,' said Leslie.

'You make me sick,' said Margo, with dignified scorn.

'Well, join little Dodo in the flower-bed.'

'Now, now,' said Mother, 'don't argue about it. It's my dog and I like her, so that's all that matters.'

So Dodo settled in, and almost immediately showed faults in her make-up which caused us more trouble than all the other dogs put together. To begin with she had a weak hind-leg, and at any time during the day or night her hip joint was liable to come out of its socket, for no apparent reason. Dodo, who was no stoic, would greet this catastrophe with a series of piercing shrieks that worked up to a crescendo of such quivering intensity that it was unbearable. Strangely enough, her leg never seemed to worry her when she went out for walks, or gambolled with elephantine enthusiasm after a ball on the veranda. But invariably in the evening when the family were all sitting quietly, absorbed in writing or reading or knitting, Dodo's leg would suddenly leap out of its socket, she would roll on her back and utter a scream that would make everybody jump and lose control of whatever they were doing. By the time we had massaged her leg back into place Dodo would have screamed herself to exhaustion, and immediately fall into a deep and peaceful sleep, while we would be so unnerved that we would be unable to concentrate on anything for the rest of the evening.

We soon discovered that Dodo had an extremely limited intelligence. There was only room for one idea at a time in her skull, and once it was there Dodo would retain it grimly in spite of all opposition. She decided quite early in her career that Mother belonged to her, but she was not over-possessive at first until one afternoon Mother went off to town to do some shopping and left Dodo behind. Convinced that she would never see Mother again, Dodo went into mourning and waddled, howling sorrowfully, round the house, occasionally being so overcome with grief that her leg would come out of joint. She greeted Mother's return with incredulous joy, but made up her mind that from that moment she would not let Mother out of her sight, for fear she escaped again. So she attached herself to Mother with the tenacity of a limpet, never moving more than a couple of feet away at the most. If Mother sat down, Dodo would lie at her feet; if Mother had to get up and cross the room for a book or a cigarette, Dodo would accompany her, and then they would return together and sit down again, Dodo giving a deep sigh of satisfaction at the thought that once more she had foiled Mother's attempts at escape. She even insisted in being present when Mother had a bath, sitting dolefully by the tub and staring at Mother with embarrassing intensity. Any attempts to leave her outside the bathroom door resulted in Dodo howling madly and hurling herself at the door-panels, which almost invariably resulted in her hip slipping out of its socket. She seemed to be under the impression that it was not safe to let Mother go alone into the bathroom, even if she stood guard over the door. There was always the possibility, she seemed to think, that Mother might give her the slip by crawling down the plug-hole.

At first Dodo was regarded with tolerant scorn by Roger, Widdle, and Puke; they did not think much of her, for she was too fat and too low slung to walk far, and if they made any attempt to play with her it seemed to bring on an attack of persecution mania, and Dodo would gallop back to the house, howling for protection. Taken all round they were inclined to consider her a boring and useless addition to the household, until they discovered that she had one superlative and overwhelmingly delightful characteristic: she came into season with monotonous regularity. Dodo herself displayed an innocence about the facts of life that was rather touching. She seemed not only puzzled but positively scared at her sudden bursts of popularity, when her admirers arrived in such numbers that Mother had to go about armed with a massive stick. It was owing to this Victorian innocence that Dodo fell an easy victim to the lure of Puke's magnificent ginger eyebrows, and so met a fate worse than death when Mother inadvertently locked them in the drawing-room together while she supervised the making of tea. The sudden and unexpected arrival of the English padre and his wife, ushering them into the room in which the happy couple were disporting themselves, and the subsequent efforts to maintain a normal conversation, left Mother feeling limp, and with a raging headache.

To everyone's surprise (including Dodo's) a puppy was born of this union, a strange, mewling blob of a creature with its mother's figure and its father's unusual liver-and-white markings. To suddenly become a mother like that, Dodo found, was very demoralizing, and she almost had a nervous breakdown, for she was torn between the desire to stay in one spot with her puppy and the urge to keep as close to Mother as possible. We were, however, unaware of this psychological turmoil. Eventually Dodo decided to compromise, so she followed Mother around and carried the puppy in her mouth. She had spent a whole morning doing this before we discovered what she was up to; the unfortunate baby hung from her mouth by its head, its body swinging to and fro as Dodo waddled along at Mother's heels. Scolding and pleading having no effect, Mother was forced to confine herself to the bedroom with Dodo and her puppy, and we carried their meals up on a tray. Even this was not altogether successful, for if Mother moved out of the chair, Dodo, ever alert, would seize her puppy and sit there regarding Mother with starting eyes, ready to give chase if necessary.

'If this goes on much longer that puppy'll grow into a giraffe,' observed Leslie.

'I know, poor little thing,' said Mother; 'but what can I *do*? She picks it up if she sees me lighting a cigarette.'

'Simplest thing would be to drown it,' said Larry. 'It's going to grow into the most horrifying animal, anyway. Look at its parents.'

'No, indeed you won't drown it!' exclaimed Mother indignantly.

'Don't be *horrible*,' said Margo; 'the poor little thing.'

'Well, I think it's a perfectly ridiculous situation, allowing yourself to be chained to a chair by a dog.'

'It's my dog, and if I want to sit here I *shall*,' said Mother firmly.

'But for how long? This might go on for months.'

'I shall think of something,' said Mother with dignity.

The solution to the problem that Mother eventually thought of was simple. She hired the maid's youngest daughter to carry the puppy for Dodo. The arrangement seemed to satisfy Dodo very well,.and once more Mother was able to move about the house. She pottered from room to room like some Eastern potentate, Dodo pattering at her heels, and young Sophia bringing up the end of the line, tongue protruding and eyes squinting with the effort, bearing in her arms a large cushion on which reposed Dodo's strange offspring. When Mother was going to be in one spot for any length of time Sophia would place the cushion reverently on the ground, and Dodo would surge on to it and sigh deeply. As soon as Mother was ready to go to another part of the house, Dodo would get off her cushion, shake herself, and take up her position in the cavalcade, while Sophia lifted the cushion aloft as though it carried a crown. Mother would peer over her spectacles to make sure the column was ready, giving a

She hired the maid's youngest daughter to carry the puppy for Dodo

little nod, and they would wind their way off to the next job.

Every evening Mother would go for a walk with the dogs, and the family would derive much amusement from watching her progress down the hill. Roger, as senior dog, would lead the procession, followed by Widdle and Puke. Then came Mother, wearing an enormous straw hat, which made her look like an animated mushroom, clutching in one hand a large trowel with which to dig any interesting wild plants she found. Dodo would waddle behind, ears protruding and tongue flapping, and Sophia would bring up the rear, pacing along solemnly, carrying the imperial puppy on its cushion. Mother's Circus, Larry called it, and would irritate her by bellowing out of the window:

'Oi! Lady, wot time does the big top go up, hey?'

He purchased a bottle of hair restorer for her so that, as he explained, she could conduct experiments on Sophia and try to turn her into a bearded lady.

'That's wot your show *needs*, lady,' he assured her in a hoarse voice – 'a bit of clarse, see? Nothing like a bearded lady for bringin' a bit o' clarse to a show.'

But in spite of all this Mother continued to lead her strange caravan off into the olive-groves at five o'clock every evening.

Human Friends

SHEILA BURNFORD

This is part of the story of an incredible 300 mile journey made by an old bull terrier, a Labrador and a Siamese cat to get home to their owners in a different part of Ontario, Canada. The road they had to travel was a wild one, fraught with dangers and it is amazing that they all survived.

Over two hundred miles now lay behind them, and as a group they were whole and intact, but of the three only the cat remained unscathed. The old dog, however, still plodded cheerfully and uncomplainingly along. It was the Labrador who was in really poor condition: his once beautiful gleaming coat was harsh and staring now, his grotesquely swollen face in horrible contrast to his gaunt frame, and the pain in his infected jaw made it almost impossible for him to open his mouth, so that he was virtually starving. The other two now allowed him first access to any newly killed and bleeding animal provided by the cat, and he lived solely on the fresh blood that could be licked from the carcass.

They had slipped into a steady routine during the day; the two dogs trotting along side by side, unconcerned and purposeful, might have seemed like two family pets out for a leisurely neighbourhood ramble.

They were seen like this one morning by a timber-cruising forester returning to his jeep along an old tote road deep in the Ironmouth Range. They disappeared round a bend in the distance, and, preoccupied with tree problems, he did not give them a second thought. It was with a considerable shock that he remembered them later on in the day, his mind now registering the fact that there was no human habitation within thirty miles. He told the senior forester, who roared with laughter, then asked him if he had seen any elves skipping around toadstools too?

But inevitably the time was drawing nearer when the disappearance of the animals must be uncovered, the hue and cry begin, and every glimpse or smallest piece of evidence be of value. The forester was able to turn the laugh a week later when his chance encounter was proved to be no dream.

At Heron Lake John Longridge and his brother were making plans for the last trip of the season. In England the excited Hunter family were packed in readiness for the voyage home. Mrs Oakes was busy in the old stone house, cleaning and polishing, while her husband stacked the wood cellar.

Soon all concerned would be back where they belonged, like pieces of a jigsaw puzzle being fitted together; and soon it must be discovered that three of the pieces were missing . . .

Sublimely unaware of the commotion and worry, tears and heartbreak that their absence would cause, the three continued on their way.

The countryside was less wild now, and once or twice they saw small lonely hamlets in the distance. The young dog resolutely avoided these, keeping always to the woods and dense bush wherever possible – much to the disgust of the old dog, who had implicit faith in the helpfulness and loving kindness of human beings. But the young dog was the leader: however longingly the bull terrier looked towards a distant curl of smoke from a chimney he must turn away.

Late one afternoon they were followed for several miles by a single timber wolf who was probably curious about the cat and was no real menace: however hungry, it would never have risked an encounter with two dogs.

Like all his kind, however, the young dog hated and feared the wolf with some deep primeval instinct which must have had its origin in those mists of time when they shared a common ancestor. He was uneasy and disturbed by the slinking grey shape that merged into the undergrowth every time he looked back to snarl at it.

Unable to shake off the hateful shadow, and aware that the sun was sinking, irritable and exhausted with pain, he chose the lesser of two evils – leaving the bush for a quiet country road with small farms scattered at lonely intervals along it. He hurried his companions on, seeking protection for the night in the form of a barn or even an open field near a farm, sensing that the wolf would not follow within sight of human habitation.

They approached a small hamlet at dusk, a few small houses clustered around a schoolhouse and a white frame church. When the young dog would have skirted this too, the old terrier suddenly turned mutinous. He was, as usual, hungry; and the sight of the warm lights streaming out from the houses convinced him that this evening there was only one sensible way of obtaining food – from the hand of a human being! His eyes brightening at the thought, he ignored the young dog's warning growl, and trotted on unheeding down the forbidden road towards the houses, his rounded porcine quarters swinging defiantly, his ears laid back in stubborn disregard.

The young dog offered no further resistance. His whole head was throbbing violently with the pain of infection from the quills, and more than anything he wanted time to scratch and scratch, to rub the burning cheek along the ground.

The rebel passed the first few cottages, so snug and inviting to his comfort-loving soul – smoke rising in the still evening air, and the reassuring smell and sounds of humans everywhere. He paused before a small white cottage, snuffling ecstatically the wonderful aroma of cooking drifting out mingled with wood smoke. Licking his chops he walked up the steps, lifted a bold demanding paw and scratched at the door, then sat down, pricking his ears expectantly.

He was not disappointed. A widening stream of light from the opening door revealed a small girl. The old dog grinned hideously in pleasure, his slanted eyes blinking strangely in the sudden light. There is little to equal a bull terrier's grin, however charmingly presented, for sheer astonishing ugliness.

There was a moment's silence, followed by an urgent wail of 'Dad . . .' Then the door slammed shut in his face. Puzzled but persistent, he scratched again, cocking his head to one side, his big triangular ears erect, listening to footsteps scurrying around within. A face appeared at the window. He barked a polite reminder. Suddenly the door was thrown open again and a man rushed out, a bucket of water in his hand, his face convulsed with fury. He hurled the water full in the face of the astonished dog, then grabbed a broom.

'Get out! Get out of here!' yelled the man, brandishing his broom so menacingly that the terrier tucked his tail between his legs and fled, soaking and miserable, towards his waiting companions. He was not afraid, only deeply offended – never in his long life had human beings reacted in such a way to his friendly overtures. Justifiable fury he knew and expected when he had terrorized their pets in the old days; laughter, and sometimes nervousness – but never a crude, uncivilized reception like this.

Baffled and disappointed, he fell meekly in behind his leader.

Two miles along the road they came to a winding cart track leading uphill to a farm. They crossed the dark fields, startling up an old white horse and some cows, heading for a group of outbuildings clustered together some distance from the farmhouse. A thin curl of smoke rose from the chimney of one. It was a smokehouse, where hams were smoking over a slow hickory fire. Pressing against the faint warmth at the base of the chimney they settled down for the night.

The young dog spent a restless night. The running sores on his face had been extended, by his continuous frantic clawing, into raw inflamed patches over the glands on one side of his neck; and the spreading infection was making him feverish and thirsty. Several times he left the others to drink from a small lake a short distance away, standing chest-deep in the cool, soothing water.

When the old dog woke shivering with cold he was alone. The cat was some distance away, belly to ground and tail twitching excitedly, stalking his breakfast. Stealing through the morning air came a familiar smell of smoke and something cooking – beckoning irresistibly.

The mists were rolling back from the valley, and a pale sun was lightening the sky when the old dog came through the windbreak of tall Norway pines and sat down outside the farmhouse door. His memory was short; already human beings were back on their rightful pedestals, cornucopias of dog food in their hands. He whined plaintively. At a second, louder whine, several cats appeared from the barn nearby and glared at him with tiger-eyed resentment. At any other time he would have put them to instant flight; now he had more pressing business and chose to ignore them. The door swung open, a wondrous smell of bacon and eggs surged out, and the terrier drew up all the heavy artillery of his charm: with an ingratiating wag of his tail he glued his ears back, and wrinkled his nose in preparation for his disastrous winning leer. There was an astonished silence, broken by the deep amused voice of a man. 'Well!' said the owner of the voice, surveying his odd visitor, whose eyes were now rolled so far back that they had almost disappeared into his head. He called into the house, and was answered by the pleasant, warm voice of a woman. There was a sound of footsteps. The tail increased its tempo.

The woman stood for a moment in the doorway, looking down in silent astonishment at the white gargoyle on the step, and when he saw her face break into a smile that past master in the art of scrounging proffered a civil paw. She bent down and shook it, laughing helplessly, then invited him to follow her into the house.

Dignified, the old dog walked in, and gazed at the stove with bland confidence.

He was in luck this time, for there could not have been pleasanter people or a more welcoming house for miles around. They were an elderly couple, James Mackenzie and his wife Nell, living alone now in a big farmhouse which still held the atmosphere of a large, cheerful family living and laughing and growing up in it. They were well used to dogs, for there had been eight children in that house once upon a time, and a consequent succession of pets who had always started their adopted life out in the yard but invariably found their way into the household on the wildest pretexts of the children: misunderstood mongrels, orphaned kittens, sad strays, abandoned otter pups – Nell Mackenzie's soft heart had been as defenceless before them then as it was now.

She gave their visitor a bowl of scraps, which he bolted down in ravenous gulps, looking up then for more. 'Why, he's starving!' she exclaimed in horror, and contributed her own breakfast. She petted and fussed over him, accepting him as though the years had rolled back and one of the children had brought home yet another half-starved stray. He basked in this affection, and emptied the bowl almost before it reached the ground. Without a word Mackenzie passed over his plate as well. Soon the toast was gone too, and a jug of milk; and at last, distended and happy, the old dog stretched out on a rug by the warmth of the stove while Nell cooked another breakfast.

'What is he?' she asked presently. 'I've never seen anything quite so homely – he looks as though he had been squeezed into the wrong coat, somehow.'

'He's an English bull,' said her husband, 'and a beauty too – a real old bruiser! I love them! He looks as though he'd been in a fight quite recently, yet he must be ten or eleven if he's a day!' And at the unqualified respect and admiration in the voice, so dear to the heart of a bull terrier – but so seldom forthcoming – the dog thumped his tail agreeably, then rose and thrust his bony head against his host's knee. Mackenzie looked down, chuckling appreciatively. 'As cocksure as the devil – and as irresistible, aren't you? But what are we going to do with you?'

Nell passed her hand over the dog's shoulder and felt the scars, then examined them more closely. She looked up, suddenly puzzled. 'These aren't from any dogfight,' she said. 'They're *claw* marks – like the ones bears leave on fresh wood, only smaller –'

In silence they looked down at the dog by their feet, digesting the implication, the unknown story behind the sinister scars; and they saw now, for the first time, the gathering cloudiness in the depths of the humorous little eyes; the too-thin neck shamed by the newly distended belly; and they saw that the indefatigable tail which thumped so happily on the floor was ragged and old, with a broken end. This was no bold, aggressive adventurer – only a weary old dog; hungry not only for food but for affection. There was no shadow of doubt in either what they would do – keep him, if he would stay, and give him what he needed.

They searched unavailingly under the white coat and in the pink ears for an identifying registered tattoo, then decided that when Mackenzie went into Deepwater to fetch some new churns later in the day he would make some inquiries there, tell the Provincial Police, and possibly put an advertisement in a city paper. And if nothing came of that ... 'Then I guess we're landed with you for good, you disreputable old hobo!' said Mackenzie cheerfully, prodding his delighted audience with an experienced foot, so that the dog rolled over on his back with a blissful sigh and invited further attention under his forearms.

When he opened the door that morning Mackenzie had seen a flight of mallards going down in the direction of the small lake fed by the creek running through the farm. It was still early enough to walk over to see if they were still there, so he put a handful of shells in his pocket, took down an old pump gun from the wall and set off, leaving Nell stepping over and around the recumbent white form of their guest as she cleared the table. He noticed that an infinitesimal slit of eye followed her every movement.

Halfway over the still misty fields he stopped to load his gun, then walked quietly toward the cover of the alders fringing the little lake. Peering through the branches, he saw six mallards about halfway across, just out of range. With the wind the way it was he might wait all day for a shot, unless something startled them on the other side.

But even as he turned away he saw a disturbance in the reeds across the water. Simultaneously, quacking loudly in alarm, the mallards took off in a body. He fired twice as they came over, one bird plummeting into the water and the other landing with a thud on the shore nearby. He picked this one up, thinking that he would have to bring the light canoe for the other, when he saw to his astonishment a large head of a dog swimming towards it.

The sound of a shot and the splash of a duck had had the same effect on the Labrador as a trumpet call to an old war horse, and drew him as irresistibly. Without a second's hesitation he had plunged in for the retrieve, only to find that he was unable to open his mouth to grasp the heavy duck properly, and was forced to tow it ashore by a wingtip. He emerged from the water twenty feet from the man, the beautiful greenhead trailing from its outstretched wing, the sun striking the iridescent plumage. The Labrador looked doubtfully at the stranger, and Mackenzie stared back in open-mouthed amazement. For a moment the two were frozen in a silent tableau, then the man recovered himself.

'Good dog!' he said quietly, holding out one hand. 'Well done! Now bring it to me.' The dog advanced hesitantly, dragging the bird.

'Give!' said Mackenzie, as the dog still hesitated.

The dog walked slowly forward, releasing his hold, and now Mackenzie saw with horror that one side of his face was swollen out of all proportion, the skin stretched so tautly that the eyes were mere slits and one rigid lip pulled back over the teeth. Sticking out like evil little pins on a rounded cushion of raw skin were several quills, deeply embedded. Every rib showed up under the wet coat, and when the dog shook himself Mackenzie saw him stagger.

Mackenzie made up his mind quickly: no matter whose, this dog was desperately in need of urgent treatment; the quills must be extracted at once before the infection spread further. He picked up the ducks, patted the dog's head reassuringly, then 'Heel!' he said firmly. To his relief the dog fell in behind unquestioningly, following him back to the farmhouse, his resistance weakened to the point where he longed only to be back in the well-ordered world of human beings, that solid world where men commanded and dogs obeyed.

Crossing the fields, the stranger padding trustingly at his heels, Mackenzie suddenly remembered the other dog, and frowned in bewilderment. How many more unlikely dogs in need of succour would he lead into the farmhouse kitchen today – a lame poodle this afternoon, a halt beagle tonight?

His long, early morning shadow fell over the woodpile, and the sleepy Siamese cat sunning himself there lay camouflaged by stillness as he passed, unobserved by the man, but acknowledged by the dog with a brief movement of his tail and head.

Mackenzie finished cleaning up the Labrador's face nearly an hour later. He had extracted the quills with a pair of pliers; one had worked its way into the mouth and had to be removed from within, but the dog had not growled once, only whimpering when the pain was most intense, and had shown pathetic gratitude when it was over, trying to lick the man's hands. The relief must have been wonderful, for the punctures were now draining freely, and already the swelling was subsiding.

All through the operation the door leading out of the kitchen to a back room had shaken and rattled to the accompaniment of piteous whining. The old dog had been so much in the way when Mackenzie was working, pushing against his hand and obviously worried that they were going to do his companion some harm, that Nell had finally enticed him out with a bone, then quickly shut the door on his unsuspecting face.

Now, still deeply suspicious of foul play, he was hurling himself against the door with all his weight, but they did not want to let him in yet until the other dog had finished a bowl of milk. Mackenzie went to wash his hands, and his wife listened to the anxious running feet and the thuds that followed until she could bear it no longer, certain that he would harm himself. She opened the door and the old dog shot out in a fury, prepared to do battle on behalf of his friend – but he drew up all standing, a comical, puzzled expression on his face as he saw him peacefully lapping up a bowl of milk. Presently they sat down together by the door and the young dog patiently suffered the attentions of the other.

It was evident by their recognition and devotion that they came from the same home – a home which did not deserve to have them, as Nell said angrily, still upset by the gaunt travesty of a dog that had appeared; but Mackenzie pointed out that they must have known care and appreciation, as both had such friendly, assured dispositions. This made it all the harder to understand why they should be roaming such solitary and forbidding country, he admitted. But perhaps their owner had died, and they had run away together, or perhaps they had been lost from some car travelling across country, and were trying to make their way back to familiar territory. The possibilities were endless, and only one thing was certain – that they had been on the road long enough for scars to heal and quills to work their way inside a mouth; and long enough to know starvation.

'So they could have come from a hundred miles away or more,' said Mackenzie. 'From Manitoba, even. I wonder what they can have lived on, all that time –'

'Hunting? Scrounging at other farms? Stealing, perhaps!' suggested Nell, who had watched with amusement in the kitchen mirror her early morning visitor sliding a piece of bacon off a plate after breakfast when he thought her back was turned.

'Well, the pickings must have been pretty lean,' said her husband thoughtfully. 'The Labrador looks like a skeleton – he wouldn't have got much farther. I'll shut them in the stable when I go to Deepwater; we don't want them wandering off again.

'Now, Nell, are you quite sure that you want to take on two strange dogs? It may be a long time before they're traced

– they may never be.'

'I want them,' she said simply, 'for as long as they will stay. And in the meantime we must find something else to call them besides "Hi!" or "Good dog." I'll think of something while you're away,' she added, 'and I'll take some more milk out to the stable during the morning.'

From his sunny observation post on the woodpile, the cat had watched Mackenzie cross the yard and usher the two dogs into a warm, sweet-smelling stable, shutting the door carefully behind him. Shortly afterwards the truck rattled down the farm road, then all was quiet again. A few curious farm cats were emboldened to approach the woodpile, resenting this exotic stranger who had taken possession of their favourite sunning place. The stranger was not fond of other cats at the best of times, even his own breed, and farm cats were beyond the pale altogether. He surveyed them balefully, considering his strategy. After two or three well-executed skirmishes the band dispersed, and the black-masked pirate returned to his lair to sleep.

Halfway through the morning he awoke, stretched, and jumped down, looking warily around before stalking over to the stable door. He bleated plaintively and was answered by a rustle of straw within. Leisurely, he gathered himself for a spring, then leaped effortlessly at the latch on the door. But he was not quite quick enough; the latch remained in position. Annoyed, unused to failure, he sprang again, this time making sure of success. For a split second, almost in the same impetus as the spring, one paw was curved around the wooden block handle supporting his weight, while the other paw released the latch above and the door swung open. Purring with restrained pleasure, the cat walked in, suffering a boisterous welcome from his old friend before investigating the empty bowl. Disappointed, he left the stable, the two dogs following him into the sunlit yard, and disappeared into the henhouse. Several enraged and squawking fowls rushed out as he made his way towards the nesting-boxes. Curving his paws expertly around a warm brown egg, he held it firmly, then cracked it with a neat sideways tap from a long incisor tooth, the contents settling intact on the straw. He had brought this art to perfection after years of egg stealing. He lapped with delicate unhurried thoroughness, helping himself to two more before retiring to his woodpile again.

When Mackenzie drove into the farmyard later on in the afternoon he was surprised to see the two dogs sleeping in the sun by the shelter of the cattle trough. They stood by the truck wagging their tails in recognition as he unloaded, then followed him into the farmhouse.

'Did you let them out of the stable, Nell?' he asked, opening a parcel at the kitchen table and sheepishly dropping a meaty bone into the sharklike mouth that had opened beside him.

'Of course not,' she answered in surprise. 'I took them out some milk, but I remember being particularly careful to close the door.'

'Perhaps the latch wasn't down properly,' said Mackenzie. 'Anyway, they're still here. The Lab's face looks better already – he'll be able to eat a decent meal by this evening, I hope; I'd like to get some meat on those bones.'

Nothing was known of the runaways in Deepwater, he reported, but they must have come from the east, for a mink breeder at Archer Creek had spoken of chasing a white dog off his doorstep the night before, mistaking it for a local white mongrel well known for his thieving ways. Most men thought the Labrador could have been lost from a hunting trip, but nobody could account for an unlikely bull terrier as his companion. The Indian Agent had offered to take the Labrador if nobody turned up to claim him, as his own hunting dog had recently died . . .

'Indeed he will not!' Nell broke in indignantly.

'All right,' said her husband, laughing. 'I told him we would never separate them, and of course we'll keep them as long as we can – I'd hate to think of one of my own dogs running loose at this time of year. But I warn you, Nell, that if they are heading somewhere with a purpose, nothing on earth will keep them here – even if they're dropping on their feet, the instinct will pull them on. All we can do is keep them shut in for a while and feed them up. Then, if they leave, at least we've given them a better start.'

After supper that night the Mackenzies and their guests moved into the little back room: a cosy, pleasantly shabby place, its shelves still filled with children's books, tarnished trophies and photographs; while snowshoes, mounted fish and grandchildren's drawings jostled one another for space on the walls with award ribbons, pedigrees and a tomahawk. Mackenzie sat at a table, puffing peacefully on a pipe, and working at the minute, intricate rigging on a model schooner, while his wife read *Three Men in a Boat* aloud to him. The replete and satisfied Labrador had eaten ravenously that evening, cleaning up bowls of fresh milk and plates of food with a bottomless appetite. Now he lay stretched full length under the table in the deep sleep of exhaustion and security, and the terrier snored gently from the depths of an old leather sofa, his head pillowed on a cushion, four paws in the air.

The only disturbance during the evening was the noise of a tremendous cat battle out in the yard. Both dogs sat up immediately and, to the astonishment of the elderly couple watching, wagged their tails in unison, wearing almost identical expressions of pleased and doting interest.

Later on they followed Mackenzie out quite willingly to the stable, where he piled some hay in a corner of a loose box for them, filled the bowl with water, then shut the door firmly behind him – satisfying himself that the latch was down and firmly in place, and would remain so even when the door was rattled. Shortly afterwards the lights downstairs in the farmhouse went out, followed in a little while by the bedroom light upstairs.

The dogs lay quietly in the darkness, waiting. Soon there was a soft scrabbling of paws on wood, the latch clicked, and the door opened a fraction, just enough to admit the slight body of the cat. He trampled and kneaded the hay for a while, purring in a deep rumble, before curling up in a ball at the old dog's chest. There were several contented sighs, then silence reigned in the stable.

When the young dog awoke in the cold hour before dawn only a few pale laggard stars were left to give the message which his heart already knew – it was time to go, time to press on westwards.

The yawning, stretching cat joined him at the stable door; then the old dog, shivering in the cold dawn wind; and for a few minutes the three sat motionless, listening, looking across the still dark farmyard, where already they could hear the slight stirrings of the animals. It was time to be gone; there were many miles to be travelled before the first halt in the warmth of the sun. Silently they crossed the yard and entered the fields leading to the dark, massed shadows of the trees in the farthermost corner, their paws making three sets of tracks in the light rime of frost that covered the field; and even as they turned on to a deer trail leading westward through the bush, a light came on upstairs in the farmhouse . . .

Ahead of them lay the last fifty miles of the journey.

The Dominant Primordial Beast

JACK LONDON

Buck was kidnapped from his comfortable home and sold as a team dog in Canada during the Gold Rush, when powerful dogs were at a premium. Pulling a sled in the frozen wastes of the north, he has to learn the art of survival fast, particularly in the pack where the dogs constantly vie for superiority.

The dominant primordial beast was strong in Buck, and under the fierce conditions of trail life it grew and grew. Yet it was a secret growth. His new-born cunning gave him poise and control. He was too busy adjusting himself to the new life to feel at ease, and not only did he not pick fights, but he avoided them whenever possible. A certain deliberateness characterized his attitude. He was not prone to rashness and precipitate action; and in the bitter hatred between him and Spitz he betrayed no impatience, shunned all offensive acts.

On the other hand, possibly because he divined in Buck a dangerous rival, Spitz never lost an opportunity of showing his teeth. He even went out of his way to bully Buck, striving constantly to start the fight which could end only in the death of one or the other. Early in the trip this might have taken place had it not been for an unwonted accident. At the end of this day they made a bleak and miserable camp on the shore of Lake Le Barge. Driving snow, a wind that cut like a white-hot knife, and darkness had forced them to grope for a camping place. They could hardly have fared worse. At their backs rose a perpendicular wall of rock, and Perrault and François were compelled to make their fire and spread their sleeping robes on the ice of the lake itself. The tent they had discarded at Dyea in order to travel light. A few sticks of driftwood furnished them with a fire that thawed down through the ice and left them to eat supper in the dark.

Close in under the sheltering rock Buck made his nest. So snug and warm was it, that he was loath to leave it when François distributed the fish which he had first thawed over the fire. But when Buck finished his ration and returned, he found his nest occupied. A warning snarl told him that his trespasser was Spitz. Till now Buck had avoided trouble with his enemy, but this was too much. The beast in him roared. He sprang upon Spitz with a fury which surprised them both, and Spitz particularly, for his whole experience with Buck had gone to teach him that his rival was an unusually timid dog, who managed to hold his own because of his great weight and size.

François was surprised, too, when they shot out in a tangle from the disrupted nest and he divined the cause of the trouble. 'A-a-ah!' he cried to Buck. 'Gif it to heem, by Gar! Gif it to heem, the dirty t'eef!'

Spitz was equally willing. He was crying with sheer rage and eagerness as he circled back and forth for a chance to spring in. Buck was no less eager, and no less cautious, as he likewise circled back and forth for the advantage. But it was then that the unexpected happened, the thing which projected their struggle for supremacy far into the future, past many a weary mile of trail and toil.

An oath from Perrault, the resounding impact of a club upon a bony frame, and a shrill yelp of pain, heralded the breaking forth of pandemonium. The camp was suddenly discovered to be alive with skulking furry forms – starving huskies, four or five score of them, who had scented the camp from some Indian village. They had crept in while Buck and Spitz were fighting, and when the two men sprang among them with stout clubs they showed their teeth and fought back. They were crazed by the smell of the food. Perrault found one with head buried in the grub-box. His club landed heavily on the gaunt ribs, and the grub-box was capsized on the ground. On the instant a score of the famished brutes were scrambling for the bread and bacon. The clubs fell upon them unheeded. They yelped and howled under the rain of blows, but struggled none the less madly till the last crumb had been devoured.

In the meantime the astonished team-dogs had burst out of their nests only to be set upon by the fierce invaders. Never had Buck seen such dogs. It seemed as though their bones would burst through their skins. They were mere skeletons, draped loosely in draggled hides, with blazing eyes and slavered fangs. But the hunger-madness made them terrifying, irresistible. There was no opposing them. The team-dogs were swept back against the cliff at the first onset. Buck was beset by three huskies, and in a trice his head and shoulders were ripped and slashed. The din was frightful. Billee was crying as usual. Dave and Sol-leks, dripping blood from a score of wounds, were fighting bravely side by side. Joe was snapping like a demon. Once, his teeth closed on the fore leg of a husky, and he crunched down through the bone. Pike, the malingerer, leaped upon the crippled animal, breaking its neck with a quick flash of teeth and a jerk. Buck got a frothing adversary by the throat, and was sprayed with blood when his teeth sank through the jugular. The warm taste of it in his mouth goaded him to greater fierceness. He flung himself upon another, and at the same time felt teeth sink in his own throat. It was Spitz, treacherously attacking from the side.

Perrault and François, having cleaned out their part of the camp, hurried to save their sled-dogs. The wild wave of famished beasts rolled back before them, and Buck shook himself free. But it was only for a moment. The two men were compelled to run back to save the grub, upon which the huskies returned to the attack on the team. Billee, terrified into bravery, sprang through the savage circle and fled away over the ice. Pike and Dub followed on his heels, with the rest of the team behind. As Buck drew himself together to spring after them, out of the tail of his eye he saw Spitz rush upon him with the evident intention of overthrowing him. Once off his feet and under that mass of huskies, there was no hope for him. But he braced himself to the shock of Spitz's charge, then joined the flight out on the lake.

Later, the nine team-dogs gathered together and sought shelter in the forest. Though unpursued, they were in a sorry plight. There was not one who was not wounded in four or five places, while some were wounded grievously. Dub was badly injured in a hind leg; Dolly, the last husky added to the team at Dyea, had a badly torn throat; Joe had lost an eye; while Billee, the good-natured, with an ear chewed and rent to ribbons, cried and whimpered throughout the night. At daybreak they limped warily back to camp, to find the marauders gone and the two men in bad tempers. Fully half their grub supply was gone. The huskies had chewed through the sled lashings and canvas coverings. In fact, nothing, no matter how remotely eatable, had escaped them. They had eaten a pair of Perrault's moose-hide moccasins, chunks out of the leather traces, and even two feet of lash from the end of François's whip. He broke from a mournful contemplation of it to look over his wounded dogs.

'Ah, my frien's,' he said softly, 'mebbe it mek you mad dog, dose many bites. Mebbe all mad dog, sacredam! Wot you t'ink, eh, Perrault?'

The courier shook his head dubiously. With four hundred miles of trail still between him and Dawson, he could ill afford to have madness break out among his dogs. Two hours of cursing and exertion got the harness into shape, and the wound-stiffened team was under way, struggling painfully over the hardest part of the trail they had yet encountered, and for that matter, the hardest between them and Dawson.

The Thirty Mile River was wide open. Its wild water defied the frost, and it was in the eddies only and in the quiet places that the ice held at all. Six days of exhausting toil were required to cover those thirty terrible miles. And terrible they were, for every foot of them was accomplished at the risk of life to dog and man. A dozen times, Perrault, nosing the way, broke through the ice bridges, being saved by the long pole he carried, which he so held that it fell each time across the hole made by his body. But a cold snap was on, the thermometer registering fifty below zero, and each time he broke through he was compelled for very life to build a fire and dry his garments.

Nothing daunted him. It was because nothing daunted him that he had been chosen for government courier. He took all manner of risks, resolutely thrusting his little weazened face into the frost and struggling on from dim dawn to dark. He skirted the frowning shore on rim ice that bent and crackled under foot and upon which they dared not halt. Once, the sled broke through, with Dave and Buck, and they were half-frozen and all but drowned by the time they were dragged out. The usual fire was necessary to save them. They were coated solidly with ice, and the two men kept them on the run around the fire, sweating and thawing, so close that they were singed by the flames.

At another time Spitz went through, dragging the whole team after him up to Buck, who strained backward with all his strength, his forepaws on the slippery edge and the ice quivering and snapping all around. But behind him was Dave, likewise straining backward, and behind the sled was François, pulling till his tendons cracked.

Again the rim ice broke away before and behind, and there was no escape except up the cliff. Perrault scaled it by a miracle, while François prayed for just that miracle; and with every thong and sled lashing and the last bit of harness rove into a long rope, the dogs were hoisted, one by one, to the cliff crest. François came up last, after the sled and load. Then came the search for a place to descend, which descent was ultimately made by the aid of the rope, and night found them back on the river with a quarter of a mile to the day's credit.

By the time they made the Hootalinqua and good ice, Buck was played out. The rest of the dogs were in like condition; but Perrault, to make up lost time, pushed them late and early. The first day they covered thirty-five miles to the Big Salmon; the next day thirty-five more to the Little Salmon; the third day forty miles, which brought them well up towards the Five Fingers.

Buck's feet were not so compact and hard as the feet of the huskies. His had softened during the many generations since the day his last wild ancestor was tamed by a cave-dweller or river man. All day long he limped in agony, and camp once made, lay down like a dead dog. Hungry as he was, he would not move to receive his ration of fish, which François had to bring to him. Also, the dog-driver rubbed Buck's feet for half an hour each night after supper, and sacrificed the tops of his own moccasins to make four moccasins for Buck. This was a great relief, and Buck caused even the weazened face of Perrault to twist itself into a grin one morning, when François forgot the moccasins and Buck lay on his back, his four feet waving appealingly in the air, and refused to budge without them. Later his feet grew hard to the trail, and the worn-out foot-gear was thrown away.

At the Pelly one morning, as they were harnessing up, Dolly, who had never been conspicuous for anything, went suddenly mad. She announced her condition by a long, heart-breaking wolf howl that sent every dog bristling with fear, then sprang straight for Buck. He had never seen a dog go mad, nor did he have any reason to fear madness; yet he knew that here was horror, and fled away from it in a panic. Straight away he raced, with Dolly, panting and frothing, one leap behind; nor could she gain on him, so great was his terror, nor could he leave her, so great was her madness. He plunged through the wooded breast of the island, flew down to the lower end, crossed a back channel filled with rough ice to another island, gained a third island, curved back to the main river and in desperation started to cross it. And all the time, though he did not look, he could hear her snarling just one leap behind. François called to him a quarter of a mile away and he doubled back, still one leap ahead, gasping painfully for air and putting all his faith in that François would save him. The dog-driver held the axe poised in his hand, and as Buck shot past him the axe crashed down upon mad Dolly's head.

Buck staggered over against the sled, exhausted, sobbing for breath, helpless. This was Spitz's opportunity. He sprang upon Buck, and twice his teeth sank into his unresisting foe and ripped and tore the flesh to the bone. Then François's lash descended, and Buck had the satisfaction of watching Spitz receive the worst whipping as yet administered to any of the team.

'One devil, dat Spitz,' remarked Perrault. 'Some dam day heem keel dat Buck.'

'Dat Buck two devils,' was François's rejoinder. 'All de tam I watch dat Buck I know for sure. Lissen: some dam fine day heem get mad lak hell an' den heem chew dat Spitz all up an' spit heem out on de snow. Sure. I know.'

From then on it was war between them. Spitz, as lead-dog and acknowledged master of the team, felt his supremacy threatened by this strange Southland dog. And strange Buck was to him, for of the many Southland dogs he had known, not one had shown up worthily in camp and on trail. They were all too soft, dying under the toil, the frost, and starvation. Buck was the exception. He alone endured and prospered, matching the husky in strength, savagery, and cunning. Then he was a masterful dog, and what made him dangerous was the fact that the club of the man in the red sweater had knocked all blind pluck and rashness out of his desire for mastery. He was pre-eminently cunning; and could bide his time with a patience that was nothing less than primitive.

It was inevitable that the clash for leadership should come. Buck wanted it. He wanted it because it was his nature, because he had been gripped tight by that nameless, incomprehensible pride of the trail and trace – that pride which holds dogs in the toil to the last gasp, which lures them to die joyfully in the harness, and breaks their hearts if they are cut out of the harness. This was the pride of Dave as wheel-dog, of Sol-leks as he pulled with all his strength; the pride that laid hold of them at break of camp, transforming them from sour and sullen brutes into straining, eager, ambitious creatures; the pride that spurred them on all day and dropped them at pitch of camp at night, letting them fall back into gloomy unrest and uncontent. This was the pride that bore up Spitz and made him thrash the sled-dogs who blundered and shirked in the traces or hid away at harness-up time in the morning. Likewise it was his pride that made him fear Buck as a possible lead-dog. And this was Buck's pride, too.

He openly threatened the other's leadership. He came between him and the shirks he should have punished. And he did it deliberately. One night there was a heavy snow-fall, and in the morning Pike, the malingerer, did not appear. He was securely hidden in his nest under a foot of snow. François called him and sought him in vain. Spitz was wild with wrath. He ranged through the camp, smelling and digging in every likely place, snarling so frightfully that Pike heard and shivered in his hiding-place.

But when he was at last unearthed, and Spitz flew at him to punish him, Buck flew, with equal rage, in between. So unexpected was it, and so shrewdly managed, that Spitz was hurled backward and off his feet. Pike, who had been trembling abjectly, took heart at this open mutiny, and sprang upon his overthrown leader. Buck, to whom fair play was a forgotten code, likewise sprang upon Spitz. But François, chuckling at the incident while unswerving in the administration of justice, brought his lash down upon Buck with all his might. This failed to drive Buck from his prostrate rival, and the butt of the whip was brought into play. Half-stunned by the blow, Buck was knocked backward and the lash laid upon him again and again, while Spitz soundly punished the many times offending Pike.

In the days that followed, as Dawson grew closer and closer, Buck still continued to interfere between Spitz and the culprits;

but he did it craftily, when François was not around. With the covert mutiny of Buck, a general insubordination sprang up and increased. Dave and Sol-leks were unaffected, but the rest of the team went from bad to worse. Things no longer went right. There was continual bickering and jangling. Trouble was always afoot, and at the bottom of it was Buck. He kept François busy, for the dog-driver was in constant apprehension of the life-and-death struggle between the two which he knew must take place sooner or later; and on more than one night the sounds of quarrelling and strife among the other dogs turned him out of his sleeping robe, fearful that Buck and Spitz were at it.

But the opportunity did not present itself, and they pulled into Dawson one dreary afternoon with the great fight still to come. Here were many men, and countless dogs, and Buck found them all at work. It seemed the ordained order of things that dogs should work. All day they swung up and down the main street in long teams, and in the night their jingling bells still went by. They hauled cabin logs and firewood, freighted up to the mines, and did all manner of work that horses did in the Santa Clara Valley. Here and there Buck met Southland dogs, but in the main they were the wild wolf husky breed. Every night, regularly at night, at twelve, at three, they lifted a nocturnal song, a weird and eerie chant, in which it was Buck's delight to join.

With the aurora borealis flaming coldly overhead, or the stars leaping in the frost dance, and the land numb and frozen under its pall of snow, this song of the huskies might have been the defiance of life, only it was pitched in minor key, with long-drawn wailings and half-sobs, and was more the pleading of life, the articulate travail of existence. It was an old song, old as the breed itself – one of the first songs of the younger world in a day when songs were sad. It was invested with the woe of unnumbered generations, this plaint by which Buck was so strangely stirred. When he moaned and sobbed, it was with the pain of living that was of old the pain of his wild fathers, and the fear and mystery of the cold and dark that was to them fear and mystery.

And that he should be stirred by it marked the completeness with which he harked back through the ages of fire and roof to the raw beginnings of life in the howling ages.

Seven days from the time they pulled into Dawson they dropped down the steep bank by the Barracks to the Yukon Trail, and pulled for Dyea and Salt Water. Perrault was carrying despatches if anything more urgent than those he had brought in; also, the travel pride had gripped him, and he purposed to make the record trip of the year. Several things favoured him in this. The week's rest had recuperated the dogs and put them in thorough trim. The trail they had broken into the country was packed hard by later journeyers. And further, the police had arranged in two or three places deposits of grub for dog and man, and he was travelling light.

They made Sixty Mile, which is a fifty-mile run, on the first day; and the second day saw them booming up the Yukon well on their way to Pelly. But such splendid running was achieved not without great trouble and vexation on the part of François. The insidious revolt led by Buck had destroyed the solidarity of the team. It no longer was as one dog leaping in the traces. The encouragement Buck gave the rebels led them into all kinds of petty misdemeanours. No more was Spitz a leader greatly to be feared. The old awe departed, and they grew equal to challenging his authority. Pike robbed him of half a fish one night, and gulped it down under the protection of Buck. Another night Dub and Joe fought Spitz and made him forgo the punishment they deserved. And even Billee, the good-natured, was less good-natured, and whined not half so placatingly as in former days. Buck never came near Spitz without snarling and bristling menacingly. In fact, his conduct approached that of a bully, and he was given to swaggering up and down before Spitz's very nose.

The breaking down of discipline likewise affected the dogs in their relations with one another. They quarrelled and bickered more than ever among themselves, till at times the camp was a howling bedlam. Dave and Sol-leks alone were unaltered, though they were made irritable by the unending squabbling.

François swore strange barbarous oaths, and stamped the snow in futile rage, and tore his hair. His lash was always singing among the dogs, but it was of small avail. Directly his back was turned they were at it again. He backed up Spitz with his whip, while Buck backed up the remainder of the team. François knew he was behind all the trouble, and Buck knew he knew; but Buck was too clever ever again to be caught red-handed. He worked faithfully in the harness, for the toil had become a delight to him; yet it was a greater delight slyly to precipitate a fight amongst his mates and tangle the traces.

At the mouth of the Tahkeena, one night after supper, Dub turned up a snowshoe rabbit, blundered it, and missed. In a second the whole team was in full cry. A hundred yards away was a camp of the Northwest Police, with fifty dogs, huskies all, who joined the chase. The rabbit sped down the river, turned off into a small creek, up the frozen bed of which it held steadily. It ran lightly on the surface of the snow, while the dogs ploughed through by main strength. Buck led the pack, sixty strong, around bend after bend, but he could not gain. He lay down low to the race, whining eagerly, his splendid body flashing forward, leap by leap, in the wan white moonlight. And leap by leap, like some pale frost wraith, the snowshoe rabbit flashed on ahead.

All that stirring of old instincts which at stated periods drives men out from the sounding cities to forest and plain to kill things by chemically propelled leaden pellets, the blood lust, the joy to kill – all this was Buck's, only it was infinitely more intimate. He was ranging at the head of the pack, running the wild thing down, the living meat, to kill with his own teeth and wash his muzzle to the eyes in warm blood.

There is an ecstasy that marks the summit of life, and beyond which life cannot rise. And such is the paradox of living, this ecstasy comes when one is most alive, and it comes as a complete forgetfulness that one is alive. This ecstasy, this forgetfulness of living, comes to the artist, caught up and out of himself in a sheet of flame; it comes to the soldier, war-mad on a stricken field and refusing quarter; and it came to Buck, leading the pack, sounding the old wolf-cry, straining after the food that was alive and that fled swiftly before him through the moonlight. He was sounding the deeps of his nature, and of the parts of his nature that were deeper than he, going back into the womb of Time. He was mastered by the sheer surging of life, the tidal wave of being, the perfect joy of each separate muscle, joint, and sinew in that it was everything that was not death, that it was aglow and rampant, expressing itself in movement, flying exultantly under the stars and over the face of dead matter that did not move.

But Spitz, cold and calculating even in his supreme moods, left the pack and cut across a narrow neck of land where the creek made a long bend around. Buck did not know of this, and as he rounded the bend, the frost wraith of a rabbit still flitting before him, he saw another larger frost wraith leap from the overhanging bank into the immediate path of the rabbit. It was Spitz. The rabbit could not turn, and as the white teeth broke its back in mid air it shrieked as loudly as a stricken man may shriek. At sound of this, the cry of Life plunging down from Life's apex in the grip of Death, the full pack at Buck's heels raised a hell's chorus of delight.

Buck did not cry out. He did not check himself, but drove in upon Spitz, shoulder to shoulder, so hard that he missed the throat. They rolled over and over in the powdery snow. Spitz gained his feet almost as though he had not been overthrown, slashing Buck down the shoulder and leaping clear. Twice his teeth clipped together, like the steel jaws of a trap, as he backed away for better footing, with lean and lifting lips that writhed and snarled.

In a flash Buck knew it. The time had come. It was to the death. As they circled about, snarling, ears laid back, keenly watchful for the advantage, the scene came to Buck with a sense of familiarity. He seemed to remember it all – the white woods, and earth, and moonlight, and the thrill of battle. Over the whiteness and silence brooded a ghostly calm. There was not the faintest whisper of air – nothing moved, not a leaf quivered, the visible breaths of the dogs rising slowly and lingering in the

They circled about, snarling

frosty air. They had made short work of the snowshoe rabbit, these dogs that were ill-tamed wolves; and they were now drawn up in an expectant circle. They, too, were silent, their eyes only gleaming and their breaths drifting slowly upward. To Buck it was nothing new or strange, this scene of old time. It was as though it had always been the wonted way of things.

Spitz was a practised fighter. From Spitzbergen through the Arctic, and across Canada and the Barrens, he had held his own with all manner of dogs and achieved to mastery over them. Bitter rage was his, but never blind rage. In passion to rend and destroy, he never forgot that his enemy was in like passion to rend and destroy. He never rushed till he was prepared to receive a rush; never attacked till he had first defended that attack.

In vain Buck strove to sink his teeth in the neck of the big white dog. Wherever his fangs struck for the softer flesh, they were countered by the fangs of Spitz. Fang clashed fang, and lips were cut and bleeding, but Buck could not penetrate his enemy's guard. Then he warmed up and enveloped Spitz in a whirlwind of rushes. Time and time again he tried for the snow-white throat, where life bubbled near to the surface, and each time and every time Spitz slashed him and got away. Then Buck took to rushing, as though for the throat, when, suddenly drawing back his head and curving in from the side, he would drive his shoulder at the shoulder of Spitz, as a ram by which to overthrow him. But instead, Buck's shoulder was slashed down each time as Spitz leaped lightly away.

Spitz was untouched, while Buck was streaming with blood and panting hard. The fight was growing desperate. And all the while the silent and wolfish circle waited to finish off whichever dog went down. As Buck grew winded, Spitz took to rushing, and he kept him staggering for footing. Once Buck went over, and the whole circle of sixty dogs started up; but he recovered himself, almost in mid air, and the circle sank down again and waited.

But Buck possessed a quality that made for greatness – imagination. He fought by instinct, but he could fight by head as well. He rushed, as though attempting the old shoulder trick, but at the last instant swept low to the snow and in. His teeth closed on Spitz's left fore leg. There was a crunch of breaking bone, and the white dog faced him on three legs. Thrice he tried to knock him over, then repeated the trick and broke the right fore leg. Despite the pain and helplessness, Spitz struggled madly to keep up. He saw the silent circle, with gleaming eyes, lolling tongues, and silvery breaths drifting upward, closing in upon him as he had seen similar circles close in upon beaten antagonists in the past. Only this time he was the one who was beaten.

There was no hope for him. Buck was inexorable. Mercy was a thing reserved for gentler climes. He manoeuvred for the final rush. The circle had tightened till he could feel the breaths of the huskies on his flanks. He could see them, beyond Spitz and to either side, half crouching for the spring, their eyes fixed upon him. A pause seemed to fall. Every animal was motionless as though turned to stone. Only Spitz quivered and bristled as he staggered back and forth, snarling with horrible menace, as though to frighten off impending death. Then Buck sprang in and out; but while he was in, shoulder had at last squarely met shoulder. The dark circle became a dot on the moon-flooded snow as Spitz disappeared from view. Buck stood and looked on, the successful champion, the dominant primordial beast who had made his kill and found it good.

Memoirs of a Yellow Dog

O. HENRY

I don't suppose it will knock any of you people of your perch to read a contribution from an animal. Mr Kipling and a good many others have demonstrated the fact that animals can express themselves in remunerative English, and no magazine goes to press nowadays without an animal story in it, except the old-style monthlies that are still running pictures of Bryan and the Mont Pelée horror.

But you needn't look for any stuck-up literature in my piece, such as Bearoo, the bear, and Snakoo, the snake, and Tammanoo, the tiger, talk in the jungle books. A yellow dog that's spent most of his life in a cheap New York flat, sleeping in a corner on an old sateen underskirt (the one she spilled port wine on at the Lady Longshoremen's banquet), mustn't be expected to perform any tricks with the art of speech.

I was born a yellow pup; date, locality, pedigree and weight unknown. The first thing I can recollect, an old woman had me in a basket at Broadway and Twenty-third trying to sell me to a fat lady. Old Mother Hubbard was boosting me to beat the band as a genuine Pomeranian-Hambletonian-Red-Irish-Cochin-China-Stoke-Pogis fox terrier. The fat lady chased a V around among the samples of gros grain flannelette in her shopping bag till she cornered it, and gave up. From that moment I was a pet – a mamma's own wootsey quidlums. Say, gentle reader, did you ever have a 200-pound woman breathing a flavour of Camembert cheese and Peau d'Espagne pick you up and wallop her nose all over you, remarking all the time in an Emma Eames tone of voice: 'Oh, oo's um oodlum, doodlum, woodlum, toodlum, bitsy-witsy skoodlums?'

From pedigreed yellow pup I grew up to be an anonymous yellow cur looking like a cross between an Angora cat and a box of lemons. But my mistress never tumbled. She thought that the two primeval pups that Noah chased into the ark were but a collateral branch of my ancestors. It took two policemen to keep her from entering me at the Madison Square Garden for the Siberian bloodhound prize.

I'll tell you about that flat. The house was the ordinary thing in New York, paved with Parian marble in the entrance hall and cobblestones above the first floor. Our flat was three – well, not flights – climbs up. My mistress rented it unfurnished, and put in the regular things – 1903 antique upholstered parlour set, oil chromo of geishas in a Harlem tea house, rubber plant and husband.

By Sirius! there was a biped I felt sorry for. He was a little man with sandy hair and whiskers a good deal like mine. Henpecked? – well, toucans and flamingoes and pelicans all had their bills in him. He wiped the dishes and listened to my mistress tell about the cheap, ragged things the lady with the squirrel-skin coat on the second floor hung on her line to dry. And every evening while she was getting supper she made him take me out on the end of a string for a walk.

If men knew how women pass the time when they are alone they'd never marry. Laura Lean Jibbey, peanut brittle, a little almond cream on the neck muscles, dishes unwashed, half an hour's talk with the iceman, reading a package of old letters, a couple of pickles and two bottles of malt extract, one hour peeking through a hole in the window shade into the flat across the air-shaft – that's about all there is to it. Twenty minutes before time for him to come home from work she straightens up the house, fixes her rat so it won't show, and gets out a lot of sewing for a ten-minute bluff.

I led a dog's life in that flat. 'Most all day I lay there in my corner watching that fat woman kill time. I slept sometimes and had pipe dreams about being out chasing cats into basements and growling at old ladies with black mittens, as a dog was intended to do. Then she would pounce upon me with a lot of that drivelling poodle palaver and kiss me on the nose – but what could I do? A dog can't chew cloves.

I began to feel sorry for Hubby, dog my cats if I didn't. We looked so much alike that people noticed it when we went out; so we shook the streets that Morgan's cab drives down, and took to climbing the piles of last December's snow on the streets where cheap people live.

One evening when we were thus promenading, and I was trying to look like a prize St Bernard, and the old man was trying to look like he wouldn't have murdered the first organ-grinder he heard play Mendelssohn's wedding-march, I looked up at him and said, in my way:

'What are you looking so sour about, you oakum trimmed lobster? She don't kiss you. You don't have to sit on her lap and listen to talk that would make the book of a musical comedy sound like the maxims of Epictetus. You ought to be thankful you're not a dog. Brace up, Benedick, and bid the blues begone.'

The matrimonial mishap looked down at me with almost canine intelligence in his face.

'Why, doggie,' says he, 'good doggie. You almost look like you could speak. What is it, doggie – cats?'

Cats! Could speak!

But, of course, he couldn't understand. Humans were denied the speech of animals. The only common ground of communication upon which dogs and men can get together is in fiction.

In the flat across the hall from us lived a lady with a black-and-tan terrier. Her husband strung it and took it out every evening, but he always came home cheerful and whistling. One day I touched noses with the black-and-tan in the hall, and I struck him for an elucidation.

'See here, Wiggle-and-Skip,' I says, 'you know that it ain't the nature of a real man to play dry nurse to a dog in public. I never saw one leashed to a bow-wow yet that didn't look like he'd like to lick every other man that looked at him. But your boss comes in every day as perky and set up as an amateur prestidigitator doing the egg trick. How does he do it? Don't tell me he likes it.'

'Him?' says the black-and-tan. 'Why, he uses Nature's Own Remedy. He gets spifflicated. At first when we go out he's as shy as the man on the steamer who would rather play pedro when they make 'em all jackpots. By the time we've been in eight saloons he don't care whether the thing on the end of his line is a dog or a catfish. I've lost two inches of my tail trying to sidestep those swinging doors.'

The pointer I got from that terrier – Vaudeville please copy – set me to thinking.

One evening about 6 o'clock my mistress ordered him to get busy and do the ozone act for Lovey. I have concealed it until now, but that is what she called me. The black-and-tan was called 'Tweetness'. I consider that I have the bulge on him as far as you could chase a rabbit. Still 'Lovey' is something of a nomenclatural tin can on the tail of one's self-respect.

At a quiet place on a safe street I tightened the line of my custodian in front of an attractive, refined saloon. I made a dead-ahead scramble for the doors, whining like a dog in the press despatches that lets the family know that little Alice is bogged while gathering lilies in the brook.

'Why, darn my eyes,' says the old man, with a grin; 'darn my eyes if the saffron-coloured son of a seltzer lemonade ain't asking me in to take a drink. Lemme see – how long's it been since I saved shoe leather by keeping one foot on the foot-rest? I believe I'll –'

I knew I had him. Hot Scotches he took sitting at a table. For an hour he kept the Campbells coming. I sat by his side rapping for the waiter with my tail, and eating free lunch such as mamma in her flat never equalled with her homemade truck bought at a delicatessen store eight minutes before papa comes home.

When the products of Scotland were all exhausted except the rye bread the old man unwound me from the table leg and played me outside like a fisherman plays a salmon. Out there he took off my collar and threw it into the street.

'Poor doggie,' says he; 'good doggie. She shan't kiss you any more. 'S a darned shame. Good doggie, go away and get run over by a street car and be happy.'

I refused to leave. I leaped and frisked around the old man's legs happy as a pug on a rug.

'You old flea-headed woodchuck-chaser,' I said to him – 'you moon-baying, rabbit-pointing, egg-stealing old beagle, can't you see that I don't want to leave you? Can't you see that we're Pups in the Wood and the missis is the cruel uncle after you with the dish towel and me with the flea liniment and a pink bow to tie on my tail. Why not cut that all out and be pards forever more?'

Maybe you'll say he didn't understand – maybe he didn't. But he kind of got a grip on the Hot Scotches, and stood still for a minute, thinking.

'Doggie,' says he, finally, 'we don't live more than a dozen lives on this earth, and very few of us live to be more than 300. If I ever see that flat any more I'm a flat, and if you do you're flatter; and that's no flattery. I'm offering 60 to 1 that Westward Ho wins out by the length of a dachshund.'

There was no string, but I frolicked along with my master to the Twenty-third Street ferry. And the cats on the route saw reason to give thanks that prehensile claws had been given to them.

On the Jersey side my master said to a stranger who stood eating a currant bun:

'Me and my doggie, we are bound for the Rocky Mountains.'

But what pleased me most was when my old man pulled both of my ears until I howled, and said:

'You common, monkey-headed, rat-tailed, sulphur-coloured

son of a door mat, do you know that I'm going to call you?'

I thought of 'Lovey', and I whined dolefully.

'I'm going to call you "Pete"', says my master; and if I'd had five tails I couldn't have done enough wagging to do justice to the occasion.

Miracle Needed

DODIE SMITH

Pongo and Missis have to rescue their thirteen puppies, kidnapped by the evil Cruella de Vil to make a fur coat. On reaching the hide-out, they are horrified to find a total of ninety-seven puppies, stolen from all over the country, who must be saved. They set out secretly on the long journey to London: not an easy venture for such a large number in the middle of winter.

'Last lap before supper,' said Pongo, as they started off again across the moonlit fields.

It was the most cheering thing he could have said for the ninety-seven puppies were now extremely hungry. He had guessed this because he was hungry himself. And so was the Missis. But she was feeling too peaceful to mind.

They went on for nearly two miles, then Pongo saw a long row of cottage roofs ahead across the fields.

'This should be it,' he said.

'What is that glow in the sky beyond the roof-tops?' asked Missis.

Pongo was puzzled. He had seen such a glow in the sky over towns which had many lights, but never over a village. And this was a very bright glow. 'Perhaps it's a larger place than we expected it to be,' he said, and did not feel it would be safe to go any nearer until some dog came to meet them. He called a halt and barked news of their arrival.

He was answered a once, by a bark that said: 'Wait where you are. I am coming.' And though he did not tell Missis, Pongo felt there was something odd about this bark that answered his. For one thing, there were no cheerful words of welcome.

Soon a graceful red Setter came dashing towards them. They guessed, even before she spoke, that something was very wrong.

'The bakery's on fire!' she gasped.

The blaze, due to a faulty chimney, had begun only a few minutes before – the fire engine had not yet arrived. No one had been hurt, but the bakehouse was full of flames and smoke – all the food spread out for the Dalmatians was burned.

'There's nothing for you to eat and nowhere for you to sleep,' moaned the poor Setter – she was hysterical. 'And the village street's full of people.' She looked pitifully at Missis. 'All your poor hungry puppies!'

The strange thing was that Missis felt quite calm. She tried to comfort the Setter, saying they would go to some barn.

'But no arrangements are made,' wailed the Setter. 'And there's no spare food anywhere. All the village dogs brought what they could to the bakery.'

Just then came a shrill whistle.

'My pet is calling me,' said the Setter. 'He's the doctor here. There's no dog at the bakery, so I was chosen to arrange everything – because I took first prize in a Dog Show. And now I've failed you.'

'You have *not* failed,' said Missis. 'No one could say the fire was act of dog. Go back to your pet and don't worry. We shall simply go on to the next village.'

'*Really?*' said the Setter, gasping again – but with relief.

Missis kissed her on the nose. 'Off with you, my dear, and don't give the matter another thought. And thank you for all you did.'

The whistle came again and the Setter ran off, wildly waving her feathered tail.

'Feather-brained as well as feather-tailed,' said Pongo.

'Just very young,' said Missis, gently. 'I doubt if she's had a family yet. Well, on to the next village.'

'Thank you for being so brave, dear Missis,' said Pongo. 'But where *is* the next village?'

'In the country, there are villages in *every* direction,' said Missis, brightly.

Desperately worried though he was, Pongo smiled lovingly at her. Then he said: 'We will go to the road now.'

'But what about traffic, Pongo?'

'We shall not be very long on the road,' said Pongo.

Then he told her what he had decided. Even if the next village should only be a few miles away, many of the pups were too tired and too hungry to get there – some of them were already asleep on the frozen ground. And every minute it got colder.

'And even if we could get to the next village, where should we sleep, Missis, what should we eat, with no plans made ahead? We must give in, my dear. Come, wake the pups! Quick march, everyone!'

The waking pups whimpered and shivered, and Missis saw that even the strongest pups were now wretchedly cold. So she helped Pongo to make them all march briskly. Then she whispered:

'But *how* do we give in, Pongo?'

Pongo said: 'We must go into the village and find the police station.'

Missis stared at him in horror. 'No Pongo, no! The police will take the puppies from us!'

'But they will feed them, Missis. And perhaps we shall be kept together until Mr Dearly has been told about us. They will have read the papers. They will know we are the Missing Dalmatians.'

'But we are not Dalmatians any more, Pongo,' cried Missis. 'We are black. They will think we are ordinary stray dogs. And we are illegal – ninety-nine dogs without collars. We shall be put in prison.'

'No, Missis!' But Pongo was shaken. He had forgotten they were now black dogs. Suppose the police did *not* recognize them? Suppose the Dearlys were never told about them? What happened to stray dogs that no one claimed?

'Please, Pongo, I beg you!' cried Missis. 'Let us go on with our journey! I *know* it will be all right.'

They had now reached the road and were on the edge of the village. Pongo was faced with a terrible choice. But it still seemed to him wiser to trust the police than to lead the hungry, exhausted puppies into the bitter winter night.

'Missis, dear Missis, we *must* go to the police-station,' he said, and turned towards the village. They could now see the burning bakery and at that moment a huge flame leapt up through the roof. By its light Pongo saw the whole village street, with the villagers making a human chain to hand along buckets of water. And he also saw something else – something which made him stop dead, shouting 'Halt!' at the top of his bark.

In front of the burning bakery was a great striped black-and-white car. And with it was Cruella de Vil – standing right up on the roof of the car, where she had climbed so as to get a good view of the fire. Her white face and absolutely simple white mink cloak no longer looked white. From head to foot she was bathed in the red-gold flicker of the flames. And as they leapt higher and higher she clapped her hands in delight.

The next instant there was a wild clamour of bells as the fire engine arrived at last. The noise, the flames, and, above all, the sight of Cruella were too much for many of the puppies. Squealing in terror, they turned and fled, with Pongo, Missis, and Lucky desperately trying to call them to order.

Fortunately, the clamour from the fire engine prevented anyone in the village hearing the barking and yapping. And after a little while, the terrified pups obeyed Pongo's orders and stopped their headlong flight. They were very shame-faced as Pongo told them that, though he quite understood how they had felt, they must never, never behave in such a panic-stricken way and must always, always obey orders instantly. Then he praised

From head to foot she was bathed in the red-gold flicker of the flames

the pups who had stuck to the Cadpig's cart, praised Patch for staying close to the Cadpig, rescued Roly Poly from a ditch, and counted the pups carefully. He did all this as hurriedly as possible for he knew now that they must press on with their journey. There was no way they could get to the police station without passing Cruella de Vil.

Their plight was now worse than ever. They not only had to face the dangers of hunger and cold; there was the added danger of Cruella. They knew from the direction her car was facing that their enemy must have already been to Hell Hall, learned that they had escaped, and now be on her way back to London. At any moment, she might leave the fire and overtake them.

If only they could have left the road and travelled by the fields again! But there were now woods on either side of the road, woods so thick that the army could not have kept together.

'But we can hide in there, if we see the car's headlights,' said Pongo, and explained this to the puppies. Then the army was on the march again.

'At least the pups are warm now,' said Missis. 'And they have forgotten how tired and hungry they are. It will be all right, Pongo.'

The pace was certainly good for a couple of miles, then it got slower and slower.

'The puppies will have to rest,' said Missis. 'And this is a good place for it.'

There was now a wide, grassy verge to the road. The moment Pongo called a halt the pups sank down on the frosty grass. Many of them at once fell asleep.

'They ought not to sleep,' said Pongo, anxiously.

'Let them, for a little while,' said Missis.

The Cadpig was not asleep. She sat up in her cart and said: 'Will there be a barn soon, with kind cows and warm milk?'

'I'm sure there will be *something* nice,' said Missis. 'Snuggle down in your hay, my darling. Pongo, how strangely quiet it is.'

They could no longer hear any sounds from the village. No breath of wind rustled the grass or stirred the trees. The world seemed frozen into a silvery, silent stillness.

Something soft and fluffy touched Pongo's head, something that puzzled him. Then, as he realized what it was, Missis whispered:

'Look, Pongo! Look at the puppies!'

Tiny white dots were appearing on the sooty black coats. Snow had begun to fall.

Missis said, smiling: 'Instead of being white pups with black spots they are turning into black pups with white spots – only soon, they will be all white. How soft and gentle the snow is!'

Pongo was not smiling. He cried: 'If they sleep on until it has covered them, they will never wake – they will freeze to death beneath that soft, gentle snow! Wake up, pups! Wake up!'

By now, every pup but Lucky and the Cadpig had fallen into a deep, exhausted sleep. Lucky helped his parents to rouse them, and the Cadpig helped, too, sitting up in her cart and yapping piercingly. The poor pups begged to be left to sleep, and those who tottered on to their feet soon tottered off them again.

'We shall never get them going,' said Pongo, despairingly.

For a moment, the Cadpig stopped yapping and there was a sudden silence. Then, from the village behind them, came the strident blare of the loudest motor-horn in England.

The pups sprang up, their exhaustion driven away by terror.

'To the woods!' cried Pongo. Then he saw that the woods were now protected by wire netting, through which not even the smallest pup could squeeze. And there was no ditch to hide in. But he could see that the woods ended, not very far ahead. 'We must go on,' he cried. 'There may be fields, there may be a ditch.'

The horn sounded again, repeatedly. Pongo guessed that the fire engine had put out the fire and now Cruella was scattering the villagers as she drove on her way. Already she would be less than two miles behind them – and the great striped car could travel two miles in less than two minutes. But the woods were ending, there were fields ahead!

'To the fields!' cried Pongo. 'Faster, faster!'

The pups made a great spurt forward, then fell back in dismay. For though the woods ended, the wire netting still continued, on both sides of them. There was still no way off the road. And the horn sounded again – louder and nearer.

'Nothing but a miracle can save us now,' said Pongo.

'Then we must find a miracle,' said Missis, firmly. 'Pongo, what *is* a miracle?'

It was at that moment that they suddenly saw, through the swirling snow, a very large van drawn up on the road ahead of them. The tailboard was down and the inside of the van was lit by electric light. And sitting there, on a newspaper, was a Staffordshire Terrier with a short clay pipe in his mouth. That is, it looked like a clay pipe. It was really made of sugar and had once had a fine long stem. Now the Staffordshire drew the bowl of the pipe into his mouth and ate it. Then he looked up from the newspaper – which he was reading as well as sitting on – and stared in astonishment at the army of pups rushing helter-skelter towards him.

'Help, help, help!' barked Pongo. 'We are being pursued. How soon can we get off this road?'

'I don't know, mate,' barked back the Staffordshire. 'You'd better hide in my van.'

'The miracle, the miracle!' gasped Pongo to Missis.

'Quickly, pups! Jump into the nice miracle,' said Missis, who now thought 'miracle' was another name for a removal van.

A swarm of pups surged up the tailboard. Up went the Cadpig's cart, pulled from the front and pushed from behind. Then more and more pups jumped or scrambled up until the entire army was in.

'Golly, there are a lot of you,' said the Staffordshire, who had flattened himself against the side of the van. 'Lucky the van was empty. Who's after you, mates? Old Nick?'

'Some relation of his, I think,' said Pongo. The strident horn sounded again and now two strong headlights could be seen in the distance. 'And she's in that car.'

'Then I'd better put the lights off,' said the Staffordshire, neatly working the switch with his teeth. 'That's better.'

Pongo's heart seemed to miss a beat. Suddenly he knew that letting the pups get into the van had been a terrible mistake.

'But the car's headlights will shine in,' he gasped. 'Our enemy will see the pups.'

'Not black pups in a black van,' said the Staffordshire.'Not if they close their eyes.'

Oh, excellent suggestion! Quickly Pongo gave the command:

'Pups, close your eyes – or they will reflect the car's headlights and shine like jewels in the darkness. Close them and do not open them, however frightened you are, until I give the word. Remember, your lives may depend on your obedience now. Close your eyes and keep them closed!'

Instantly all the puppies closed their eyes tight. And now the car's headlights were less than a quarter of a mile away.

'Close your eyes, Missis,' said Pongo.

'And don't forget to close your own, mate,' said the Staffordshire.

Now the car's powerful engine could he heard. The strident horn blared again and again, as if telling the van to get out of the way. Louder and louder grew the noise from the engine. The glare from the headlights was now so intense that Pongo was conscious of it through his tightly shut eyelids. Would the pups obey orders? Or would terror make them look towards the oncoming car? Pongo, himself, had a wild desire to do so and a wild fear that the car was going to crash into the van. The noise of horn and engine grew deafening, the glare seemed blinding, even to closed eyes. Then, with a roar, the great striped car was on them – and past them, roaring on and on into the night!

'You may open your eyes now, my brave obedient pups,' cried Pongo. And indeed they deserved praise for not one eye had been opened.

'That was quite a car, mate,' said the Staffordshire to Pongo. 'You must have quite an enemy. Who are you, anyway? The local pack of soot-hounds?' Then he suddenly stared very hard at Pongo's nose. 'Well, swelp me if it *isn't* soot! And it doesn't fool me. You're the Missing Dalmatians. Want a lift back to London?'

A lift? A lift all the way in this wonderful van! Pongo and Missis could hardly believe it. Swiftly the pups settled to sleep on the rugs and blankets used for wrapping round furniture.

'But why are there so many pups?' said the Staffordshire. 'The newspapers don't know the half of it, nor the quarter, neither. They think there are only fifteen missing.'

Pongo started to explain but the Staffordshire said they would talk during the drive to London. 'My pets will be out of that house there any minute. Fancy us doing a removal on a Sunday – *and* Christmas Eve. But the van broke down yesterday and we had to finish the job.'

'How many days will the journey to London take?' asked Missis.

'Days?' said the Staffordshire. 'It won't take much more than a couple of hours, if *I* know my pets. They want to get home to finish decorating their kids' Christmas trees. Sssh, now! Pipe down, both of you.'

A large man in a rough apron was coming out of a near-by house, Missis thought: 'As soon as one danger is past, another threatens.' Would they all be turned out of the miracle?

The Staffordshire, wagging his tail enthusiastically, hurled himself at the man's chest, nearly knocking him down.

'Look out, Bill!' said the man, over his shoulder. 'The Canine Cannon Ball's feeling frisky.'

Bill was an even larger man, but even he was shaken by the Staffordshire's loving welcome.

'Get down, you Self-launched Bomb,' he shouted, with great affection.

The two men and the Staffordshire came back to the van and the Staffordshire jumped inside. The sooty Dalmatians, huddled together, were invisible in the darkness.

'Want to ride inside, do you?' said Bill. 'Well, it *is* cold.' He put the tailboard up and shouted: 'Next stop, St John's Wood.' A moment later, the huge van took the road.

St John's Wood! Surely, that was where the Splendid Vet lived – quite close to Regent's Park! What wonderful, wonderful luck, thought Pongo. Just then he heard a clock strike. It was still only eight o'clock.

'Missis!' he cried. 'We shall get home tonight! We shall be home for Christmas!'

Clancy

JAMES HERRIOT

As the faint rumbling growl rolled up from the rib cage into the ear pieces of my stethoscope the realization burst upon me with uncomfortable clarity that this was probably the biggest dog I had ever seen. In my limited past experience some Irish Wolfhounds had undoubtedly been taller and a certain number of Bull Mastiffs had possibly been broader, but for sheer gross poundage this one had it. His name was Clancy.

It was a good name for an Irishman's dog and Joe Mulligan was very Irish despite his many years in Yorkshire. Joe had brought him in to the afternoon surgery and as the huge hairy form ambled along, almost filling the passage, I was reminded of the times I had seen him out in the fields around Darrowby enduring the frisking attentions of smaller animals with massive benignity. He looked like a nice friendly dog.

But now there was this ominous sound echoing round the great thorax like a distant drum roll in a subterranean cavern, and as the chest piece of the stethoscope bumped along the ribs the sound swelled in volume and the lips fluttered over the enormous teeth as though a gentle breeze had stirred them. It was then that I became aware not only that Clancy was very big indeed but that my position, kneeling on the floor with my right ear a few inches from his mouth, was infinitely vulnerable.

I got to my feet and as I dropped the stethoscope into my pocket the dog gave me a cold look – a sideways glance without moving his head; and there was a chilling menace in his very immobility. I didn't mind my patients snapping at me but this one, I felt sure, wouldn't snap. If he started something it would be on a spectacular scale.

I stepped back a pace. 'Now what did you say his symptoms were, Mr Mulligan?'

'Phwaat's that?' Joe cupped his ear with his hand. I took a deep breath. 'What's the trouble with him?' I shouted.

The old man looked at me with total incomprehension from beneath the straightly adjusted cloth cap. He fingered the muffler knotted immediately over his larynx and the pipe which grew from the dead centre of his mouth puffed blue wisps of puzzlement.

Then, remembering something of Clancy's past history, I moved close to Mr Mulligan and bawled with all my power into his face. 'Is he vomiting?'

The response was immediate. Joe smiled in great relief and removed his pipe. 'Oh aye, he's womitin' sorr. He's womitin' bad.' Clearly he was on familiar ground.

Over the years Clancy's treatment had all been at long range. Siegfried had told me on the first day I had arrived in Darrowby two years ago that there was nothing wrong with the dog which he had described as a cross between an Airedale and a donkey, but his penchant for eating every bit of rubbish in his path had the inevitable result. A large bottle of bismuth, mag carb mixture had been dispensed at regular intervals. He had also told me that Clancy, when bored, used occasionally to throw Joe to the ground and worry him like a rat just for a bit of light relief. But his master still adored him.

Prickings of conscience told me I should carry out a full examination. Take his temperature, for instance. All I had to do was to grab hold of that tail, lift it and push a thermometer into his rectum. The dog turned his head and met my eye with a blank stare; again I heard the low booming drum roll and the upper lip lifted a fraction to show a quick gleam of white.

'Yes, yes, right, Mr Mulligan,' I said briskly. 'I'll get you a bottle of the usual.'

In the dispensary, under the rows of bottles with their Latin names and glass stoppers I shook up the mixture in a ten ounce bottle, corked it, stuck on a label and wrote the directions. Joe seemed well satisfied as he pocketed the familiar white medicine but as he turned to go my conscience smote me again. The dog did look perfectly fit but maybe he ought to be seen again.

'Bring him back again on Thursday afternoon at two o'clock,' I yelled into the old man's ear. 'And please come on time if you can. You were a bit late today.'

I watched Mr Mulligan going down the street, preceded by his pipe from which regular puffs rose upwards as though from a departing railway engine. Behind him ambled Clancy, a picture of massive calm. With his all-over covering of tight brown curls he did indeed look like a gigantic Airedale.

Thursday afternoon, I ruminated. That was my half day and at two o'clock I'd probably be watching the afternoon cinema show in Brawton, with Helen.

The following Friday morning Siegfried was sitting behind his desk, working out the morning rounds. He scribbled a list of visits on a pad, tore out the sheet and handed it to me.

'Here you are, James, I think that'll just about keep you out of mischief till lunch time.' Then something in the previous day's entries caught his eye and he turned to his younger brother who was at his morning task of stoking the fire.

'Tristan, I see Joe Mulligan was in yesterday afternoon with his dog and you saw it. What did you make of it?'

Tristan put down his bucket. 'Oh, I gave him some of the bismuth mixture.'

'Yes, but what did your examination of the patient disclose?'

'Well now, let's see.' Tristan rubbed his chin. 'He looked pretty lively, really.'

'Is that all?'

'Yes . . . yes . . . I think so.'

Siegfried turned back to me. 'And how about you, James? You saw the dog the day before. What were your findings?'

'Well it was a bit difficult,' I said. 'That dog's as big as an elephant and there's something creepy about him. He seemed to me to be just waiting his chance and there was only old Joe to hold him. I'm afraid I wasn't able to make a close examination but I must say I thought the same as Tristan – he did look pretty lively.'

Siegfried put down his pen wearily. On the previous night, fate had dealt him one of the shattering blows which it occasionally reserves for vets – a call at each end of his sleeping time. He had been dragged from his bed at 1 a.m. and again at 6 a.m. and the fires of his personality were temporarily damped.

He passed a hand across his eyes. 'Well God help us. You, James, a veterinary surgeon of two years' experience and you, Tristan, a final year student can't come up with anything better between you than the phrase "pretty lively". It's a bloody poor thing! Hardly a worthy description of clinical findings is it? When an animal comes in here I expect you to record pulse, temperature and respiratory rate. To auscultate the chest and thoroughly palpate the abdomen. To open his mouth and examine teeth, gums and pharynx. To check the condition of the skin. To catheterize him and examine the urine if necessary.'

'Right,' I said.

'O.K.,' said Tristan.

My partner rose from his seat. 'Have you fixed another appointment?'

'I have, yes.' Tristan drew his packet of Woodbines from his pocket. 'For Monday. And since Mr Mulligan's always late for the surgery I said we'd visit the dog at his home in the evening.'

'I see.' Siegfried made a note on the pad, then he looked up suddenly. 'That's when you and James are going to the young farmers' meeting, isn't it?'

The young man drew on his cigarette. 'That's right. Good for the practice for us to mix with the young clients.'

'Very well,' Siegfried said as he walked to the door. 'I'll see the dog myself.'

On the following Tuesday I was fairly confident that Siegfried would have something to say about Mulligan's dog, if only to point out the benefits of a thorough clinical examination. But he was silent on the subject.

It happened that I came upon old Joe in the market place sauntering over the cobbles with Clancy inevitably trotting at his heels.

I went up to him and shouted in his ear. 'How's your dog?'

Mr Mulligan removed his pipe and smiled with slow benevolence. 'Oh foine, sorr, foine. Still womitin' a bit, but not bad.'

'Mr Farnon fixed him up, then?'

'Aye, gave him some more of the white medicine. It's wonderful stuff, sorr, wonderful stuff.'

'Good, good,' I said. 'He didn't find anything else when he examined him?'

Joe took another suck at his pipe. 'No he didn't now, he didn't. He's a clever man, Mr Farnon – I've niver seen a man work as fast, no I haven't.'

'What do you mean?'

'Well now he saw all he wanted in tree seconds, so he did.'

I was mystified. 'Three seconds?'

'Yes,' said Mr Mulligan firmly. 'Not a moment more.'

'Amazing. What happened?'

Joe tapped out his pipe on his heel and without haste took out a knife and began to carve a refill from an evil looking coil of black twist. 'Well now I'll tell ye. Mr Farnon is a man who moves awful sudden, and that night he banged on our front door and jumped into the room.' (I knew those cottages. There was no hall or lobby – you walked straight from the street into the living room.) 'And as he came in he was pullin' his thermometer out of its case. Well now Clancy was lyin' by the fire and he rose up in a flash and he gave a bit of a wuff, so he did.'

'A bit of a wuff, eh?' I could imagine the hairy monster leaping up and baying into Siegfried's face. I could see the gaping jaws, the gleaming teeth.

'Aye, just a bit of a wuff. Well, Mr Farnon just put the thermometer straight back in its case, turned round and went out the door.'

'Didn't he say anything?' I asked.

'No, divil a word. Just turned about like a soldier and marched out the door, so he did.'

It sounded authentic. Siegfried was a man of instant decision. I put my hand out to pat Clancy but something in his eyes made me change my mind.

'Well, I'm glad he's better,' I shouted.

The old man ignited his pipe with an ancient brass lighter, puffed a cloud of choking blue smoke into my face and tapped a little metal lid on the bowl. 'Aye, Mr Farnon sent round a big bottle of the white stuff and it's done 'im good. Mind yous,' he gave a beatific smile, 'Clancy's allus been one for the womitin', so he has.'

Nothing more was said about the big dog for over a week, but Siegfried's professional conscience must have been niggling at him because he came into the dispensary one afternoon when Tristan and I were busy at the tasks which have passed into history – making up fever drinks, stomach powders, boric acid pessaries. He was elaborately casual.

'Oh by the way, I dropped a note to Joe Mulligan. I'm not entirely convinced that we have adequately explored the causes of his dog's symptoms. This womiting . . . er, vomiting is almost certainly due to depraved appetite but I just want to make sure. So I have asked him to bring him round tomorrow afternoon between two and two thirty when we'll all be here.'

No cries of joy greeted his statement, so he continued. 'I suppose you could say that this dog is to some degree a difficult animal and I think we should plan accordingly.' He turned to me. 'James, when he arrives you get hold of his back end, will you?'

'Right,' I replied without enthusiasm.

He faced his brother. 'And you, Tristan, can deal with the head. O.K.?'

'Fine, fine,' Tristan muttered, his face expressionless.

His brother continued, 'I suggest you get a good grip with your arms round his neck and I'll be ready to give him a shot of sedative.'

'Splendid, splendid,' said Tristan.

'Ah well, that's capital.' My partner rubbed his hands together. 'Once I get the dope into him the rest will be easy. I do like to satisfy my mind about these things.'

It was a typical Dales practice at Darrowby; mainly large animals and we didn't have packed waiting rooms at surgery times. But on the following afternoon we had nobody in at all, and it added to the tension of waiting. The three of us mooched about the office, making aimless conversation, glancing with studied carelessness into the front street, whistling little tunes to ourselves. By two twenty-five we had all fallen silent. Over the next five minutes we consulted our watches about every thirty seconds, then at exactly two thirty Siegfried spoke up.

'This is no damn good. I told Joe he had to be here before half past but he's taken not a bit of notice. He's always late and there doesn't seem to be any way to get him here on time.' He took a last look out of the window at the empty street. 'Right we're not waiting any longer. You and I, James, have got that colt to cut and you, Tristan, have to see that beast of Wilson's. So let's be off.'

Up till then, Laurel and Hardy were the only people I had ever seen getting jammed together in doorways but there was a moment when the three of us gave a passable imitation of the famous comics as we all fought our way into the passage at the same time. Within seconds we were in the street and Tristan was roaring off in a cloud of exhaust smoke. My colleague and I proceeded almost as rapidly in the opposite direction.

At the end of Trengate we turned into the market place and I looked around in vain for signs of Mr Mulligan. It wasn't until we had reached the outskirts of the town that we saw him. He had just left his house and was pacing along under a moving pall of blue smoke with Clancy as always bringing up the rear.

'There he is!' Siegfried exclaimed. 'Would you believe it? At the rate he's going he'll get to the surgery around three o'clock. Well we won't be there and it's his own fault.' He looked at the great curly-coated animal tripping along, a picture of health and energy. 'Well, I suppose we'd have been wasting our time examining that dog in any case. There's nothing really wrong with him.'

For a moment he paused, lost in thought, then he turned to me.

'He does look pretty lively, doesn't he?'

Natuk

Experiences in the life of Dr H. G. Esmonde,
told by
MAJOR GEORGE BRUCE

[Maga, February, 1944.]

Most people know something of the North-west Mounted Police. Novels and films have made them familiar with the dashing horsemen in red coats and Stetson hats. But not everyone realizes that in the Far North of Canada the dashing horseman does not exist. On rare occasions of ceremony at some big post, we of the Mounted Police might turn out in boots and spurs; but our ordinary work in those latitudes was done in summer by canoe or on foot, in winter by dog-team sledge.

North of Lat. 60° the country could never have been opened up by white men, had it not been for that splendid creature the husky, who is just the timber-wolf, domesticated for ages by the Eskimo and the Indian. Fitted by nature to live under conditions of severest hardship, few animals, if any, can match him in courage and endurance. It is no exaggeration to say that Canada owes more to the husky dog than to any man in her history. And I myself owe my life to the best husky I ever owned.

I was on the Porcupine River, some fifty miles north of Rat

Lake, well on the cool side of the Arctic Circle, but just then we were having our short hot summer. The day temperature often rose to 80°, and in the evenings there seemed to be more mosquitoes than fresh air. My cabin stood by a small lake from which a stream ran down to the river, among low hills covered with spruce forest. I spent many hours roaming through that forest, or sitting still, watching the wild life that filled it. Among bracken and brambles, fallen trees and branches, it was easy to find a hiding-place from which one could see all round. There was plenty to see, if a man stayed quiet and kept his eyes open: birds of many sorts, foxes, martens, squirrels, mink, the friendly little chipmunks, perhaps a deer, perhaps a she-wolf with a small cub, a lumbering bear in search of food, or a porcupine stripping the rough outer bark from a sapling spruce, to feed on the succulent inner skin.

One day I had been for a long walk through the woods and was on my way back when I came upon a wolverine trap. It had been sprung, and in it, lying dead, was a beautiful husky bitch. She must have run away from some Indian camp, the call of her wolf ancestors in her blood, and taken to the woods.

The trap had been set for wolves or wolverines, pestilent brutes both, and it was clearly right that I should set it again. I forced down the spring till I could open the powerful spiked jaws, and was pulling out the dead husky when I heard a whimper. Out from under the body crawled a little pup, only a few weeks old. I tucked him into the breast of my coat and re-set the trap, after which I skinned the husky, thinking that her pelt would make a good rug for my cabin, and then started for home.

My dogs were tied up, but when I put the pup down and began to open the cabin door they evidently scented him, and a savage growl arose, a growl that told of their smelling possible food. The pup sensed danger and huddled close to my feet as I entered the cabin.

I fed him on condensed milk till he was old enough to eat solid food, and at night he would curl into my bunk with me. Before long he would follow me everywhere unless I had to go out for the day, when he would settle down on the rug beside my bed, the rug I had made out of his mother's skin. Evidently he found some friendly influence in it; for while I was away he would lie there quite happy and never move.

After the first week I introduced him formally to the sledge dogs. They sniffed him over, each in turn, and then accepted him as a regular member of the household. Soon he would take all manner of liberties with them, usually borne with amused tolerance, but if he went too far – if, for example, he tugged too vigorously with his sharp little teeth at a big dog's ear – a growl and a warning snap of teeth would follow. The pup would flee in any direction and lie low till the atmosphere cleared, when he would come back and play more gently.

My team leader especially became very attached to the youngster. When I took the sledge out I would put the pup on top of the load, and the team leader soon recognized this as part of the regular routine. Before starting he would look round to see that the pup was on the load. If he was not, no shouts or whip-cracks would induce the leader to start till the pup was duly installed in his proper place.

From the first I decided that he was not to be a sledge dog, but was to be my personal companion; and a splendid companion he proved. He came with me on all my rambles through the woods, and if I was looking for meat he would put up rabbits for me to shoot. I soon trained him not to chase them, and as his intelligence developed I taught him many things. I would leave some article on the doorstep and send him back to fetch it, till he would do so from a long distance. Later I would give him something, a glove or mitten perhaps, sending him home to leave it on the doorstep and return.

Perhaps because he was never treated as harshly as one has to treat sledge dogs, he showed a sensitive nature such as I have known in no other husky. I never once had to beat him: a tap of my fingers on his nose was the utmost correction he needed, and he would look up with a pathetic expression as much as to say, 'What have I done wrong?' As a watch-dog he was unsurpassed.

No stranger could approach the cabin unless I introduced him, when the dog would sniff him all over with a low throaty growl, and would never fail to know him if he came again.

By the time he had grown to his full size, a magnificent dog, we were inseparable companions. He would hardly let me out of his sight: wherever I went he followed close at my heels. I called him 'Natuk', which in the West Eskimo language means 'shadow'. We lived alone, far from any human society, and our comradeship grew closer and closer as time went on, till I used to feel that he knew exactly what I was thinking about.

A handsome animal was Natuk, about thirty inches at the shoulder and weighing close on nine stone. His colour was that of a sable collie, but a few shades lighter, with dark tips to the long hair, especially on his flanks, while his broad chest was almost white. Probably his sire was a timber-wolf, for he had the true wolf head with sharp prick-ears, though a white blaze on his face suggested a strain of Newfoundland in his dam, which may have accounted for his weight and strength. His bushy tail was carried in proper husky style, close-curled over his back.

My position in the Mounted Police was officially that of doctor, but in that sparsely populated region the calls for medical or surgical help were few, and unofficially I did a good deal of regular police work, especially in the matter of keeping an eye on any strangers who might drift into the country, and finding out all about them. Some fifty miles away lived a friend of mine, a Dogrib Indian, whom I found very useful in getting me information of this kind, information which I passed on to the proper quarter.

Early in October a rumour reached me of two newcomers to the district who did not sound desirable visitors. I decided to look up my Indian friend and see what he could tell me about them. The first snow had already fallen, and as usual, before the weather grows really cold, it was soft and yielding. Snow of that kind makes bad travelling for a dog sledge, and fifty miles being a short journey as we reckon things in the North, I planned to do it on foot, pulling a light toboggan with the few things I needed –

rifle, blankets, grub, and a small shelter-tent. Natuk, of course, would come with me, and my Indian chore-boy would look after the sledge dogs till my return.

Above twenty-five miles out, half-way to my destination, was the cabin of my nearest neighbour, a Swedish trapper and a good friend of mine. Ole Oleson was a man with more education than the average trapper, and a better philosophy of life. In the spring, when he took his winter's harvest of furs to the trading-post, instead of spending the proceeds in a riotous orgy he would bank most of the money and come back to the North to earn more. He was now a well-to-do man. His cabin was comfortable beyond the ordinary standard; he was intelligent and a good talker, and I always enjoyed an evening with him.

Starting early, Natuk and I made Ole's cabin late in the afternoon. We had a hearty welcome from the trapper, and spent a pleasant evening. Next morning after breakfast I began to pack my gear on the toboggan, when Ole begged me not to go.

'There's a blizzard coming,' he said. 'Stop here today, and you can go when it has blown over.'

Ole was an experienced backwoodsman, but so was I, having been born and brought up in that country. I looked at the sky and could see no sign of an approaching storm.

'I reckon you're wrong, Ole,' I said.

'I'm not,' said he. 'It's sure coming. I can smell it.'

I did not believe him, and I said so. I was anxious to push on, as I felt it was important to see the Indian and lay him on to those two strangers before they could start any funny business. But Ole insisted, and the end of it was that we lit our pipes and sat talking and smoking till well after mid-day. Then I decided that I could delay no longer, so I finished packing the toboggan and said –

'Well, Ole, if I *do* get into a jam, I'll send Natuk back to you and he'll guide you to wherever I happen to be.'

Natuk and I set out, taking a trail that led through the upper hills where the spruce forest was thin and open. The sun went down about three o'clock, and with its setting a wind sprang up, growing rapidly stronger. I began to think that Ole might be right about the blizzard, and turned downhill towards the thick spruce in the valley, which would give some shelter. I was going as fast as I could when suddenly the ground gave way under my feet, and dropped into space. Throwing out my hands instinctively to save myself, I let go the rope, and the toboggan skidded away among the trees.

In a moment I realized what had happened. I had fallen into an Indian bear-trap, scores of which were to be found in these hills. A wide pit is dug, about eight feet deep, one or more pointed stakes fixed in the bottom, the top crossed by stretchers of young saplings, over which is laid a cover of small branches and brushwood. The snow had hidden the trap effectively, and I had walked straight into it.

Not having the weight or bulk of a bear, I had not gone to the bottom. I was caught round the waist by a mass of jagged sticks, the upper part of my body free, but on kicking about to try for some foothold I found that the pit was full of brambles and dead twigs that had fallen through the cover. This meant that the trap was an old one, perhaps several years old.

That set me thinking. Probably the stretchers covering the trap were pretty rotten. If I struggled too violently, the whole thing might collapse and land me at the bottom of the pit, where the pointed hardwood stakes might still be sound enough and sharp enough to impale me. Even if they were not, it would be impossible to climb out, and I should starve to death miserably in that tangle of dead sticks and brambles.

Cautiously I tried to work my way out of the raffle of spiky branches that gripped me, but in vain. I had no foothold to give me a purchase, and my efforts only resulted in my sinking a few inches lower. The wind was blowing a gale now, and I could hear dead trees falling far and near. Suddenly a sharp crack sounded close by. A dead spruce, split by the frost of some previous winter, broke off, the whole top of one half falling across the bear-trap and pinning me down. I was not much hurt, but only my right arm remained free: my left arm and my body were held as in a vice among the network of broken boughs and débris.

All this time Natuk had been jumping round me, scratching in the snow, trying to dig me out, and pulling at sticks with his teeth. Several times he broke through the top crust, but having four legs he was able to scramble out. Now that I was helplessly pinioned, it flashed into my mind that he might really be able to assist me. I had said in joke to Ole that if I got into a jam I would send Natuk to fetch him. That joke could be turned into reality if Natuk was as clever as I believed him to be.

When I came in from a journey I would often get him to pull off my big moose-hide mittens, and now I called him, holding out my free right hand till he caught the end of the mitten in his teeth. As he pulled if off I said, 'Take it back and get help, Natuk!' waving my hand in the direction of Ole's cabin. Natuk looked at me as if trying to grasp what I was saying; then, as I repeated the order and pointed to the way, he seemed to catch the idea. With one snap he gripped the mitten firmly in his mouth and set off at a loping wolf-canter on the line that I had given him.

There I was, left all alone, with plenty of time to think things over. I began to calculate when I might expect help to come. We had covered about ten miles when I turned off the trail. With the wild animal's instinct for short-cuts, Natuk should bring that down to seven miles at most, and could do that in an hour. It should not take Ole more than an hour and a half to harness up his dog-team and come out. So in two hours and a half, three hours at most, I might expect to be released.

The wind dropped as quickly as it had risen, and in an hour's time the air was again perfectly still. Not a sound of any kind in the woods, only the dead silence of an Arctic winter night. Though there was no moon it was by no means dark, as the brilliance of the stars in that clear air, refracted from the snow, gives light enough to see things fairly well at a short distance.

In my constrained position, half lying with my feet unsupported, I grew very stiff and cold, especially my right arm. When the tree fell I had thrown it up to guard my head, with the result

'Take it back and get help, Natuk!'

that a forked branch had trapped it so that I could not bring my hand lower than my shoulder. Now that the heavy moose-hide mitten was gone, I had no protection for that hand but the woollen inner mitten. Lucky for me that the wind had dropped, or I should have been frost-bitten. Round me was a cage of bare branches; in front of me the long split trunk of the spruce, its flat upper side showing white in the starlight.

Slowly the time crawled on, while I tried to picture my dog racing through the woods to the trapper's cabin; Ole's face when he saw him; the hurried harnessing of the dog-team to the sledge and the Swede dashing along the trail; Natuk, ahead of the team, going all out to bring help to his master and friend.

Then through the profound silence of the winter woods rang a blood-freezing cry, the howl of a lone wolf. There is a difference between the howl of a wolf that leads a pack, on first scenting his quarry, and that leads a pack, on first scenting his quarry, and that of a solitary beast, the ex-leader of a pack, driven from his position by a younger and stronger rival. The difference is not to be described in words, but the lone wolf's howl has an indefinable quality which a trained ear cannot mistake, an aggressive and defiant note, as if voicing the bitterness that rankles in the heart of the deposed leader. That sense of defeat, joined to the craft and cunning which years of leadership have given him, makes the lone wolf the most dangerous beast in all the North.

I could hear that cry now, its low cadence gradually working up to the full-throated howl, then dying away. A long pause, ten minutes at least, and it came again, this time nearer and louder. Once more it sounded, nearer still, and then the deep silence of the night. I listened with every nerve strung. Was it my scent that the hunter had winded, or that of some night-roaming animal?

Near the butt of the fallen spruce I suddenly saw two points of green light. They moved forward, and behind them I could just make out a ghostly form creeping along the tree-trunk. I shouted, and the brute backed away; but before long he crept forward again. Again I shouted, and again, and each time he drew back. Once or twice he disappeared for a short time, but returned. I kept on shouting till my voice dropped to a hoarse croak. The wolf grew bolder, and came on slowly till he was no more than ten or twelve feet away.

In spite of the peril of my position I could not help feeling the grim humour of it. Here was I, a grown man in full health and strength, at the mercy of a beast not half my size. Born and reared in these northern forests, trained from childhood in all the woodcraft and hunting lore of the Indians, I felt that the rawest tenderfoot could not have got himself into a worse mess. My revolver, a Colt's .45, capable of killing six wolves in ten seconds, hung from my belt fully loaded. But I could not get either hand down to draw it, and the wolf was master of the situation. The thing was just absurd.

Absurd or not, however, I must do what I could while any hope remained. Indian hunters had often told me that a wolf will never attack so long as a man keeps up some rhythmic motion. I began to wave my right hand in a measured swing from side to side, and I could see the wolf's head and eyes following the movement. He stood there half crouched, a lean hungry-looking brute, saliva dripping from his jaws, and those baleful green eyes glowing dimly in the starlight; but he came no nearer. I was numb with cold, and my arm grew so weary with the steady movement that I began to wonder how long I could keep it up. The chill of utter exhaustion was creeping over me. Soon I should be unable to swing my hand any more, and then . . .

Three shots rang out – distant, but clear in the still night air. Ole was firing to signal his coming. A rush of hope surged through me, lending a momentary spasm of energy to my weary arm. But the sound of those shots seemed to rouse the wolf from his inaction, as if he felt that his time was short and that he must get to work. With fangs bared he began to creep nearer. My strength was almost gone; another moment and those fangs would be in my throat.

A heavy body hurtled through the air. Natuk, his teeth buried in the wolf's shoulder, flung him off the tree, and the two were locked in a fierce grapple in the hollow of the bear-trap. The snow flew in showers as the fight maddened to fury. Both fought mute after the manner of wolves, not a sound but the snap and slash of teeth and the dull rip of skin and flesh. If ever I prayed in my life, I prayed in those moments that my dog might win.

The duel went on, fierce and deadly, both combatants fighting to kill. If Natuk was a shade the heavier, the wolf was an experienced brute that had fought his way to the head of the pack and kept his position for years by dint of ferocity and fangs. My vision was so cramped and their movements so quick that for a time I could not tell which was getting the better of it.

At length the wolf bounded out of the hollow on to the level ground. Natuk leaped after him, and the death-worry began again. I saw Natuk grip the wolf by the side of the neck and throw him clean over his back. Then I must have fainted, for I knew no more till I heard the crack of a pistol close at hand – Ole finishing off the wolf.

It seemed ages before Ole dragged me clear of the bear-trap. I was too spent to give him any help, and it needed all his great strength to pull me out. My first thought was to look at Natuk. He lay on the blood-soaked snow, hideously mauled, a mass of wounds. Both shoulders were torn to the bone, one ear was slashed off, his flank ripped open to the ribs, and the entrails sagging out. But his eyes spoke to me dumbly, and he tried to lick my hand.

We of the North have not much use for sentiment. Life is too hard and death too near at all times to encourage any soft-hearted emotions, and my bringing-up among the Indians had case-hardened my feelings since childhood. But the sight of my friend and comrade lying there in such agony brought me nearer to a breakdown than ever before or since. Yet the wolf was in a worse state, and it can hardly have needed Ole's bullet to give him the *coup de grâce*. Natuk was dying, but he had won the battle.

I knew too much of wounds to have any hope. The only

kindness I could show Natuk was to put him out of his pain. I drew my revolver, but the look in the dog's eyes was too much for me, and I dropped it back into the holster. 'Ole,' I said, 'I'll leave it to you to do him the good turn.'

Sick at heart, I crept away among the bushes, pulling my coat over my head, till through the heavy fur I heard a muffled report and knew that all was over. We put Natuk on the sledge, and next day I buried him in a clearing near the trapper's cabin, where the sun would shine upon his grave. At its head I placed a heavy wooden slab, and on it cut three words deeply with my knife –

NATUK MY SHADOW.

Montmorency

JEROME K. JEROME

Montmorency, the author's infamous fox terrier, goes along as mascot to his young master and two friends when they set off one summer in the 1880s on what has become an historic boat trip up the Thames.

To look at Montmorency you would imagine that he was an angel sent upon the earth, for some reason withheld from mankind, in the shape of a small fox-terrier. There is a sort of Oh-what-a-wicked-world-this-is-and-how-I-wish-I-could-do-something-to-make-it-better-and-nobler expression about Montmorency that has been known to bring the tears into the eyes of pious old ladies and gentlemen.

When first he came to live at my expense, I never thought I should be able to get him to stop long. I used to sit down and look at him, as he sat on the rug and looked up at me, and think: 'Oh, that dog will never live. He will be snatched up to the bright skies in a chariot, that is what will happen to him.'

But, when I had paid for about a dozen chickens that he had killed; and had dragged him, growling and kicking, by the scruff of the neck, out of a hundred and fourteen street fights; and had had a dead cat brought round for my inspection by an irate female, who called me a murderer; and had been summoned by the man next door but one for having a ferocious dog at large, that had kept him pinned up in his own tool-shed, afraid to venture his nose outside the door for over two hours on a cold night; and had learned that the gardener, unknown to myself, had won thirty shillings by backing him to kill rats against time, then I began to think that maybe they'd let him remain on earth for a bit longer, after all.

We got up tolerably early on the Monday morning at Marlow, and went for a bathe before breakfast; and, coming back, Montmorency made an awful ass of himself. The only subject on which Montmorency and I have any serious difference of opinion is cats. I like cats; Montmorency does not.

When I meet a cat, I say, 'Poor Pussy!' and stoop down and tickle the side of its head; and the cat sticks up its tail in a rigid, cast-iron manner, arches its back, and wipes its nose up against my trousers; and all is gentleness and peace. When Montmorency meets a cat, the whole street knows about it; and there is enough bad language wasted in ten seconds to last an ordinary respectable man all his life, with care.

I do not blame the dog (contenting myself, as a rule, with merely clouting his head or throwing stones at him), because I take it that it is his nature. Fox-terriers are born with about four times as much original sin in them as other dogs are, and it will take years and years of patient effort on the part of us Christians to bring about any appreciable reformation in the rowdiness of the fox-terrier nature.

I remember being in the lobby of the Haymarket Stores one day, and all round about me were dogs, waiting for the return of their owners, who were shopping inside. There were a mastiff, and one or two collies, and a St Bernard, a few retrievers and Newfoundlands, a boar-hound, a French poodle, with plenty of hair round its head, but mangy about the middle; a bulldog, a few Lowther Arcade sort of animals, about the size of rats, and a couple of Yorkshire tykes.

There they sat, patient, good, and thoughtful. A solemn

peacefulness seemed to reign in that lobby. An air of calmness and resignation – of gentle sadness pervaded the room.

Then a sweet young lady entered, leading a meek-looking fox-terrier, and left him, chained up there, between the bulldog and the poodle. He sat and looked about him for a minute. Then he cast up his eyes to the ceiling, and seemed, judging from his expression, to be thinking of his mother. Then he yawned. Then he looked round at the other dogs, all silent, grave, and dignified.

He looked at the bulldog, sleeping dreamlessly on his right. He looked at the poodle, erect and haughty, on his left. Then, without a word of warning, without the shadow of a provocation, he bit that poodle's near fore-leg, and a yelp of agony rang through the quiet shades of that lobby.

The result of his first experiment seemed highly satisfactory to him, and he determined to go on and make things lively all round. He sprang over the poodle and vigorously attacked a collie, and the collie woke up, and immediately commenced a fierce and noisy contest with the poodle. Then Foxey came back to his own place, and caught the bulldog by the ear, and tried to throw him away; and the bulldog, a curiously impartial animal, went for everything he could reach, including the hall-porter, which gave that dear little terrier the opportunity to enjoy an uninterrupted fight of his own with an equally willing Yorkshire tyke.

Anyone who knows canine nature need hardly be told that, by this time, all the other dogs in the place were fighting as if their hearths and homes depended on the fray. The big dogs fought each other indiscriminately; and the little dogs fought among themselves, and filled up their spare time by biting the legs of the big dogs.

The whole lobby was a perfect pandemonium, and the din was terrific. A crowd assembled outside in the Haymarket, and asked if it was a vestry meeting; or, if not, who was being murdered, and why? Men came with poles and ropes, and tried to separate the dogs, and the police were sent for.

And in the midst of the riot that sweet young lady returned, and snatched up that sweet little dog of hers (he had laid the tyke up for a month, and had on the expression, now, of a new-born lamb) into her arms, and kissed him, and asked him if he was killed, and what those great nasty brutes of dogs had been doing to him; and he nestled up against her, and gazed up into her face with a look that seemed to say: 'Oh, I'm so glad you've come to take me away from this disgraceful scene!'

She said that the people at the Stores had no right to allow great savage things like those other dogs to be put with respectable people's dogs, and that she had a great mind to summon somebody.

Such is the nature of fox-terriers; and, therefore, I do not blame Montmorency for his tendency to row with cats; but he wished he had not given way to it that morning.

We were, as I have said, returning from a dip, and half-way up the High Street a cat darted out from one of the houses in front of us, and began to trot across the road. Montmorency gave a cry of joy – the cry of a stern warrior who sees his enemy given over to his hands – the sort of cry Cromwell might have uttered when the Scots came down the hill – and flew after his prey.

His victim was a large black Tom. I never saw a larger cat, nor a more disreputable-looking cat. It had lost half its tail, one of its ears, and a fairly appreciable proportion of its nose. It was a long, sinewy-looking animal. It had a calm, contented air about it.

Montmorency went for that poor cat at the rate of twenty miles an hour; but the cat did not hurry up – did not seem to have grasped the idea that its life was in danger. It trotted quietly on until its would-be assassin was within a yard of it, and then it turned round and sat down in the middle of the road, and looked at Montmorency with a gentle, inquiring expression, that said:

'Yes! You want me?'

Montmorency does not lack pluck; but there was something about the look of that cat that might have chilled the heart of the boldest dog. He stopped abruptly, and looked back at Tom.

Neither spoke; but the conversation that one could imagine

was clearly as follows:

The Cat: 'Can I do anything for you?

Montmorency: 'No – no, thanks.'

The Cat: 'Don't you mind speaking, if you really want anything, you know.'

Montmorency (*backing down the High Street*): 'Oh, no – not at all – certainly – don't you trouble. I – I am afraid I've made a mistake. I thought I knew you. Sorry I disturbed you.'

The Cat: 'Not at all – quite a pleasure. Sure you don't want anything, now?'

Montmorency: (*still backing*): 'Not at all, thanks – not at all – very kind of you. Good morning.'

The Cat: 'Good morning.'

Then the cat rose, and continued his trot; and Montmorency, fitting what he calls his tail carefully into its groove, came back to us, and took up an unimportant position in the rear.

To this day, if you say the word 'Cats!' to Montmorency, he will visibly shrink and look up piteously at you, as if to say:

'Please don't.'

The Partnership Begins

SHEILA HOCKEN

My first walk with Emma came that afternoon, and it was immediately evident why we had to have a month's training with the dogs. Although Emma took to me, and we got on well together, she would not do a thing I told her. She would obey no one but Brian. Attachment and obedience to me would clearly come only with training.

I put Emma's harness on, and we started off down a quiet road near the centre. Brian was standing next to us. He gave the command to go forward, but before he even got the '-ward' bit out we were off, several miles down the road it seemed, and I was galloping along, hanging on grimly to the harness.

'I'll never keep this up,' I managed to gasp.

'Oh, you'll soon get used to it,' said Brian. 'You'll get fitter as you go along. The trouble is you've been accustomed to walking so slowly.'

A guide-dog's pace apparently averages about four miles an hour. This compares with an ordinary sighted person's two to three miles an hour. So what kind of speed I used to achieve before, I have no idea, but it was obviously not competitive even with that of the snail population. At last I began to settle down to the fast rhythm, and was just beginning to think I might enjoy it after all, when, without any warning whatsoever, Emma stopped. I was off the pavement before I could pull up. Emma had sat down on the kerb, and I heard Brian laughing.

'Don't go without your dog, that's Lesson Number One,' Brian said. 'If you go sailing on when she stops at the kerb, you'll get run over. She stops, you stop.'

'Well, I didn't know she was going to stop, did I? And you didn't tell me.'

'No, you're right. But you've got to learn to follow your dog.'

Brian was about twenty-eight at the time, very pleasant and with a great sense of humour. I imagined him good-looking with fair hair and glasses. I liked him especially because he refused to make concessions to our blindness. He expected us to be independent. Rather than mop us up, and say, 'There, there,' when we fell off the kerb, he would turn it into a joke, which was the best medicine. At least it was for me. It certainly made me get up and think, 'Right. I'll show you who can be a good guide-dog owner.'

So on this occasion I got back behind Emma, took up the harness again, and said, 'What next?'

'You've got to cross this road. First you listen for any traffic. If it's quiet, you give Emma the command to go forward.'

When I could hear no traffic, this is what I did. But nothing happened.

Brian said, 'She knows that you're behind her and not me. You've got to encourage her, to make her want to take you over the road.'

'Good girl, Emma,' I said, 'there's a clever dog.' And after a little more of this persuasion, and the word 'Forward', thrown in from time to time, she finally took me across the road.

Crossing the road with a guide-dog is a matter of teamwork: whatever you do, you do it together. I have met sighted people with such weird ideas about this. Either they think the dogs are not very clever, but just wear the harness to show their owner is blind – a sort of plea for help – or they think the dogs are superhuman, and the blind people idiots who are being taken round for a walk rather as other people take their dogs. The importance of partnership, or even its existence, never seems to occur to most people. My job when crossing a road was to listen and Emma's was to look. Only when I could hear nothing should I give her the command to cross. But if I was wrong in my assessment of the traffic, and she could see something coming, she would wait until it was clear.

Guide-dogs are taught to stop and sit down at every kerb and wait for the next command. The four basic commands are, 'Right', 'Left', 'Back', and 'Forward'. And you have to position yourself with your dog so that you give her every opportunity to obey the right command. For instance, when the command to go forward is given, it is accompanied by an indication in that direction with the arm. It is also important to keep talking to the dog, and Brian reminded me of this on our first walk, just after we had crossed the road.

'Don't stop talking, or Emma'll think you've fallen asleep.'

'What do I say?' I asked rather stupidly.

'It doesn't matter, as long as you make it interesting. Tell her what you had for breakfast if you like.'

So there I was, galloping along a street in Leamington discussing bacon and eggs with a chocolate-coloured Labrador. Brian went on, 'You're working together, and if you stop talking, she'll stop working. You've got to keep her interest. She's a dog, and there are lots of nice, interesting smells all round, and things passing that you can't see. So unless you talk to her, she'll get distracted, and stop to sniff a lamp post.' I was quite hoarse by the time we had finished our first walk together.

I owe a great deal to Brian, not only for his training, but also for matching Emma and me together. His assessment of all he knew about us resulted in an inspired pairing, as time was to prove.

One day I remember asking him where Emma came from. What I really meant was, how did the centres come by the guide-dogs? Brian explained that they came to Leamington, or one of the other centres, after being puppy-walked. The Guide-Dog Association has a big breeding and puppy-walking centre at Tollgate House, near Warwick. They own a number of brood bitches and stud dogs that are let out to people as pets, because, naturally, a permanent kennel life is not desirable, and living with a family is a much happier arrangement. At the same time the Association controls which dog should mate with which. When the litters come along, it picks the dogs or bitches required for training. At about eight weeks old, a puppy undergoes various tests to see if it is basically bold and friendly, and capable of being trained as a guide-dog. Dogs bred in this way form about sixty per cent of the total, and there are now about two thousand guide-dog owners in the country. The remaining forty per cent come to the Association either by purchase or donation from breeders or private individuals. But the rejection rate is high. Dogs are kept on approval for about three weeks to see if they are suitable. If they're not, they're returned to their owners. In all cases the dogs chosen are usually female, because the male dog has a rather different outlook and nature, including a territorial instinct, and is not as tractable as the female, who in any case is spayed for the purposes of being a guide-dog. About seventy per cent of the breeds used are Labradors, like Emma – though I prefer to think she is unique, even among Labradors – and the remainder Alsatians, Collies, Golden Retrievers, and crosses from all of these.

Once the selection is made, the puppies go to people called puppy-walkers, who live around the training centres, and give homes to potential guide-dogs for about a year. In this time they have to teach the dog the basics. The dogs learn how to be well-mannered and clean in the house, to keep off furniture, not to beg for food, and to obey commands such as 'Sit', 'Stay', 'Down', 'Come', and so on. They are taught to walk on a lead, but not at heel, because of course they will eventually be required to walk in front of a blind man or woman. In general, the puppy-walkers are expected to take the dog everywhere with them, so that the dog is not shy of traffic, buses or trains, or the sort of sudden noises that sometimes occur in the street, such as pneumatic drills. They are also specifically instructed to take the dogs shopping. During this phase the puppy grows up and becomes used to urban life, and at the same time should remain bold and friendly.

At this point, Brian told me, they come to the centres for guiding training, which lasts about five months. The puppy-walkers do a wonderful job. I couldn't do it myself: have a dog for a year, then part with it; then have another, and see it go, and so on, and I really admire those who do so much to forge the first essential link between dog and blind person.

Naturally, when Brian told me all this, I wanted to know who had puppy-walked Emma, and he said, 'Someone called Paddy Wansborough. She's a marvellous woman. She's given nine or ten dogs to the Association after puppy-walking them. In fact, Emma wasn't bred by the Association. She was bought by Paddy as a puppy, given her basic year, and then donated to the Association.'

I determined that one of the first things I would do when I got home would be to contact Paddy Wansborough.

Next day, I was out with Emma again. As the training progressed I gradually got more used to her. We used a minibus to get us about Leamington, and this played a big part in the training, because it taught us how to use public transport. When we were on the bus and the dogs under the seats, I heard a great bellow from Brian, 'I can see two brown paws sticking out.' Brown paws, I thought, that must be Emma.

He went on, 'Do you want somebody to stand on her?'

'No, of course I don't.'

'Well, do something about it.'

I began to wonder if my first impressions of Brian had been wrong. But though he was shouting at me a lot, he must have guessed what I was thinking.

'No one else is going to tell you these things, Sheila. If you don't learn here, Emma'll be the one that suffers, not you.'

My trust in Emma grew daily, but I really knew she had

transferred her affections from Brian to me on about the tenth day of my stay at the centre. Up to then, she had always slept until morning in her dog-bed on the other side of the room. But on this particular evening, she refused to go to her bed. Instead, she curled up on the floor as near to my pillow as she could get. I felt then that we had made it. We were a team, each needing the other's company. I woke the following morning with an odd sensation. It felt as if there were a steamroller on my chest. Emma was sitting on top of me, pushing with her nose, telling me, I have no doubt at all, that it was time for us both to get up. She was full of life and exuberance, and could not wait to start the day. When I did get up, I could hear her shake herself in anticipation, and stand wagging her tail near the door.

One of the centre's ingenious ways of familiarizing us with the day's programme was by using tactile maps. Pavements, buildings, and so on were raised on a wooden map of Leamington, so we could feel our way over the routes beforehand, right down to the zebra crossings and the bus stops. Emma would find these things for me, but I had to be in the right road, and the map helped enormously to make sure we did not miss our way. Our walks became more and more complicated, and Brian would try to find places where there were road works, to ensure we had mastered the business of getting round them, as well as other obstacles. Bus trips and shopping expeditions were also in the curriculum, and I really enjoyed shopping with Emma. She would not only find the shop, but also take me up to the counter. I began to forget I was blind. No one fussed round me any longer. They were all too interested in Emma.

But things did not always go smoothly. I was not keen on the obstacle course we had to practise. Emma always reacted very quickly, and usually I was not fast enough to follow. She would see the obstacle, assess it, and take a snap decision which way to go. Before I knew what was happening she would have changed course to one side or the other, and I would be left in a trail of harness and confusion. Brian always seemed to be on hand when I made mistakes, even if I thought he was following some other student. I would suddenly hear a great shout; 'When your dog jumps, you jump.'

It was easier said than done. On occasions like this, Emma would lose confidence and sit down immediately. It was almost as if she were saying, 'It's no good me doing my bit, if all you can do is to trail behind and finish up in a heap.' Literally the only way I could get her back to work again was to apologize and promise to do better next time.

It was while we were doing the obstacle course that I learned one of Emma's aversions. It came to our turn and we were going through the obstacles fairly well. All at once Emma shot off like a rocket, and I felt myself being taken at right angles up a steep grass bank. As we went, I heard Brian hysterical with laughter. When we finally came to a stop, I said rather breathlessly, 'What was all that about? Whatever did she do that for?'

'Oh, it's Napoleon.'

'Napoleon? What do you mean, Napoleon?' I thought Brian had suddenly gone out of his mind.

'You know,' he said, 'the cat. Napoleon, the cat.'

'Oh,' I said. But I still did not know why Emma had shot up the bank.

Brian, still laughing, explained that Emma could not stand cats. She knew better than to chase them, but if she saw one, she would take off in the opposite direction – the opposite direction in this case having been the steep grassy bank. Still, Brian did congratulate me on my alacrity and speed in following, and promised to keep us in mind if there was ever a guide-dog expedition to Everest. At the same time, I thought that the only way to cure Emma of her dislike of cats would be to get one, and I put that on my list of resolutions for when I got home.

That evening as we were sitting in the lounge, Brian came in and we laughed again about Emma and the cat. Then I asked him something that fascinated me more and more the longer the course went on. How did they train dogs to accomplish the amazing things they did for us? I knew a little about dog training from the experience I had had with them, but I could not fathom some of the dogs' abilities. After all, it is a fairly simple matter to train a dog to sit at a kerb every time, but how do you train them to disobey you? I asked Brian, 'For instance, I told Emma to go forward yesterday, when I hadn't heard a car coming, and she wouldn't go because she'd seen one. How on earth do you train them to do that?'

Brian replied, 'Once you've got a dog basically trained, and you're waiting to cross the road, you see a car coming and tell the dog to go forward. The dog, naturally, obeys immediately, but you don't move, and the car – other trainers drive them for these exercises – hoots, and makes a lot of noise, and the dog comes back on the pavement; by repetition of this sort of thing it is conditioned to associate the moving vehicle with danger, and therefore, despite all instinct to obey, refuses to move even when the command is given. Of course, only fairly intelligent dogs will respond like this, and that's why we have to be very stringent with our tests of character and aptitude to begin with.'

'What about obstacles?' I asked.

Brian explained that the principle behind teaching dogs not to walk their owners into obstacles was to get the dog to associate an obstacle with displeasure – to use a mild word – and also distress. A start is made with something simple such as a post. The dog walks the trainer into the post, is immediately stopped, the post is banged to draw attention to it, and the right way, allowing room, is shown. The next time a forceful 'NO' is shouted when the post is collided with, and the right way is shown again. So by repetition the dog eventually gets the message, and at the same time, the range of obstacles is extended to include the most frequent pavement obstacles of all, people.

It sounded simple in a way, but I knew a lot of hard work and talented training went into all this. The trainers, Brian told me, worked with a blindfold on when they considered the dogs had reached a certain standard of proficiency. They did this for about a fortnight to create real working conditions for the dogs, and give them confidence through working with someone they knew.

It was interesting to hear Brian explain it all, and particularly, in the light of what followed in the last stage of the course, the disobedience part. We were nearing the end of our month at Leamington, and went out once more in the mini-bus. Emma's paws, by now, were always well tucked away. Brian told us we were going to the railway station as a final test.

I have always loathed railway stations because of the noise, the hundred and one different obstacles, and the general sense of bustle which, if you are blind, is scaring. I got to dislike them so much I would never go into one, still less travel by train, even if there were a sighted person to take me. But Brian was adamant. 'Well, you know, you've got to get used to it. You might want to go by rail one day, or meet somebody off a train, and you've got Emma to guide you now. She knows her way around. There's nothing to it.'

I was not convinced. We got to the station, and I put Emma's harness on. Brian said, 'Right. I'll just go and park. You go in; Emma knows the way. I'll be with you in a minute or two.'

Emma took me through the doors, down a couple of flights of steps, in and out between people on the platform and sat down. I had no idea where I was. I just stood and waited for Brian. He was there within a couple of minutes. 'Right,' he said, 'Emma's sitting bang on the edge of the platform. There's about a six-foot drop in front of you to the railway line. Now tell her to go forward.'

I was petrified, and could feel my spine tingle. 'You must be joking,' I said.

'No, go on. Tell her to go forward.'

I stood there, not knowing what to do. This really was a terrible test. Dare I do it? I was so scared, I felt sick. In that moment I really did not want a guide-dog. Everything I had heard about them, all the training we had done, all I felt about Emma flashed through my mind, and it meant nothing. I just wanted, there and then, to lay the harness handle on Emma's back, and leave, get out, escape, anything. But, in a sort of hoarse whisper, I heard myself saying, 'Forward.'

Immediately, up she got, and almost in the same motion

pushed herself in front of my legs. Then she started pushing me back, right away from the edge of the platform.

I have never felt so ashamed in all my life. I felt about an inch tall. How could I possibly have been so doubting, so unworthy of Emma? I was utterly humiliated. Brian said, 'There you are. I told you Emma would look after you, whatever you do. Whatever you tell her to do, if there's any danger in front of you, she'll push you away.'

So that was it. We had made it. The sense of freedom was incredible. I got over my awful feelings of shame, because I sensed that Emma understood and forgave. That afternoon I walked with her down the Parade in Leamington, the busy main road, crowded with shoppers. I walked with a great big smile on my face, weaving in and out of all those people, and feeling: I don't care if you can *see* I'm blind. I can see too: I've got Emma, and she's all I need.

All too soon the day came when we were to go home, Emma and I. It was, oddly enough, very sad. It happened to be raining – pouring down – and the weather matched my mood. Even though I could not see the rain, I felt very grey and depressed. I hated the idea of having to leave the centre and all the friends I had made. Even more, I really did not want to go home, although I now had Emma, and kept trying to convince myself that things back in Nottingham were *bound* to be different. I was afraid that somehow I might be enveloped in the old ways again, despite Emma. I had not yet grasped to what an enormous extent she was about to change my life. I still had to learn to put my confidence in her.

Heavy with misgivings, I left Leamington with Emma on her harness beside me. The two of us arrived in Nottingham, were met and taken home. Once home, I let Emma off the lead and took off her harness: she went wild. Everyone was immediately taken with her. She bounded all over the place, through every room, round and round; I could hear her tearing about, sending rugs flying, stopping to sniff each chair and table leg. The air swished to the wagging of her tail, and resounded with her snortings and sniffings. This, she obviously realized, was where she was going to live. It was such a different Emma from the sober responsible animal on the harness, and for the first time I appreciated that there were two distinct sides to her character: one when she was working, and in charge of me, and the other when she was off the harness, totally joyous, full of fun and energy, and as far from any sense of responsibility as a clown. My misgivings began to evaporate.

That first night back, Emma slept at the bottom of the bed; she had decided that there was no other place good enough for her, and in the morning she woke me with her usual insistence. It struck me that this morning we were really starting a new life together. We would be going out into Nottingham on our own. I got out of bed and started dressing. This was not my usual form, because I'm normally a very slow, sleepy starter, but on this day of all days I could not wait to find out how Emma and I, put to the test, would get on together.

Over breakfast I decided we would go to visit some old friends, Norman and Yvonne, whom I hadn't seen recently and who lived quite near. In the decision itself lay the prospect of freedom. With Emma, I would be able to go all over Nottingham!

I had the directions worked out in my mind after a telephone consultation. They presented no problems: all I had to do was to go out of our front gate, tell Emma to turn right to the top of the road, a main road, turn right again, go straight to the bottom, turn left, and ask Emma to find the first gate. So, off we went.

Twenty minutes after setting out, we were standing in the porch of Norman and Yvonne's house, and I was feeling for the bell. We had done it. To anyone walking down that Nottingham street of detached houses, lined with trees and built in the 1920s, there may have appeared nothing out of the ordinary about a girl and a dog standing in a doorway waiting for the bell to be answered. But inside me was a huge sense of triumph: it was a milestone. 'Good girl, Emma,' I kept saying. I was so proud of her.

Norman and Yvonne were naturally delighted to see me, and they were even more thrilled to meet Emma. They made a great fuss of her. Several hours later we set off home, and found our way back to the main road. Then came a terrible realization. In my excitement that everything was going so well with Emma, I had forgotten to count how many intersections we had crossed. There had been no need to count on the way there because we went as far as the road went, up to a T-junction. But I should have counted for getting back. And I hadn't. So there I was with no idea where I should tell Emma to turn left. After a whole month of training, I had straightaway forgotten one of the cardinal principles: always count the roads as you go.

What could I do? I thought: Here I am, and there's no trainer to save me. Emma, all unknowing, was taking me along at her furious pace, and I felt as if I were in an endless race to nowhere. Not only that, but I felt I had let Emma down. I seemed alienated from her through my own eagerness and thoughtlessness; I was sure, too, that she would never commit a mistake that would put us both in jeopardy. Emma wasn't in the least daunted, however, and, ignoring my commands, started taking me down a side road. I tried to stop her. 'No, Emma. No! Go back, go back!' But she paid no attention. In turn, I dared not let go of her, so I had to follow. At last she turned left again, and sat down. Instinctively I put my hand out. I felt leaded-lights and painted wood with one or two blisters. It was my back door. If I had forgotten to count the roads on the way out, Emma certainly hadn't!

Not long after we were home from Leamington I wrote to Paddy Wansborough, the marvellous woman who had puppy-walked Emma. By 'wrote' I mean, technically speaking, that I sent a tape-recorded cassette to tell her how much Emma had come to mean to me, and to thank her for giving Emma as a guide-dog after puppy-walking her. That was the beginning of a correspondence by cassette, and of a friendship that continues to this day.

Through this correspondence I learned all sorts of little details about Emma. Paddy had her from the age of eight weeks, and she sent me a photograph taken at this time. Although I had to rely on other people's descriptions of the photograph it was splendid to have a picture of Emma as she was when she was first picked out of the litter to be a guide-dog. She was already eighteen months old when I first met her, so of course I missed all her puppy ways, but to hear Paddy describe them on cassette was the best possible substitute. She said that Emma had always seemed a busy dog, was interested from the beginning in doing things constructively, and always gave the impression of having something on her mind. This confirmed what I knew of her.

On one cassette Paddy told me a story that I possibly found more amusing than she had at the time. One day Paddy planted some hundred and fifty bulbs in her garden. She had then gone indoors, leaving Emma still playing on the lawn. After about half an hour, Emma came in looking extremely pleased with herself. When Paddy happened to look out of the window a moment or so later, she was confronted with a a huge pile of bulbs neatly stacked on the back doorstep. Emma had dug each one up with loving care and immense energy, and was thrilled to have been such a help in restoring them to their owner.

Before long, Paddy asked me to visit her in Yorkshire. They were having a small function to raise money for guide-dogs at a local fête and she rightly thought I would like to go with Emma. Through our cassette correspondence, I felt I already knew Paddy, but I wondered if Emma would remember her. As we got off the coach I heard Paddy's voice greeting us, 'Hello, Sheila. How are you?' And it was the signal for Emma to go wild. She leaped all over Paddy, but although she was delighted to see her again, she kept coming back to me as if to say, 'Well, I'm pleased to be here, but I haven't forgotten that I'm your dog.'

Emma and I started to go to work together as soon as we were settled again. At that time I lived in Carlton, on one side of Nottingham, and I worked right over the other side, the Bulwell side of the city. I had to catch two buses, with a walk across the Market Square in the middle of Nottingham in between. The terminus for the first bus was at the bottom of our road, so that part was easy. Emma trotted down the road with her tail in the air – I could feel it brushing my hand as we went along – and, at the same time, I began to learn how sensitive it was possible to be, via the harness, to what she was doing. Through it I could tell whether her ears were up or down, whether she was turning her head left or right, and all sorts of little movements.

We found the stop, and from that moment Emma loved going on buses. It was not just the bus itself, however. One important factor was the admiration she received that morning, and every time we got on a bus henceforth: 'Oh, what a lovely dog. Oh, what a beautiful colour.' And so on. I could sense Emma basking in the glory. She had picked the second seat on the right for me. For some reason, this was the place she always chose on this particular bus. I sat down, and Emma went under the seat. Strangely, this was the only bus on which she had such a preference: it always had to be the same one. After we had been going to work together for about three weeks, we were nearing the bus one morning when I began to pick up the sound of a great commotion going on inside it. As we came alongside I could hear a woman's muffled shout: 'You'll have to get up you know. You can't sit there, I tell you it's Emma's seat. Come on – they'll be here in a minute.'

On other buses, Emma simply went for any empty seat, preferably – in the winter at least – one near the heaters. But since we normally travelled in the rush-hour the buses, apart from our first one, were very often full, so she had to use a different technique. She would drag me along the aisle, nosing everyone else out of the way if there were standing passengers, decide on where she wanted to sit, then stare at whoever was sitting there until they gave way. To be fair, they normally gave the seat up very quickly, and before the bus was in an uproar. This, of course, appealed to the exhibitionist in Emma. When she was sure she had got her audience, she would turn to me, lay her head across my knee, looking, I imagined, specially devoted and possibly a little pathetic. By this time the entire bus was hers.

But to get back to that first morning. When I walked into the office there was a reception committee waiting. While everyone said 'Hello' to me, they were clearly more interested in seeing what Emma was like. Emma once again responded with great delight, and when I had taken her harness off, took it round, her tail wagging, to show everyone in turn.

So she was a hit straight away, and when the others had gone she inspected her basket, played for a while with a rubber toy I had brought with me to occupy her, then settled down. The telephone had already started going, and soon it was like old times – with the tremendous difference of that reassuring sleeping form under my desk. The morning went on, and in a lull, thinking what a good quiet dog Emma was being, I put my hand down to pat her head. But, where her head should have been, there was nothing. I felt round in a wider circle. Emma had disappeared! I immediately got up and went to feel if my office door was open; sure enough, it was. I called her. No response. All sorts of anxieties began to crowd in on me. Had she got out? What if she had gone into the street? What if she were lost . . . what . . . then I heard the sound of paws coming down the corridor. Thank goodness. In came Emma. 'Emma,' I said, 'where *have* you been?' Her reply was to push something into my lap. I did not want to believe my fingers. It was a purse. I was horrified. 'Emma! Where did you get that from?' Her reply this time was to do her tattoo bit, bouncing up and down on her forelegs, and swishing me furiously with her tail. The message was clear: 'How about that for brilliance! I've brought you somebody's purse.' Fleetingly, the thought of a four-legged Artful Dodger came to mind. I took the purse from her, and hoped that someone would come and claim it, and accept my excuses.

The owner concerned eventually found out what had happened, and came to claim the purse. But no one would believe that I had not taught Emma to perform the trick, which did nothing to ease my mind about the prospect of the afternoon, or indeed of continuing to work for Industrial Pumps. It was a relief to take Emma out of the office for a run in the local park. This was something I had decided I must do every day. Since she worked hard it was only fair that she should have a free run whenever possible.

I sat myself on a bench with my sandwiches, let her off the lead, and she went charging across the grass. I soon heard barking in the distance, and recognized Emma. But every so often she would come back to me, touch my hands with her nose, and then scamper off again. It was something that she never failed to do whenever we went to the park from then on. She was reassuring me: 'I'm here, and I haven't forgotten you.'

That afternoon I sat down at the switchboard, and, in between calls, waited uneasily for the sound of Emma bringing me another gift. But she settled down and slept, and after that did not bring any more presents – at least, not in the office. Perhaps it was her way of making a mark, and returning her welcome. Whatever it was, I was pleased it was over.

The first week went by very happily. Travelling to and from work, in fact, became easier every day. I did not have to give Emma all the lefts and rights in the Square because she soon began to take me straight to the right road and across to the forty-three bus stop. I started to appreciate, and this was something that established itself firmly as time went on, that Emma had only to take any route once and she knew it. I had no sooner discovered this than I found there was a drawback in having such an intelligent dog.

About the middle of the second week we set off for work as usual. I merely said to Emma that we were going to work, and, by now, knew she could do this without any corrections or promptings. We got our first bus, and reached the Market Square. Everything was fine. But when we got to the first road to cross in the Square, Emma sat down instead of going forward. I listened for traffic, and when I thought it was clear, told her to go forward. But she would not move. She simply continued to sit. I could not understand what was going on. I thought that perhaps I had misjudged the traffic, so when it was quiet I told her again. Still she would not go forward. Instead, she got up and turned right, and started taking me along the pavement. 'Emma,' I said, rather desperately, as I was being dragged along, 'where are you taking me? Where's the bus stop? Come on. Bus stop . . .' But no, she would not listen, or if she did listen she certainly did not take any notice. We went on, across a road, made a sharp left turn, and crossed another road. Then she sat down again. I had no idea where we were. I had completely lost my sense of direction and was utterly confused about the pattern I had to keep in my mind in order to reach the bus stop; this was the equivalent of the checks that sighted people, probably unconsciously, make when they are getting from A to B: right at St Mary's Church, past W. H. Smith's, left at the Royal Oak, and so on.

I was not only disappointed in Emma, but slightly upset and annoyed with her as well. 'Emma,' I said crossly, 'we shall be late for work.' How do you tell the boss that it was the dog who made you late? Thinking back, it must have looked a rather comic scene to anyone passing by. 'Excuse me,' I said as the next footsteps approached, 'can you tell me how to get to the forty-three bus stop, please?' There was a silence for a second or two, during which time I thought: they don't know, we really are lost. Then a man's voice, obviously puzzled, said, 'Forty-three bus stop? You're *at* the forty-three bus stop. Your dog's at the foot of the post.' I was relieved, astonished, and utterly baffled. We got on the bus when it came along, and I put the incident out of my mind. Until the following morning.

This time Emma went left instead of right, crossed another road, turned right, crossed a further road, walked along and sat down. We were at the forty-three bus stop again. I was unnerved, but by now getting used to the feeling. At work, I asked Carol, a friend who I knew came to the office via the Market Square, if there were any roadworks on the route I had originally mapped out. She said no, and no new buildings either, or any kind of obstruction.

I was totally at a loss. I thought and thought, and then the only possible explanation came to me: Emma, having learnt a route, became bored with having to follow it every day. So she invented variations. From then on she found a series of routes round the the Market Square quite independently of any guidance from me, and chose one of them every day. I soon became resigned to this and got up ten minutes earlier just to allow for Emma's possibly making a mistake. But, of course, she never did.

The Dogsbodies

KENNETH BIRD

Himself is a very unusual and enterprising dog who, unknown to most people, can understand and even talk in human speech. He leads a lively and varied existence, wandering round Ireland with his tinker master, Timothy Hogan, in an old caravan drawn by an extremely stubborn mule called Milligan.

It was the longest night Timothy could ever remember. An hour of it was spent stretching a tarpaulin over the top of the caravan to serve as a makeshift roof. The wind did everything in its power to thwart him, and he was nearly exhausted by the time he managed to secure the tarpaulin at the four corners.

'We can't spend another night like this,' Himself grumbled. 'You'll have to get a new roof as soon as 'tis light.'

'What am I supposed to use for money?' Timothy inquired bitterly. 'Isn't there less than two pounds in the kitty?'

'Then you will have to find a job.'

Jobs and money, as far as Himself was concerned, were as plentiful as buttercups in a meadow. He had never had any difficulty in raising thousands of pounds for Clongarrie Monastery when it was needed, so what was there to stop Timothy earning the pin-money for a new roof just as easily?

Alas, it was not as simple as that. Nobody seemed to want any pots and pans mended and jobs were hard to come by in this part of Ireland. Besides, thought Timothy, wouldn't it be more sensible to go to Clongarrie where my brother, Michael, will be only too pleased to look after us until I can afford to repair the roof?

An ideal solution, no doubt about that, yet Timothy knew he would be wasting words if he put it to Himself. Both he and Milligan would never dream of leaving their beloved Kerry until the cold breath of winter coated the caravan window with frost. What was more, they would oppose any attempt to do so by every means in their power.

'Sometimes life can be very hard,' sighed Timothy before dropping off to sleep.

Next morning he had more troubles to contend with. The gale had kept Milligan awake and he didn't take kindly to being backed between the shafts by his inconsiderate master. When, after a long struggle, Timothy finally got his own way, Milligan retaliated by refusing to budge an inch.

The battle had been fought many times before, and there was only one way round it. Timothy tied his last banana on the end of a stick and dangled it in front of Milligan's nose. The ruse worked, and ten minutes later the red and brown caravan was in the market square in Pollnooth. There, with steam rising from his flanks, Milligan was allowed to swallow the banana, skin and all.

'Let's look for a carpenter,' said Timothy to Himself.

They found one in a side street behind the church. Mr Murphy, a kindly man, agreed to put on a new roof for twenty-five pounds and to wait a week for Timothy to earn the money. But that was easier said than done.

The hotels in Pollnooth had all the waiters and odd-job men they needed. No drovers were wanted at the cattle market and the stationmaster had more than enough porters already. So, much against his will, Timothy took the only course left open to him – he wrote to his brother, Michael the monk, warning him that he might soon be needing a loan of twenty-five pounds.

Then he looked around for Himself. But his pet was nowhere to be seen. 'I'll bet he's job-hunting,' said Timothy with a wry grin. 'Sure, and he has never trusted me to find work on my own. He'll scour the town till dusk, then home he'll come with his head full of wild tales about millionaires looking for butlers and ship-owners crying out for captains.'

In one way Timothy was right – Himself *was* job-hunting, or at least he had been until a hullabaloo in Pollnooth Stadium attracted his attention. He put his head on one side and listened to the hoarse cries coming from the building.

'Go on, O'Dowd, kill the Crusher!'

'That's it, O'Dowd, massacre the spalpeen!'

Kill! Massacre! What on earth was going on in there? At that moment somebody opened a door and the noise became deafening. Himself wriggled between someone's legs and went inside.

At first all he could see were rows of people with their backs to him. Some screamed and shook their fists, others had their hands over their faces as though they could not bear to watch what was going on.

Well, what *was* going on?

Himself ventured along a broad aisle until he had a view of a raised platform surrounded by ropes. Inside the ropes were two men wearing only shorts. A fair-haired man lay on his face; the other, a monster with black hair on his chin and none on his head, seemed to be trying to tie his companion's arms and legs into fancy knots.

'Isn't the Kerry Crusher the dirtiest fighter in all Ireland?' a woman howled and she shook her brolly at the bearded wrestler.

'Get up, O'Dowd, and tear him apart!' roared someone else.

But O'Dowd had had enough. To the disappointment of the crowd he begged the referee to stop the contest while his arms and legs were still in one piece.

The referee obliged. O'Dowd scrambled to his feet and limped back to his corner. The Crusher strutted around the ring snarling defiance at those who were booing him.

'Stop your noise!' he thundered, and the hubbub died down a little. 'If you're so brave, why doesn't one of ye come into the ring and take me on, eh? Five hundred pounds of my own money is waiting for the fellow who can prove himself a better wrestler than myself.'

Nobody accepted his challenge. Himself heard somebody whisper that no living soul would stand a chance against the Kerry Crusher. Hadn't he the strength of a wild bull and wasn't the referee a friend of his and always ready to turn a blind eye to the Crusher's dirty tricks?

That was the end of the wrestling. Doors opened, people started to go home. Himself fought his way through a forest of legs until he reached the street.

'Shame on people for watching such a disgraceful spectacle,' he muttered. 'Haven't they anything better to do with their time?'

He resumed his search for a job for Timothy, stopping every now and then to listen to what passers-by were saying. After all, he reasoned, if you don't listen you don't find out. And sooner or later wasn't someone bound to say how badly he was needing an ostler, a gardener or a hotel waiter?

Tonight, however, his luck seemed to be out. The sole topic of conversation seemed to be the wicked ways of the Kerry Crusher, and Himself was soon sick of hearing the man's name.

He was on the point of giving up when he spotted a large building at the end of a narrow, cobbled street. It was like dozens of other buildings in Pollnooth, except for one thing – the door was wide open.

Jobs, he mused, are to be found in the most unlikely places, and that's an unlikely place if ever I've seen one. Timothy, of course, would pass it by without a second glance, but that's where he differs from me. I'm a persistent dog; I go where humans fear to tread and I won't take no for an answer.

Himself climbed two steps and trotted into a hall ablaze with lights. So dazzling were the lamps in the ceiling that he couldn't see whether the place was empty or full of people. All he heard was a foot tapping on the floor and somebody saying: 'A-one, a-two, a-three . . .'

What happened next gave Himself the shock of his life. A tidal wave of music suddenly engulfed him. It seemed to come up from the floor, down from the ceiling, in through the walls – a mixture of jungle drums, yelling tribesmen, twanging telephone wires and a church organ with a sore throat.

Himself shrank back in horror. He caught a glimpse of faces festooned in hair, of guitars flashing like the sequins on a circus girl's gown. Then he turned and fled from the torrent of sound which battered his ears.

The door slammed as he reached it. Himself scratched the woodwork and whimpered. He tried to fasten his teeth around the door handle. All in vain. He, a life-long hater of music, was trapped in a hall full of mad musicians.

Opening his mouth, he gave vent to his feelings.

'Woooooh!' howled Himself.

In the past his mournful wail had surprised many people, simply because they could not believe that such a small animal could make such a loud noise. But tonight it passed unnoticed, drowned by music which went on and on as though nothing short of an earthquake could stop it.

The Blast-Offs – for they were the ones rehearsing in the parish hall – strummed their guitars and thumped their drums till the windows rattled protestingly. Then, to add to Himself's anguish, Hoppy began singing a solo.

'I'm going to write myself a letter . . .'

'Weeeeeooooh!' howled Himself.

'Mebbe make myself feel better . . .'

'Wooooohoooooeeee!'

He made his mark at last. The music began to die away. Hoppy, Little Lemon, Windy and Stix stared wide-eyed at the intruder. Each was thinking the same thing – that a new sound, the one Plunk and the world were waiting for, had just exploded into their music like a bombshell. A sound so way-out, so different, that it would take the fans by storm.

'Man, it's worked!' Little Lemon exclaimed. 'The four-leaf

clover has delivered the goods.'

'A groovey dog that understands music!' gasped Hoppy, and he tossed his hair back from his eyes so as to get an uninterrupted view of the creature who was about to turn the bitter dregs of failure into success.

'He's a natural,' Windy agreed. 'Smack on the beat he was. With that dog we'll be top of the charts by the autumn.'

Himself could make no sense of their gibberish. Now he was more certain than ever that he had strayed into an asylum for musicians who had been driven mad by the sound of their own music.

'The Dogsbodies!' Stix spoke so rarely that his companions stared at him in surprise.

'Did you say something, Stix?'

'The Dogsbodies,' Stix repeated. 'A new name for the four of us and the dog.'

'Man, that's just great!' the others chorused jubilantly. 'The Blast-Offs are dead and buried. Long live The Dogsbodies!'

The young men slapped each other on the back and rubbed their hands. Himself watched in growing alarm. Suddenly Hoppy frowned.

'Not so fast,' he said. 'Suppose the dog belongs to somebody. We can't just steal him.'

Little Lemon was quick to point out that the dog had no collar. Didn't that prove he was a stray and wouldn't they be doing him a favour by giving him a home?

'We'll do more than give him a home,' laughed Windy. 'Man, we're going to turn that pooch into a star.'

Himself bared his teeth as the four young men moved towards him. Perhaps they weren't musicians at all, but *magicians*. After all, nobody but a magician could transform a dog into a twinkling star. Well, he would fight like a tiger rather than let them cast a spell on him.

'Grrrr,' he growled.

'Leave him to me.' Little Lemon, the practical member of the group, took command. Picking up a rug, he threw it over

'A groovey dog that understands music!' gasped Hoppy

Himself's head. Then, with help from the others, he wound the rug around his captive until he was like a hot dog trapped inside a bread roll.

'He's ours!' Windy cried triumphantly. 'Now we've got to put him on the road to fame and fortune.'

Timothy was worried. The church clock had long since chimed ten and still his pet had not returned to the caravan. That he should have gone for a walk on his own was not surprising; that he should stay away for two hours most certainly was. Few things in a town interested him, apart from lamp-posts and dustbins, and he soon tired of those.

So what was keeping him? Or was he being kept against his will?

In the past Himself had been kidnapped several times by men who scented a fortune in a dog with a human tongue. Timothy tried to quieten his forebodings with the thought that nobody in Pollnooth knew Himself could talk and that his dog had learnt from harsh experience never to speak in front of strangers. Sure, but suppose he had had the ill luck to meet Charles Egan or Thomas Doyle...?

Timothy buttoned up his green tinker's jacket and went out into the cool night air. Hadn't Egan, the ringmaster, vowed that one day he would have the World's Only Talking Dog in his circus? And wouldn't Doyle, the animal trainer who had taught Himself to talk, do anything to recover his brightest pupil?

Himself was nowhere to be seen in the main street, nor was he foraging in dustbins outside Pollnooth Stadium. Timothy asked a passer-by if he had seen a white terrier with a black patch over one eye.

''Tis strange ye should be mentioning it,' the man replied. 'For didn't I notice such a creature at the wrestling?'

'The wrestling!' cried Timothy in astonishment.

'Watching the Kerry Crusher he was, and looking as disgusted as the rest of us. Ah, Mister, 'twas a shameful spectacle to be sure. The Crusher up to all his usual dirty tricks, kicking, gouging, biting and . . .'

Timothy thanked the man, made an excuse, and continued on his way. What, he wondered, had prompted Himself to go to a wrestling match?

He looked anxiously up and down the street. Four young men with long hair came out of a hall and slammed the door behind them. One of them carried a rolled-up rug under his arm. Nothing suspicious in that. Timothy listened to their footsteps dying away. Then, just before they turned a corner, one of them spoke, and the breeze carried his words to the little tinker.

'Where is he going to sleep tonight? Shan't we be thrown out of our digs if Mother Murphy sees him?'

'He'll be just great under my bed, man.'

'What if he barks?'

Barks! Timothy sprinted after the four young men and their innocent looking bundle. Turning a corner, he found himself in a square in front of the church. People were pouring out of a cinema and cars were reversing and backfiring. There was no sign of the kidnappers.

Timothy ran this way and that, peering into the shadows. Then he stopped an old woman and asked her if she knew where Mother Murphy lived.

'Wisha! Aren't half the people in Pollnooth named Murphy?'

'I think this one lets rooms.'

'Ah, then 'tis Anastasia Murphy ye'll be wanting.' She directed Timothy to Number 17 in a street of large, terraced houses. He marched up to the front door and banged the iron knocker. The door was opened by a woman as broad as she was tall. Her hair was in curlers and she had a blanket wrapped around her stocky shoulders.

'A tinker is it, at this time o' night?' she growled. 'Be off wid ye till mornin'.'

''Tis not pots and pans I've come for,' Timothy explained, 'I'm wanting my dog back.'

'Your dog?' Mother Murphy shrilled. 'Well, ye'll not be findin' any dogs in this house. Strictly forbidden they are.'

'I know that,' said Timothy. 'Isn't that why they've wrapped him in a rug and smuggled him inside?'

'They? Who are they?'

'Four young men with long hair.'

'The Blast-Offs!' Mother Murphy's nostrils quivered and her eyes smouldered. 'Tryin' to deceive me, are they? Well, tinker, if 'tis the truth you're tellin', those pop singers will soon be thinkin' a chimney stack has fallen on 'em!'

She pounded upstairs, muttering threats under her breath. Timothy started to follow her, then changed his mind. Mother Murphy didn't need any help.

He was right. Cries of alarm from the depths of the house told Timothy that the Blast-Offs had been caught red handed. Then came a noise like a chest of drawers overturning. A door opened and Himself shot downstairs two at a time. He yelped with relief on seeing his master in the porch.

'Oh, Timothy,' he wailed, 'haven't I suffered terrible torments? Guitars, drums, an organ ... sure, and you'd never believe what a noise those magicians make!'

'Musicians not magicians,' said Timothy, hugging his pet.

'No, magicians is what they are. Didn't they say they were going to turn me into a star?'

'A star?' Suddenly Timothy looked suspicious. 'Himself, don't tell me you *talked* to them?'

''Tis nothing to do with talking,' cried Himself. 'They kidnapped me for my howl, only *they* call it singing. They want me to sing with them.'

Suitcases thrown into the street stopped Timothy from trying to make sense of what his pet was saying. Then the four pop singers were bundled out of the house by an irate Mother Murphy.

''Twill teach ye to obey the rules in future!' she shouted after them.

Hoppy looked reproachfully at Timothy. 'This wouldn't have happened if your dog had worn a collar,' he complained. 'How were we to know he wasn't a stray?'

Timothy didn't argue with him. He wasn't angry with the Blast-Offs any longer. They looked friendly fellows, not the kind who would knowingly steal somebody else's dog.

'Why did you make off with him?' he asked curiously.

Hoppy, Little Lemon and Windy told him how their search for a brand new pop sound had ended when that little dog at his feet had added his fine soprano voice to their music.

'I expect he was howling,' said Timothy with a grin.

'Man, that was no howl!' Little Lemon looked shocked. 'That dog is real groovey. You should have heard him picking up the beat. I tell you he'll put us, The Dogsbodies, right back in the charts.'

'The Dogsbodies? I thought you were the Blast-Offs?'

'We were,' Hoppy answered. ''Twas your dog that made us change our name. Just think, man – I'm going to write numbers specially for him. Doggy numbers, and after he's recorded them he'll be a star.'

'But . . .'

'Thirty pounds, man, that'll be your down payment on his first two tracks.'

Timothy was flabbergasted. Thirty pounds . . . he could hardly believe it. Nor could Himself. Until tonight people had hurled old boots at him when he howled. Yet now these young men were saying that the self-same howl was his passport to fame and fortune.

He was flattered, of course. Didn't this discovery of a new, unsuspected talent prove that there was more to him than met either the eye or the ear? If a dog who could speak was . . . well, unusual . . . wasn't a dog who could sing as well as talk doubly remarkable?

Himself even began to fancy himself in the role of singer. It was, after all, something he had never done before. And as a budding artist, had he any right to deny his musical gifts to the world? The only snags were the bangings and twangings that were part and parcel of his new profession.

'What do you say, man?' Windy asked Timothy.

All Timothy would say was that he needed time to think about it. What he didn't tell The Dogsbodies was that the decision, when all was said and done, did not rest with him.

'We'll come to your caravan first thing in the morning,' Hoppy promised, and he and the others went off in search of somewhere to spend the night.

In the caravan Timothy lit his lantern and undressed in silence. He had no intention of persuading his pet to do anything he didn't want to. All the same, he kept his fingers crossed as he snuggled down in his bunk.

The minutes ticked away. Then a gruff voice whispered in his ear: 'Timothy, I'll do it for the sake of the caravan roof.'

'Bless your heart!' cried Timothy joyfully. 'Aren't you the most wonderful dog in the world?'

Maybe I am, thought Himself, but he was too modest to say so out loud.

Chiquitito-Brown

PHILIPPA PEARCE

After a long period of longing for a dog, at last it looks as if Ben Blewitt will have his wish fulfilled. His family is thinking of moving near Hampstead Heath and his grandfather's dog, Tilly, has some puppies, one of which has been earmarked for Ben. But this puppy is a very different specimen from Chiquitito, the aristocratic little chihuahua Ben had brought to life in his imagination when he had no hope of owning a real dog.

Of course, being a Londoner, he had heard of Hampstead Heath, and several times recently Charlie, May, or Dilys had mentioned its nearness to their part of North London; but Ben had paid no particular attention. He had even been on the Heath once, years before, when he was very little. Mr and Mrs Blewitt had taken their three eldest children (Paul and Frankie were not yet born) to the August Bank Holiday Fair, held on part of the Heath.There had been merry-go-rounds and coconut shies and crowds through which May and Dilys had dragged him, each holding one of his hands. That was really all he remembered.

This time there was no fair, no dense crowds of people: he was on his own on the open Heath.

For a while he would follow a path, never asphalted or gravelled, never ruled straight to any plan. The ways across Hampstead Heath are mostly tracks that go where Londoners' feet have made them go, muddy in winter, dusty and scuffed in summer. Then he would cut across grass and through bushes to reach some point of vantage: there were no notices prohibiting it. The grass on Hampstead Heath is tough, tousled, wild, free – green and springy at the time of year when Ben trod it; later, brown and trampled and tired, longing for the repose of winter, whose damps also rot away the litter left by careless people. The trees and bushes on the Heath seem to grow where they themselves have chosen, and in irregular shapes comfortable to themselves. Ben liked them like that.

There are slippery slopes and potholes, which the wary avoid, for fear of twisting an ankle; but Ben was agile. There are marshy places in hollows, with no notices warning people that they may get their feet wet. Ben got his feet wet, and did not care.

He wandered up and down, round and round, further and further. He came to the slow, wide dip of heathland beyond which Kenwood House presents its bland front. He stared, and then turned away, and on. Wherever he went he saw people – plenty of people on such a fine afternoon; but the Heath is never overcrowded. The sun was hot for the time of year, and some people were even lying on the grass: elderly men on spread-out waterproofs, Sunday newspapers over their faces; young lovers in their embraces, careless of rheumatism from damp grass or dazzle from the sun. A mother sat knitting while her baby practised walking. A boy flew a kite. Children at play called to each other over wide spaces. And Ben saw dogs – dogs that ran freely, barking without correction. You were not even sure to whom any particular dog belonged until a distant shout recalled him.

Ben roved on, by a stretch of water and men fishing in it and a public house beyond. Then he climbed a slope up to a road and traffic – traffic that moved on all sides of a pond where fathers and children sailed boats. Beyond this a flagstaff and flag reared itself up; and beyond again was more grass, with bushes, sloping away to more tree-tops. So the Heath still went on.

But Ben paused. From the feel of his legs, he knew that he had come a long way, and he knew that the time was late from the feel of his stomach, which was empty for May's tea. Besides, he had seen enough already; the place was big enough – fast and wild. And it still went on.

He turned round, set off impetuously back, realized that he did not know the way after all his indirect wanderings, and then saw the keeper – the first he had seen since entering upon the Heath. He must be some kind of park-keeper, from his brown uniform and the metal badge on the front of his hat. He had just strolled up one of the paths and was now standing a moment, watching the people or nothing in particular.

In the ordinary course of things, Ben would not have asked his way of a park-keeper. He did not like them. But now he wanted to lead up to a more important – a vital question which only a park-keeper could answer with authority.

He edged up to him: 'Please!'

'Yes?'

'Please, could you tell me the way to get back?' Ben described the railway bridge, the sports pavilion and playground, the grassy hill –

'You want Parliament Hill,' said the keeper, and pointed his direction out to him.

Ben thanked him, set off slowly, came back, and said: 'Please!'

'What is it now?'

But Ben lacked the courage for the real question. He invented a substitute: 'I wanted to know what flag it is up there – please.'

'It's our flag – the London County Council house-flag.'

'Oh. Why is it flying to-day?'

'We fly it every day, unless we fly the Union Jack instead. Anything else you want to know?'

Yes, indeed, if only he dared ask; but – 'No, thank you – no – at least, that is – what do you fly the Union Jack for, then?'

'Special occasions: anniversary of the accession of the Queen;

Queen's birthday; Queen's wedding-day; birthday of Queen Elizabeth the Queen Mother; openings of Parliament –' He was slowing up in his list, eyeing Ben.

'Thank you very much,' said Ben.

Now or never: if he hesitated again, the keeper would decide that he was thinking up questions just to be impertinent. He would ask Ben why he didn't go home, now that he knew the direction. He would send him packing, with the really important question unasked, unanswered.

So, for the third time, and very quickly, this time: 'Please!'

'Now, look here –'

'Please – *please*: can anyone take a dog on the Heath and just let him run free? Are there no rules saying that dogs mustn't do things?'

The park-keeper looked horrified. 'No rules – no by-laws? Of course there are by-laws! We can't have dogs getting out of control on the Heath.' As the keeper spoke, two dogs – one in pursuit of the other - tore up the path on which he was standing. He stepped slightly aside to let them pass, never removing his frowning gaze from Ben.

'But how exactly must they not get out of control?' Ben asked.

'Biting people, mainly.'

Well, that was quite a reasonable rule: Ben began to feel cheerful.

'Mind you, there's one pretty severe regulation for some dogs. Have you a dog?'

It was a difficult question that the librarian had once asked – difficult, now, in a different way. 'I *own* a dog,' said Ben; 'but I haven't got it.'

'What kind?'

Ben thought of Chiquitito-Brown, and of his parentage. 'It's difficult to say. You see, –'

'Is it greyhound breed?'

Ben thought of Tilly and then of Toby: either of them might have some greyhound-blood coursing secretly in their veins, but on the whole – 'No, not greyhound.'

'Your dog's lucky. On Hampstead Heath greyhounds must wear muzzles.'

'And other breeds of dogs, and just mongrels?'

'Needn't. Provided they're kept under reasonable control, of course, as I've said.'

The same two dogs as before tore past again in the same pursuit, except that one was gaining on the other.

'And no leads?' asked Ben.

'No. I've told you: provided they're kept under control.'

A few yards from where Ben and the keeper stood, one of the two dogs had caught the other up, and they were now rolling and growling in a play-fight. Such an incident was beneath the keeper's notice. He said to Ben: 'Just remember, always under proper control on this Heath. And now cut along home the way I told you to go.'

Ben went running, light as air from the joy he felt.

He was very late for tea, of course. Everyone had finished, except for Paul and Frankie, who were being held back from the remains saved for Ben. Everyone was cross with him: Paul and Frankie for his having come back at all, the others for his being so late. He explained that he had been walking around and forgotten the time.

They resumed conversation, and, when he had a moment free from eating cold, butter-soggy toast, Ben asked about the flat seen that afternoon: had they decided to take it?

'Well. . . .' said Mrs Blewitt.

In short, they hadn't decided. May and Dilys said it was a good flat, not expensive, especially for those parts; and Charlie said that if they didn't take it, someone else soon would; and Mr Blewitt said that they might as well move there, if they had to move at all. But Mrs Blewitt was full of doubts. The place was poky, for one thing.

'I didn't see anything wrong with it,' said Ben. 'You said that little room was poky, but I didn't think so. I'd like to sleep there: I like the house: I like where it is.' He wanted them to know; he wanted to do all that lay within his poor means: *'I'd like to live there.'*

'My!' said May; and Charlie said, 'You'll soon have a voice as loud and clear as Big Ben's!'

Everyone laughed at that; and Ben was glad that he had not spoken of wanting to live within reach of the Heath. They might have laughed at that, too. His family were not unsympathetic; but they would not see the overwhelming importance of living near the Heath. Paul and Frankie might have a glimmering understanding; but not his mother and father. His mother wanted a flat or house comfortable for the family and easy to run; his father wanted somewhere handy for his job. Of course, they would enjoy going on the Heath occasionally – on fine Sunday afternoons for a family stroll, for instance. But Ben would be on the Heath every morning before breakfast, every evening after school, every weekend, every day of the holidays. The Heath was a necessity to Ben – to Ben and his dog, the second and no less wonderful Chiquitito, Tilly's puppy.

But nothing at all was decided yet.

There was only one more thing Ben could do to help forward his hopes. That evening, at home, he wrote a postcard to his grandfather: 'Please keep my puppy for me. Will write more later.' He posted the card on Monday morning; it would arrive with the Fitches on Tuesday.

On Tuesday Mrs Blewitt received a letter written by her father, with a long message for Ben. No less than three of Tilly's remaining puppies had been disposed of: Spot, to the caretaker of the chapel in Little Barley; Cloudy to Mrs Perkins's mother in Yellow Salden; and Mat to a friend of Bob Moss's in Castleford.

That left only one puppy: Chiquitito-Brown.

'Chiquitito!' Ben whispered to himself, catching his breath at the narrowness of the shave; but he knew that he had been in time. His card must have crossed Grandpa's letter in the post. Grandpa would be warned by now.

That Tuesday morning old Mr Fitch read Ben's postcard aloud to his wife. Neither of them questioned keeping the puppy: it was Ben's. 'As long as he takes it away some day,' said Granny. 'That's all.'

'Well,' said Grandpa, 'it sounds to me as if he hopes to keep a dog in London, after all.' The idea gripped him: he smiled; his fingers tapped a cheerful beat on the postcard; he was brimming with optimism and happiness for Ben.

'All I hope is that he's not due for any disappointment,' said Mrs Fitch.

When Ben had been much younger – and Frankie probably still did this; perhaps even Paul – he used to hold his breath when he wanted something badly. He held it, for instance, when they were passing a plate of cakes round and there was only one of his favourite kind.

Now, when he wanted something more than he had ever wanted anything else in all his life, he felt as if he were holding his breath for days on end – for weeks.

His parents could still not make up their minds to take the flat they had seen that Sunday. It was now exactly what Mrs Blewitt had hoped for, she said. On the other hand, she had to admit that other flats were usually more expensive, or less convenient, or further from May and Dilys. She admitted all that; and the admitting made her incline increasingly – but still hesitantly – towards taking the flat. Slowly, slowly she was veering around to it.

Ben listened to his parents' discussions. He saw the way that things were going; but he could not be sure that they were going that way fast enough. For Charlie Forrester had said that if the Blewitts did not take that particular flat, then somebody else would, soon enough. The Blewitts would lose their chance, through indecision and delay.

So Ben held his breath. He would not allow himself to show emotion – almost, to feel it. He determined not to count upon having a dog; he would not hope for a dog – even think of a dog. Yet, equally, he could not think of anything else properly at all. The dog that he chased absolutely from his thoughts in the daytime stole back at night, into his dreams: Tilly's tiny, pale brown puppy, who was also the minute – the minimal, fawn-coloured, intrepid, and altogether extraordinary Chihuahua named Chiquitito. Ben called him by that name as, in his dreams, they roamed Hampstead Heath together.

Even when Mrs Blewitt came to her decision, and, after all, the flat had not been snapped up yet by anyone else, so the Blewitts could have it – even then, Ben hardly dared breathe freely. So much might still go wrong.

But when the date of house-removal was actually fixed, and Mrs Blewitt was altering the curtains to fit the new windows, Ben said: 'By the way, I could have a dog when we're living there, couldn't I?'

Mrs Blewitt stopped whirring the sewing-machine, 'Ben!'

'Really, I could!' Ben explained what his mother had never realized – the closeness of the new home to the Heath. He could exercise a dog properly, easily, regularly; he himself would see to its feeding and washing; he would see that it did not bring mud into the house or leave hairs there – Ben over-rode all objections to a dog even before they could be made.

'But, Ben!' said his mother. 'If you *can* have a dog, I want you to. In spite of your granny's scolding, we always had a dog when we were children. A family of children should have a dog, if possible.' Ben suddenly leaned over the sewing-machine and kissed his mother. 'Mind you! You must talk to your father, of course.'

And she went back to her whirring.

When Mr Blewitt came in, he saw the justice of Ben's case: there was no reason why Ben should not keep a dog in the part of London they were moving to. But where would Ben get his dog, and how much – on top of all the expenses of house-removal – would it cost?

'Nothing,' said Ben, 'because Grandpa and Granny have been keeping one of Tilly's puppies for me, just in case. They'll give it to me as soon as I ask for it, for a birthday present.'

'Your birthday's some way ahead yet.'

'Well, really, it would be for my last birthday.'

'And, although the dog will belong to Ben,' Mrs Blewitt said, 'all the family will enjoy it.'

'As we all enjoyed Frankie's white mouse when it last got loose – you especially, Lil.'

'Oh, no!' Ben said eagerly. 'It won't be like having a white mouse – truly.'

'I daresay not. Bigger, for one thing.' But, in spite of his sardonic speech, Mr Blewitt accepted the idea, as his wife had done; and Paul and Frankie eagerly welcomed it.

'What is your dog like?' Frankie asked. They had not seen any of Tilly's puppies.

'Very, very small.'

'When you last saw it, Ben,' said Mrs Blewitt. 'Remember that puppies grow fast.' But Ben paid no attention.

'Go on, Ben,' said Paul. 'What colour is it?'

'Brown – a lightish brown.' He hesitated, then said boldly: 'Well, really, a pinky-fawn.' That was the colour it must be – Chiquitito-coloured.

'Go on.'

'And it's very bold and brave.'

Mr Blewitt asked what Ben was going to call his dog. Again he hesitated (but not because he had not made up his mind), and at once the others began making suggestions: Rover, Plucky, Wagger –

'No,' said Ben. 'None of those. He's got his own name already.'

'Well, what?'

He knew that they would object, so he began, 'Well, Grandpa has been calling him Brown –'

'Sensible,' said Mr Blewitt.

'But his real name is Chiquitito.'

A hush fell, 'Chicky *what*?' asked Mr Blewitt. He did not remember – none of them did – that this had been the name on the back of the woolwork picture.

'–Tito,' said Ben. 'Chiquitito.'

'You can't call him that, Ben,' said Mr Blewitt. He meant that the thing was – not forbidden, of course – just impossible. 'His name is Brown.'

'Chiquitito,' said Ben.

Then they all pointed out to Ben what an unhandy, absurd, unthinkable name that was for a dog. They argued with him and laughed at him. He stuck by what he had said. In the end they gave up without giving way, and they forgot the dog for the time being. After all, it had been decided that Ben should not fetch his dog until after the house-removal.

The Blewitts moved house. When all the bumping and muddle and dust and crossness were over, and they were really settled into the new flat, Ben – with his parents' agreement – wrote to his grandfather and grandmother. He arranged to go down for the day to fetch his dog.

Ben travelled down to Castleford alone, on a day-excursion ticket. He took a carrier-bag of home-made cooking from his mother, and his father had bought him a dog's lead and a leather collar with a silver name-and-address plate on it. His grandfather had asked him to bring the lead and the collar, and he had also written at the end of his last letter: BRING MRZZL FOR JURNEY. This was a British Railways regulation for dogs; and Ben had bought the muzzle out of his own money, and been proud to do so.

'For a very small dog,' he had said.

'Bad-tempered?' the shopman had asked sympathetically.

'No. Just fierce when provoked.'

Now, carrying all these things, he stepped out of the train at Castleford; and there were his grandfather and Young Tilly waiting for him. No other dog; but his grandfather said at once: 'He's waiting at home for you.'

Nothing now – surely nothing – could go wrong.

Even the weather was perfect, and the hawthorn was already out along the driftway hedges as they walked up from where the Castleford bus had dropped them. The Fitches' little half-house was sunning itself, with the front door stopped open. Granny was sitting on a chair outside, very slowly shelling peas into a colander that glinted like silver in the sunshine.

'Well!' she said, as they came up; and almost at once a dog

began barking. Ben saw him come bounding out from behind the back of the house, barking jollily. He saw that he was large – almost as large as Tilly herself – and coloured a chestnut brown.

The dog saw Ben. He stopped. He stared at Ben; and Ben was already staring at him.

'He's not used to strangers up the driftway,' Grandpa said softly. 'He never sees 'em. He's a bit nervous – timid. Call him, Ben.' Then, after a pause: 'He's your dog: why don't you call him to you?'

Ben said: 'He's so big, and brown – I didn't expect it.'

'Call him.'

Ben wetted his lips, glanced sideways at his grandfather, and called: 'Chiquitito!' His tongue tripped over the syllables: the name turned out to be terribly difficult to call aloud.

The dog had taken a step or two backwards. Ben called again. The dog turned round altogether and fled round the corner of the house, out of sight.

'*What* did you call him?' asked Grandpa.

But Granny knew. 'Why do you call him after Willy's dog?'

Not after Willy's dog, but Ben's dog – the dog so small you could only see it with your eyes shut: the minute, fawn-coloured, brave Chiquitito. 'Because he's going to be Chiquitito – he *is* Chiquitito.'

'He's *Brown*,' said Grandpa. 'You can't change a dog's name like that – it only confuses him. Besides,' – he used Ben's own emphasis – 'he *is* Brown. You can't change that any more than you can change his nature. Call him again, boy – call him Brown.'

But Ben's mouth had closed in a line of deep obstinacy.

Chiquitito-Brown was playing with his liver-and-white sister, Tilda from next door. They chased and pounced and barked in the Fitches' little front garden. Tilly, their mother, lay in the sun on the front doorstep, her forepaws crossed, watching. Whenever one of the young dogs flounced too near her, she grumbled in her throat.

'They get on her nerves nowadays,' said Grandpa, '– puppies

of that size and spirit. They know she'll stand no nonsense from them, but sometimes they over-excite each other and then they forget. Then Till gives a nip or two, to remind 'em. She'll do much better when there's only one to manage – when Brown's gone.'

Ben and his grandparents had finished their dinner, and soon it would be time for Ben to take the afternoon bus back to Castleford. His grandfather was not accompanying him, but – of course – Chiquitito-Brown was. So far Ben had not spoken to his dog again, and had not even touched him. Gloomily, from the shadow of indoors, he had watched him playing in the sunlight with Tilda.

Now Grandpa called Chiquitito-Brown to him, and held him while he directed Ben to fasten the collar round the dog's neck. This was the first time that Chiquitito-Brown had felt a collar, and he hated it.

'You'll have to scratch his name and address on the plate as soon as you get home,' Grandpa said. 'Or you could do it here and now. It wouldn't take long for a boy with schooling to scratch "Brown" –'

'No,' said Ben; 'not here and now.'

Then Grandpa held the dog by the collar, while Ben clipped on the lead; and Chiquitito-Brown hated that too. He felt himself in captivity, and feared his captor – a stranger, whose voice and hands were without friendliness.

Ben, having said his goodbyes, set off for the bus, but Chiquitito-Brown would go with him only by being dragged in a half-sitting position at the end of the lead. Tilly watched, unmoved; Tilda, in astonishment.

Grandpa called after them:'Pick him up, boy, and carry him.' Ben muttered, but picked him up. The dog was heavy to carry, and he struggled; but Ben held him firmly, grimly. So they went down the driftway.

Granny shaded her eyes, looking after them. 'People get their heart's desire,' she said, 'and then they have to begin to learn how to live with it.'

The weather had been perfect in London, too: office-girls, blooming in coloured cotton dresses and white sandals, had eaten their mid-day sandwiches on park benches in the sun; City business men had ventured out for the whole day without umbrellas.

After her morning's housework, Mrs Blewitt had washed all the loose-covers, and pegged them out in the little back garden in the sun. Frankie and Paul had helped. Then it was dinner-time; and after that the two boys went out on to the Heath.

'Be sure you're back in good time for tea,' Mrs Blewitt told them. 'Remember, Ben will be bringing his dog; everyone will be here to see it.' Mr Blewitt would be back for tea, and May and Charlie and Dilys were calling in.

'We'll be back,' said Paul.

'We'll come back by the Tube-station,' said Frankie. 'We might meet him.'

They nearly did. Ben, coming out of the Tube-station with the brown dog under his arm, saw the two of them peering into a sweet-shop window – they had been dawdling and window-gazing for nearly half an hour. He knew, as soon as he saw them, that he did not want to meet them; not with this dog.

He slipped quickly round a street-corner, out of sight. Then he set the dog on the pavement, with the dry remark, 'We can both walk now.' But where? He did not want to go home – not with this dog.

The brown dog dragged reluctantly at the end of the lead as Ben went up the asphalted way to Parliament Hill. On the top of the Hill, Ben stopped and unfastened the lead. He felt a bitter relief that he was free of the dog now. He gave it a push: 'Go away then, you! Go!'

The brown dog, nameless because no longer named, moved away a little and then sat down. Ben tried to shoo him, but he simply moved out of reach and sat down again. Then Ben set off angrily over the Heath; the brown dog got up and followed him at a little distance. He knew by now that Ben did not want him, and so he did not really want Ben; but Ben was all he had. So the

'Go away then, you! Go!'

two of them went across the Heath, together but not in companionship.

Ben walked steadily, but he had neither destination nor purpose. He walked away the worst of his anger, and also what was left of the afternoon. There had been a good many people on the Heath when he first came, but now they were going home. It was late for their teas, or even time for their suppers.

He topped a rise and saw the landmark of the flagstaff by the pond. It was flying the Union Jack, and he remembered what the keeper had said: that the Union Jack was flown only to celebrate special days. Perhaps this was a royal birthday: but, seeing the flag, Ben was reminded that this was to have been a day of celebration for him. This was the wonderful day when he got his dog. As he gazed, the flag of joy began to descend. A keeper was lowering it: he detached it altogether, furled it, and carried it off; and that was that. Ben turned abruptly back over the Heath.

The flag on Hampstead Heath – the Union Jack or LCC house-flag – is run down at sunset. The people who had not been drawn home to teas and suppers were now leaving the Heath because of chilliness and the fall of evening. Only Ben wandered further and further over the Heath; and the brown dog still followed him, but at a greater distance now, more laggingly.

There was solitude, stillness of evening, dusk that was turning the distant trees from green to black. . . . Ben slowed his pace; he sat down on a slope commanding a wide expanse. He was alone on the Heath now, except for the brown dog. The dog had sat down in the middle distance and was gazing at Ben.

Ben knew that, if he called the dog by the name he was used to, he would surely come; but Ben did not call him. And if he never called him, in time the dog would get up and wander away. He would be lost on Hampstead Heath – a nameless, ownerless brown puppy-dog for some policeman to take in charge at last.

Did Ben care? He remembered his shame on the bus, when the brown dog sat trembling on his knee and the conductress had said, 'He needs a bit of cuddling; he's scared to death.' He remembered taking the dog into the guard's-van of the train at

Castleford: he had been about to put on the muzzle, according to regulations, when the guard had said, 'Don't you bother with that. The animal looks more afraid of being bitten than likely to bite.' Ben had been humiliated; for the whole journey he sat at a distance, on a crate of chickens, his face turned away from the dog. Their arrival at Liverpool Street Station, the escalators, the Tube train – all of London that this dog first encountered terrified him. Ben had had to carry that heavy, trembling weight everywhere. He did so without tenderness or pity. He felt a disappointment that was cruel to him and made him cruel.

No Chiquitito . . . Ben let his head fall forward upon his knees and wept for that minute, intrepid, fawn-coloured dog that he could not have. Other people had the dogs they wanted: the Codling boy and the Russian huntsmen and people he had seen on the Heath this very afternoon – and, long ago, in Mexico, the little girl in the white dress with long, white, ribboned sleeves.

But Ben – no Chiquitito. . . .

He shut his eyes tight, but he could see no invisible dog nowadays. He opened his eyes, and for a moment he could see no visible dog either. So the brown dog had gone at last. Then, as Ben's eyes accustomed themselves to the failing light, he could pick him out after all, by his movement: the dog had got up; he was moving away; he was slipping out of sight.

Then, suddenly, when Ben could hardly see, he saw clearly. He saw clearly that you couldn't have impossible things, however much you wanted them. He saw that if you didn't have the possible things, then you had nothing. At the same time Ben remembered other things about the brown dog besides its unChiquitito-like size and colour and timidity. He remembered the warmth of the dog's body against his own, as he had carried him; and the movement of his body as he breathed; and the tickle of his curly hair; and the way the dog had pressed up to him for protection and had followed him even in hopelessness.

The brown dog had gone further off now, losing himself in dusk. Ben could not see him any longer. He stood up; he peered over the Heath. No . . .

Suddenly knowing what he had lost – *whom* he had lost, Ben shouted, 'Brown!'

He heard the dog's answering barks, even before he could see him. The dog was galloping toward him out of the dusk, but Ben went on calling: 'BrownBrownBrownBrown!'

Brown dashed up to him, barking so shrilly that Ben had to crouch down and, with the dog's tongue slapping all over his face, put his arms round him and said steadyingly, 'It's all right, Brown! Quiet! quiet! I'm here!'

Then Ben stood up again, and Brown remained by his side, leaning against his leg, panting, loving him; and lovingly Ben said, 'It's late, Brown. Let's go home.'

Rex

D. H. LAWRENCE

Since every family has its black sheep, it almost follows that every man must have a sooty uncle. Lucky if he hasn't two. However, it is only with my mother's brother that we are concerned. She had loved him dearly when he was a little blond boy. When he grew up black, she was always vowing she would never speak to him again. Yet when he put in an appearance, after years of absence, she invariably received him in a festive mood, and was even flirty with him.

He rolled up one day in a dog-cart, when I was a small boy. He was large and bullet-headed and blustering, and this time, sporty. Sometimes he was rather literary, sometimes coloured with business. But this time he was in checks, and was sporty. We viewed him from a distance.

The upshot was, would we rear a pup for him. Now my mother detested animals about the house. She could not bear the mix-up of human with animal life. Yet she consented to bring up the pup.

My uncle had taken a large, vulgar public-house in a large and vulgar town. It came to pass that I must fetch the pup. Strange for me, a member of the Band of Hope, to enter the big, noisy, smelly plate-glass and mahogany public-house. It was called The Good Omen. Strange to have my uncle towering over me in the passage, shouting 'Hello, Johnny, what d'yer want?' He didn't know me. Strange to think he was my mother's brother, and that he had his bouts when he read Browning aloud with emotion and éclat.

I was given tea in a narrow, uncomfortable sort of living-room, half kitchen. Curious that such a palatial pub should show such miserable private accommodations, but so it was. There was I, unhappy, and glad to escape with the soft fat pup. It was winter-time and I wore a big-flapped overcoat, half cloak. Under the cloak-sleeves I hid the puppy, who trembled. It was Saturday, and the train was crowded, and he whimpered under my coat. I sat in mortal fear of being hauled out for travelling without a dog-ticket. However, we arrived, and my torments were for nothing.

The others were wildly excited over the puppy. He was small and fat and white, with a brown-and-black head: a fox terrier. My father said he had a lemon head – some such mysterious technical phraseology. It wasn't lemon at all, but coloured like a field bee. And he had a black spot at the root of his spine.

It was Saturday night – bath-night. He crawled on the hearth-rug like a fat white teacup, and licked the bare toes that had just been bathed.

'He ought to be called Spot,' said one. But that was too ordinary. It was a great question, what to call him.

'Call him Rex – the King,' said my mother, looking down on the fat, animated little teacup, who was chewing my sister's little toe and making her squeal with joy and tickles. We took the name in all seriousness.

'Rex – the King!' We thought it was just right. Not for years did I realize that it was a sarcasm on my mother's part. She must have wasted some twenty years or more of irony on our incurable naïveté.

It wasn't a successful name, really. Because my father and all the people in the street failed completely to pronounce the monosyllable Rex. They all said Rax. And it always distressed me. It always suggested to me seaweed, and rack-and-ruin. Poor Rex!

We loved him dearly. The first night we woke to hear him weeping and whinnying in loneliness at the foot of the stairs. When it could be borne no more, I slipped down for him, and he slept under the sheets.

'I won't have that little beast in the beds. Beds are not for dogs,' declared my mother callously.

'He's as good as we are!' we cried, injured.

'Whether he is or not, he's not going in the beds.'

I think now, my mother scorned us for our lack of pride. We were a little *infra dig.*, we children.

The second night, however, Rex wept the same and in the same way was comforted. The third night we heard our father plod downstairs, heard several slaps administered to the yelling, dismayed puppy, and heard the amiable, but to us heartless, voice saying 'Shut it then! Shut thy noise, 'st hear? Stop in thy basket, stop there!'

'It's a shame!' we shouted, in muffled rebellion, from the sheets.

'I'll give you shame, if you don't hold your noise and go to sleep,' called our mother from her room. Whereupon we shed angry tears and went to sleep. But there was a tension.

'Such a houseful of idiots would make me detest the little beast even if he was better than he is,' said my mother.

But as a matter of fact, she did not detest Rexie at all. She only had to pretend to do so, to balance our adoration. And in truth, she did not care for close contact with animals. She was too fastidious. My father, however, would take on a real dog's voice, talking to the puppy: a funny, high, sing-song falsetto which he seemed to produce at the top of his head. ''S a pretty little dog! 's a pretty little doggy! – ay! – yes! – he is, yes! – Wag thy strunt, then! Wag thy strunt, Rexie! – Ha-ha! Nay, tha munna –' This last as the puppy, wild with excitement at the strange falsetto voice, licked my father's nostrils and bit my father's nose with his sharp little teeth.

''E makes blood come,' said my father.

'Serves you right for being so silly with him,' said my mother. It was odd to see her as she watched the man, my father, crouching and talking to the little dog and laughing strangely when the little creature bit his nose and toused his beard. What does a woman think of her husband at such a moment?

My mother amused herself over the names we called him.

'He's an angel – he's a little butterfly – Rexie, my sweet!'

'Sweet! A dirty little object!' interpolated my mother. She and he had a feud from the first. Of course he chewed boots and worried our stockings and swallowed our garters. The moment we took off our stockings he would dart away with one, we after him. Then as he hung, growling, vociferously, at one end of the stocking, we at the other, we would cry:

'Look at him, mother! He'll make holes in it again.' Whereupon my mother darted at him and spanked him sharply.

'Let go, sir, you destructive little fiend.'

But he didn't let go. He began to growl with real rage, and hung on viciously. Mite as he was, he defied her with a manly fury. He did not hate her, nor she him. But they had one long battle with one another.

'I'll teach you, my Jockey! Do you think I'm going to spend all my life darning after your destructive little teeth! I'll show you if I will!'

But Rexie only growled more viciously. They both became really angry, whilst we children expostulated earnestly with both. He would not let her take the stocking from him.

'You should tell him properly, mother. He won't be driven,' we said.

'I'll drive him further than he bargains for. I'll drive him out of my sight for ever, that I will,' declared my mother, truly angry. He would put her into a real temper, with his tiny, growling defiance.

'He's sweet! A Rexie, a little Rexie!'

'A filthy little nuisance! Don't think I'll put up with him.'

And to tell the truth, he was dirty at first. How could he be otherwise, so young! But my mother hated him for it. And perhaps this was the real start of their hostility. For he lived in the house with us. He would wrinkle his nose and show his tiny dagger-teeth in fury when he was thwarted, and his growls of real battle-rage against my mother rejoiced us as much as they angered her. But at last she caught him *in flagrante*. She pounced on him, rubbed his nose in the mess, and flung him out into the yard. He yelped with shame and disgust and indignation. I shall never forget the sight of him as he rolled over, then tried to turn his head away from the disgust of his own muzzle, shaking his little snout with a sort of horror, and trying to sneeze it off. My sister gave a yell of despair, and dashed out with a rag and a pan of water, weeping wildly. She sat in the middle of the yard with the befouled puppy, and shedding bitter tears she wiped him and washed him clean. Loudly she reproached my mother. 'Look how much bigger you are than he is. It's a shame, it's a shame!'

'You ridiculous little lunatic, you've undone all the good it would do him, with your soft ways. Why is my life made a curse with animals! Haven't I enough as it is –'

There was a subdued tension afterwards, Rex was a little white chasm between us and our parent.

He became clean. But then another tragedy loomed. He must be docked. His floating puppy-tail must be docked short. This time my father was the enemy. My mother agreed with us that it was an unnecessary cruelty. But my father was adamant. 'The dog'll look a fool all his life, if he's not docked.' And there was no getting away from it. To add to the horror, poor Rex's tail must be *bitten* off. Why bitten? we asked aghast. We were assured that biting was the only way. A man would take the tail and just nip it through with his teeth, at a certain joint. My father lifted his lips and bared his incisors, to suit the description. We shuddered. But we were in the hands of fate.

Rex was carried away, and a man called Rowbotham bit off the superfluity of his tail in the Nag's Head, for a quart of best and bitter. We lamented our poor diminished puppy, but agreed to find him more manly and *comme il faut*. We should always have been ashamed of his little whip of a tail, if it had not been shortened. My father said it had made a man of him.

Perhaps it had. For now his true nature came out. And his true nature, like so much else, was dual. First he was a fierce, canine little beast, a beast of rapine and blood. He longed to hunt, savagely. He lusted to set his teeth in his prey. It was no joke with him. The old canine Adam stood first in him, the dog with fangs and glaring eyes. He flew at us when we annoyed him. He flew at all intruders, particularly the postman. He was almost a peril to the neighbourhood. But not quite. Because close second in his nature stood that fatal need to love, the *besoin d'aimer* which at last makes an end of liberty. He had a terrible, terrible necessity to love, and this trammelled the native, savage hunting beast which he was. He was torn between two great impulses: the native impulse to hunt and kill, and the strange secondary, supervening impulse to love and obey. If he had been left to my father and mother, he would have run wild and got himself shot. As it was, he loved us children with a fierce, joyous love. And we loved him.

When we came home from school we would see him standing at the end of the entry, cocking his head wistfully at the open country in front of him, and meditating whether to be off or not: a white, inquiring little figure, with green savage freedom in front of him. A cry from a far distance from one of us, and like a bullet he hurled himself down the road, in a mad game. Seeing him coming, my sister invariably turned and fled, shrieking with delighted terror. And he would leap straight up her back, and bite her and tear her clothes. But it was only an ecstasy of savage love, and she knew it. She didn't care if he tore her pinafores. But my mother did.

My mother was maddened by him. He was a little demon. At the least provocation, he flew. You had only to sweep the floor, and he bristled and sprang at the broom. Nor would he let go. With his scruff erect and his nostrils snorting rage, he would turn up the whites of his eyes at my mother, as she wrestled at the other end of the broom. 'Leave go, sir, leave go!' She wrestled and stamped her foot, and he answered with horrid growls. In the end it was she who had to let go. Then she flew at him, and he flew at her. All the time we had him, he was within a hair's-breadth of savagely biting her. And she knew it. Yet he always kept sufficient self-control.

We children loved his temper. We would drag the bones from his mouth, and put him into such paroxysms of rage that he would twist his head right over and lay it on the ground upside-down because he didn't know what to do with himself, the savage was so strong in him and he must fly at us. 'He'll fly at your throat one of these days,' said my father. Neither he nor my mother dared have touched Rex's bone. It was enough to see him bristle and roll the whites of his eyes when they came near. How near he must have been to driving his teeth right into us, cannot be told. He was a horrid sight snarling and crouching at us. But we only laughed and rebuked him. And he would whimper in the sheer torment of his need to attack us.

He never did hurt us. He never hurt anybody, though the neighbourhood was terrified of him. But he took to hunting. To my mother's disgust, he would bring large dead bleeding rats and lay them on the hearth-rug, and she had to take them up on a shovel. For he would not remove them. Occasionally he brought a mangled rabbit, and sometimes, alas, fragmentary poultry. We were in terror of prosecution. Once he came home bloody and feathers and rather sheepish-looking. We cleaned him and questioned him and abused him. Next day we heard of six dead ducks. Thank heaven no one had seen him.

But he was disobedient. If he saw a hen he was off, and calling would not bring him back. He was worst of all with my father, who would take him walks on Sunday morning. My mother would not walk a yard with him. Once, walking with my father he rushed off at some sheep in a field. My father yelled in vain. The dog was at the sheep, and meant business. My father crawled through the hedge, and was upon him in time. And now the man was in a paroxysm of rage. He dragged the little beast into the road and thrashed him with a walking stick.

'Do you know you're thrashing that dog unmercifully?' said a passerby.

'Ay, an' mean to,' shouted my father.

The curious thing was that Rex did not respect my father any the more, for the beatings he had from him. He took much more heed of us children, always.

But he let us down also. One fatal Saturday he disappeared. We hunted and called, but no Rex. We were bathed, and it was bed-time, but we would not go to bed. Instead we sat in a row in our nightdresses on the sofa, and wept without stopping. This drove our mother mad.

'Am I going to put up with it? Am I? And all for that hateful little beast of a dog! He shall go! If he's not gone now, he shall go.'

Our father came in late, looking rather queer, with his hat over his eye. But in his staccato tippled fashion he tried to be consoling.

'Never mind, my duckie, I s'll look for him in the morning.'

Sunday came – oh, such a Sunday. We cried, and didn't eat. We scoured the land, and for the first time realized how empty and wide the earth is, when you're looking for something. My father walked for many miles – all in vain. Sunday dinner, with rhubarb pudding, I remember, and an atmosphere of abject misery that was unbearable.

'Never,' said my mother, 'never shall an animal set foot in this house again, while I live. I knew what it would be! I knew.'

The day wore on, and it was the black gloom of bedtime, when we heard a scratch and an impudent little whine at the door. In trotted Rex, mud black, disreputable, and impudent. His air of off-hand 'How d'ye do' was indescribable. He trotted around with *suffisance*, wagging his tail as if to say, 'Yes, I've come back. But I didn't need to. I can carry on remarkably well by myself.' Then he walked to his water, and drank noisily and ostentatiously. It was rather a slap in the eye for us.

He disappeared once or twice in this fashion. We never knew where he went. And we began to feel that his heart was not so golden as we had imagined it.

But one fatal day reappeared my uncle and the dog-cart. He whistled to Rex, and Rex trotted up. But when he wanted to examine the lusty, sturdy dog, Rex became suddenly still, then sprang free. Quite jauntily he trotted round – but out of reach of my uncle. He leaped up, licking our faces, and trying to make us play.

'Why, what ha' you done wi' the dog – you've made a fool of him. He's softer than grease. You've ruined him. You've made a damned fool of him,' shouted my uncle.

Rex was captured and hauled off to the dog-cart and tied to the seat. He was in a frenzy. He yelped and shrieked and struggled, and was hit on the head, hard, with the butt-end of my uncle's whip, which only made him struggle more frantically. So we saw him driven away, our beloved Rex, frantically, madly fighting to get to us from the high dog-cart, and being knocked down, whilst we stood in the street in mute despair.

After which, black tears, and a little wound which is still alive in our hearts.

All You Need is Patience

ERNEST DUDLEY

Brett is a beautiful and intelligent Border collie puppy, promising in every way except that she is completely stone deaf. Ignoring everyone's advice to put her down, Seth, a sheep-dog trainer, is determined to teach her to work with sheep despite her handicap.

It was the first week in September, and Brett was now six months old. Some handlers might have told Seth that to start training her at such a young age was much too soon, weeks too soon. But they didn't know Brett, they hadn't watched her from the start the way Seth had. And he reckoned, if he was going to get anywhere with her, he'd have to start when she was young, and not wait till she got older. She had it in her favour that she was physically strong, she was a fine-looking youngster. And as for intelligence, well, Seth knew she was way ahead of any other dog he'd known at that age.

He had no fixed plan in his mind. He had tried to formulate some method and had talked it over with Ruth, but she had felt, as he had, that since he was up against something totally new in his experience, there was nothing he could refer to and no one could be expected to advise him. He would have to rely on his response as he went along. He couldn't do anything but agree with her. The only thing was, he was much more aware of Brett's intelligence than was his wife. He had seen it at work. It was going to be a matter of his intelligence combined with Brett's, which it was up to him to organize so that it worked.

He was going to take on a fight against nature. It was in the nature of Brett that she should listen to his commands, to do what he told her. But as she couldn't hear, she was going to have it drilled into her that it wasn't a damn bit of use using her ears, and that instead she should use her eyes. She had to be taught to look for commands, for hand-signals, which went right against her natural instincts. It was against Seth's natural impulse, also, not to tell her what he wanted her to do. Instead he had to work out hand-signals to speak for him. He reckoned he was going to have to do a lot of learning along with her.

He hadn't a clue how long it was going to take him to train her to the standard he had reached with a bright dog with normal hearing. But he knew one thing: if it took him two months or two years, he was going to do it. She was going to be a different dog when he was through with her. And he, though he hadn't reckoned on this, was going to be a different man.

Meg's two remaining pups had been taken by their respective purchasers, both of whom were, as was to be expected considering the amount of work Seth had put into them, thoroughly pleased with their new youngsters. This left Seth with just Brett on his hands. He was glad of this, he would be able to concentrate on her. He did not intend to take on any more dogs to train until he had done his utmost with Brett.

Training her was going to be very different from the way he had handled all the previous dogs he'd had to deal with. He would have to alter his entire technique, change his methods totally. It meant he would have to find out for himself, as he proceeded with every phase of her training, what method worked, and what didn't.

When he took her into the field where the sheep were, he knew she wouldn't turn to him with a look to see what he wanted her to do. She would have all her attention fixed on the sheep. She would be all set to work them. What Seth required of her was that she should lie down close to him and await his instructions.

It was a clear, crisp morning, with a typical touch of autumn in the air. Brett was eager, up on her toes, as she came out of the stables. Seth held her on a lead, which was a rope some thirty feet in length, and kept her close to him as he took her along to the field. He knew she knew where he was taking her to, all right. She was all alert, fairly bouncing along, her eyes shining up at him, and she tugged at the rope, eager to reach the field and get working. But first she had to learn to lie down and pay attention to his commands. And obey. That meant he had to get her to look at him, which was unnatural for her since she would have her eyes on the sheep. Like any other sheep-dog.

The half-dozen sheep were on the other side of the field, where several trees hung over the hedge, which ran round the field. He closed the gate behind him, and took her a few yards towards the sheep. She tugged at the lead, which he had shortened to keep her close to him. He pulled on the lead and, when she was back on her haunches, pushed her down. He pushed her down hard. She resisted, but in a few moments seemed to get the idea, and sprawled herself out beside him. Her eyes remained fixed on the sheep the other side of the field.

He bent and held her under the jaw so that she was looking up at him. Her expression was puzzled. He let go her head, and at once her jaw sank to the ground, as she switched her attention back to the sheep. After all, that's where a dog's world lies – a foot or two off the ground. It isn't shoulder high, like a human being's. It's the scents that are low down, from rabbits to sheep, that make up a dog's world. You have to bear this in mind when you're training a dog, and make allowances. He held her under the jaw again, pulling her face up so that she was looking at him. Bending down gave him some nasty twinges of pain in his back, and he hoped he wouldn't have too much of this to do. He had to hold on to his stick to lever himself upright again. He could have knelt beside her, it would have been less painful for him, but that would have meant she wouldn't have to look up at him so much. And she had got to learn to look up at him to take her attention off the sheep or whatever, whenever he wanted her to, and look at him. That was the only way he could use hand-signals to control her. He hung tightly on the lead, continuing to hold her close to him, otherwise she would have been shooting off across the field to the sheep. It was the natural thing for her to want to do. At first, every time he gave her head a shove down, he heard himself saying: 'Lie down', automatically, which was a waste of time and breath, and he managed to stop himself. That way he could concentrate on putting all he could into hand-signals. He was learning as well as she was. He reckoned that the more he stopped putting his thoughts into words, the more strongly he could get through to her.

It took him over half-an-hour before he felt she had got the message that she was to give all her attention to him, until he signalled her to carry on with the job. When he thought she'd had enough of it – a dog can't concentrate for anything like as long as a human being – he pointed his right hand back towards the stables. He was signalling her that she was to go back home. She stared at him, her expression very puzzled and then glanced back at the sheep. He took her by the jaw once more, pulled her face round to him, and pointed with his right hand again in the direction of the stables. Finally, hoping he had got through to her, he stood up, gave a short, sharp tug on the rope and started walking. His back was giving him a bit of hell, but he knew he'd have to put up with it if he was going to get anywhere with Brett. She had her natural instincts to cope with, he had his back. That made it even between them.

He took off his cap and wiped his brow with the back of his hand. It made you sweat, all this concentrating on getting through to Brett. He reckoned he was going to sweat off a few pounds weight by the time he'd finished. Brett was as fresh as a daisy.

Seth followed the same routine for the next three mornings. Take Brett out to the field with the rope held short, so that she was kept close to you. When she reached the field, she always looked for the sheep, and then you had to give her a tug on the rope to make her look at you. But she learned to do just that, to turn and look up as if waiting for her next command. Seth realized on that fourth morning of training what an extraordinary bitch she was. He had succeeded in teaching her something which ran totally against her instincts and now, by using her intelligence, she knew what he wanted her to do.

The next thing was to send her towards the sheep, but stop her before she reached them. You had to teach her to stop when you wanted her to and not in her own time, for once she reached the sheep, she wouldn't stop working them. This was what had worried and puzzled Seth when he tried to stop her by vocal commands before he realized she was deaf.

This was going to be the most difficult of all commands to get her to obey.

When he and Brett reached the field, he didn't hang about, but gave her the command by pointing with his right hand in the direction of the sheep. Nothing very sensational about that, any dog naturally looks in the direction you point. So Seth could pretty well rely on Brett's reaction to his pointed hand. His hopes would have sunk into his boots if she hadn't reacted as predicted. She was watching him intently, waiting for what she knew he was going to command her to do. The moment he pointed across the field she turned and ran towards the sheep. When she reached the end of the thirty-foot rope, she was stopped with a jerk, and at the same moment he put up his right hand. Now, would she turn round to see what it was all about and look at Seth and see his signal?

She didn't turn to look at him. He hadn't expected her to, not the first time. He knew it would have been the end of the world if she had stopped and looked away from the sheep to him at that point. Every instinct in her, every fibre of her being was impelling her to reach those sheep as it should be. He gave a tug on the rope, and put up his right hand again as a signal for her to stop. She didn't switch her attention from the sheep. Another tug on the rope, a bit harder this time. Again he shot up his right hand. She turned and looked at him. By her expression she was asking him what he wanted her to do. It was almost as if she was saying, didn't he want her to work the sheep, to gather them in and bring them to him?

He beckoned her and slapped the side of his leg. It was the sort of invitation you would give to any dog that you wanted to come to you, and Brett duly relaxed and came towards him. When she reached him, he patted her on the head and made a bit of a fuss of her. She showed she was glad about it, and wagged her tail. She had obeyed the first hand-signal he had given her. She had used her eyes where a dog with normal hearing would have obeyed his spoken command. Seth felt pleased about it, though he realized that he had a long way to go before he could let her off the rope, and then get her to obey his command to stop and to come to him. If there wasn't a rope which he could tug, how was he going to get her attention when it would be fixed on the sheep?

He sent her off again towards the sheep, which had moved round the field a dozen yards, and stood bunched together as before. None of them appeared to have taken any notice of Brett. The end of the rope on her collar stopped her. Seth gave it a tug. Brett still eyed the sheep. Another tug, harder this time, and she half-turned her head to him. He raised his hand. Another tug, and her head came round. He beckoned her, and slapped the side of his leg as before. She hesitated a moment, glancing back at the sheep, but came straight on towards him when he beckoned her to him again. He patted and fussed her to show he was pleased she had obeyed him, and she wagged her tail in response.

Seth gave her nearly an hour of the exercise. Each time she obeyed the tug on the rope and his hand-signal. Each time she came back to him, to be rewarded with a pat on the head and a fuss to show he was pleased with her. When he shortened the rope so that she would be close to him as he took her home, she looked back across the field at the sheep and then she turned to look up at him with an expression, which you could only describe as wistful – if dogs possessed any wistful feelings – and then he gave a tug at the lead, and she came along.

Seth considered he had done well enough for that day. He wondered if perhaps he was pushing her too hard, if it was taking it out of her as much as it was taking it out of him. Was she concentrating on the signals as much as he was when he was giving them? He frowned as he looked at her. What was going on in that strange, lonely world of hers? He tried to imagine what she was thinking, and tried to put himself in her place, just as a teacher would with a deaf child. He remembered the deaf girl and her parents, how they had emphasized that you needed patience and love, and understanding – above all, he told himself, you needed patience. Any amount of it.

He decided he would halve the time of each daily exercise – better give her a week of half-hours at a time than three days of an hour. To stop when he told her was the most important command she had to learn and it was better not to rush her. She was only a youngster, you couldn't expect her to remember everything the way you could a fully adult dog. He wondered if she gave any thought to what he was trying to teach her when she was back in the stables. Did she go back over the work she'd put in when she was alone? Or was her mind completely empty, until it was time for her to go through the exercise again?

He took two weeks over this exercise. Wet or fine, windy or calm, it made no difference, but he didn't always take her out to the field at the same time each day. It could be in the morning, the afternoon, or even early evening. He didn't want her to treat it as a routine business. He wanted the exercise to be fresh to her every day he put her through it, and changing the times was one way of achieving this. Brett certainly wasn't bothered – she was on her toes whatever the time of day. Fresh as could be, eager, and ready to work the whole day through if he asked it of her.

He didn't make such a fuss of her now. A pat on the head when she got back to you, that was all. He didn't want her to get the idea she was doing something that was marvellous every time she obeyed him. So far he was winning the fight with nature. She'd got the message. She was doing what he wanted her to do. She was coming straight back to him now, without hesitating. It was quite unnatural for her to give her attention to him and look away from the sheep, when all her instincts told her she shouldn't take her eyes off them for one instant. As he watched her, as she obeyed his hand signal, he wondered again and again what was going on inside her head.

Seth reckoned she was now ready to be let off the rope. He felt that if now wasn't the time to put her to the test of obeying his signals without the tug of the rope to stop her, it never would be.

There was some mist clinging to the hedgerows and the trees as Seth and Brett reached the field that morning. He held her close to him by the rope as he opened the gate and they went into the field. He stopped and unleashed her, coiling the rope in his left hand. She lay down close by his feet and he let her stay there for several moments. This was it, this was the acid test. The sheep were spread out a little in the corner of the field to his left. They stood out clear against the misty hedge.

He was sweating, but he could feel his mouth was dry. He ran his tongue across his lower lip. Then he raised his right hand and pointed in the direction of the sheep.

Brett promptly took off. Seth's left hand was clenched firmly around the coil of rope, his right hand round his stick. He could feel the muscles across his stomach tighten. He judged the exact second when he felt she would be expecting his command to stop. Now. He raised his right hand high. Her attention seemed totally concentrated on the sheep. He couldn't understand how she would ever see his signal out of the corner of her eye. But, she stopped. She stopped neatly in her tracks, as if she had been prepared for his raised right hand. She had obeyed him without any trouble. Seth could feel the tension run out of his nerve-ends. He was filled with exultation. All the hard graft, on her part as well as his, had paid off.

He beckoned her to him, slapping the side of his leg, and at once she ran unhurriedly towards him, just as if he had given her a tug on the rope. He remembered merely to give her a pat when she reached him, though he could have hugged her, he was so filled with triumph. As she lay at his feet he tried to understand how she had seen his signal when she was heading towards the sheep. He felt certain her eyes must have been fixed on them, and yet she had seen his hand go up. It must have been out of the corner of her eye, and yet that had been all she needed to obey him.

He put her through the exercise five more times. The sheep had moved out from the hedge and away to his left round the field, but this made no difference to Brett's reaction to his signal. Each time her attention seemed totally fixed on the sheep, yet each time he raised his right hand, she stopped and turned to him. She answered his beckoning hand and slap on his leg by running at an easy lope towards him. There was not the faintest doubt in his mind that she had got the exercise off pat. The trickiest part of the training, when he might have expected her to take several weeks before catching on, had in fact taken only two. The rest of the training was going to be easy by comparison, he told himself.

He was full of it when he got back to the house, and the exciting news made Ruth as happy for him as could be.

He tried her out again the next afternoon. The skies were overcast and there was a feel of thunder in the air as he took her out of the stables a few minutes after three o'clock. He unloosened his collar, which felt a bit sweaty round his neck, but Brett seemed quite unconcerned about the heaviness in the atmosphere. She could be going out in a blinding snowstorm for all the weather seemed to bother her.

He had noted before that she appeared unaffected by weather conditions. It had been different with the other dogs he had trained. Almost always, he could remember, the dogs would act sluggishly on a day such as this. He'd had to work twice as hard to get any sense into them. On a windy day they had been even more difficult because the wind would play tricks with his voice and throw his commands all over the place. But, of course, he didn't have that trouble with Brett. The wind could blow like a hurricane, it wouldn't bother her.

The trees that leaned over the hedge in the field didn't stir, their branches hung listlessly in the still air. The sheep were directly opposite the gate this afternoon and seemed to be grazing automatically, as if they weren't really interested in feeding. As he closed the gate behind him and Brett, Seth felt a twinge in his back. It was the sort of weather that didn't do much for that, as he knew from experience.

He unleashed Brett and she lay beside his feet for a minute or two. Then, Seth pointed to the sheep with his right hand and Brett was off. A few moments later he signalled her to stop and she obeyed him at once. She turned to him, and he beckoned her, slapping the side of his leg. She was panting, he noticed, as she ran towards him – the heavy atmosphere was affecting her too.

He thought he'd take it easy with her this afternoon and not work her too hard. Once more she lay at his feet. He let several minutes pass, then he pointed as usual at the sheep. Immediately she was up and racing off towards them. He put up his hand to signal her to stop at the correct moment, but this time she ran on.

Seth let out a curse of dismay and anger. He forgot her deafness and shouted at her to stop. The sheep saw her racing at them and split up, rushing off in a muddle this way and that. Seth ran after Brett, still shouting at her as if to emphasize the shaking of his right hand clenching his stick. She had turned aside after one of the sheep, but, on seeing Seth, hesitated in her run and then turned back to him. He still ran at her. He had stopped shouting, but his face was full of mingled fury and dismay and he raised his stick at her threateningly. The effect upon her was dramatic.

A kind of frightened whine gurgled at the back of her throat, and she grovelled at Seth's feet, then turned on her back. He stared down at her white, unprotected throat and belly. He knew what her behaviour meant. She was telling him she knew she had done wrong in some way unknown to her, and at the same time she was prepared to accept any punishment he cared to hand out. She was submitting to his authority as best she knew how. He was her acknowledged master, and she was accepting his superiority in the only instinctive way she knew.

When he had watched Brett as a pup playing games with Meg's four other pups, Seth knew that what she, and the others, were really engaged in was preparation for adult life. Instinctively, Brett knew that adult life was going to be hard, tough going and that she would have to be ready to fight for her life, for the territory which she had marked out for herself, and for her offspring. In the case of the male, he had to be prepared to fight for his chosen mate. Dogs once ran in packs, with an acknowledged leader that led them out on the hunt. Any dog who tried to boss the leader would have to fight until one of them accepted defeat, and rolled on its back to expose its unprotected throat and belly to the victor. The loser submitted to the winner. This was something that Meg's family acted out as they instinctively prepared for the facts of adult life in the raw.

Seth was shocked and upset at Brett's behaviour. He cursed himself for giving way to that show of anger by threatening her with his stick. In an attempt to prove to her that he wasn't really angry with her and that it had been no more than a momentary irritation, he deliberately threw the stick aside. He came back for it later, but he never carried it again when he was out with Brett. He patted her head and fussed over her. She reacted slowly. She got to her feet, but still cringed before him. There was going to be no more training that day and he turned for home, beckoning her to follow him.

At the very beginning of her training, in the earliest stages, he had recognized that Brett was of a temperament that matched his. This was what had appealed to him so powerfully about her.

She was neither a 'hard' nor a 'soft' dog, she was in between the two, as were Seth's methods of teaching. What this amounted to was that Brett possessed an extra-sensitive nature. Where your 'hard' dog wasn't troubled by a bit of stick when it did wrong, any sort of punishment, even the threat of his raised hand holding the stick, had completely demoralized Brett. He had become a 'hard' man all of a sudden and she hadn't recognized him. Who was this stranger who had turned on her in such threatening anger? Where your 'soft' dog would have yelped at a taste of punishment, and then forgotten all about it in five minutes, Brett had taken Seth's anger very much to heart and her sensitive nature had been deeply hurt. He had to win back her confidence in him. His face was dark with a worried frown. He was well aware that there were snags about training a dog of exceptional intelligence such as Brett. It was almost a certainty that the more intelligent the dog, the more problems you were liable to have if the relationship between you went awry. And that was what had happened between him and Brett. He felt worried as hell about it.

She followed him slowly, reluctantly. He turned several times to beckon her to follow, and she began to quicken her pace. She followed him into the stables, and lay down in her corner. He bent down and patted her, and he could feel her half-draw away from him. He fussed over her. She cringed a little and didn't respond. He could see in her eyes that she was still scared of him, and ready to accept any punishment he wanted to inflict on her.

What was it that had caused her to disobey him so blatantly? He hadn't been to blame, he was certain of that. He had given her the hand-signal as clearly as he had done a dozen times before. There was the heaviness in the atmosphere, he knew, which might have tired her so that she had momentarily lost her concentration. But somehow he didn't think it was that. It could only be that there was some quirk in her nature which he had not realized before.

Seth gave a deep sigh, and shook his head. It had been a bad day for him and Brett. He didn't know how he was going to repair the damage he had done. As he went back to the house, he pondered on whether he should continue her training, carry on as if nothing had happened, or whether he should give it a rest for a day or two. Leave Brett alone, in the hope that she would forget what had happened that afternoon. He still hadn't made up his mind which was the best thing to do, when he got to the kitchen door.

Ruth was as dismayed as he had been, when he gave her an account of what had happened. He didn't mention anything about the touch of pain in his back, which might have added to his anger with Brett. He didn't want Ruth to worry about that. There was quite enough to worry about over Brett. He admitted to her that he had been very much in the wrong to show his anger when Brett had disobeyed him but, as he tried to explain, it had come as such a shock to him, shock mingled with dismay, that he just hadn't been able to control his emotions.

She sympathized with him. She understood the amount of work he put into training Brett, and that it was no easy job to build up the right kind of relationship between himself and the bitch. It took it out of him, emotionally, and for once he'd been caught off-guard by Brett's totally unexpected reaction.

How should he carry on, now? Should he leave it for a day or two, or pick it up tomorrow, continue the routine?

His wife reminded him that it wasn't the first time a dog he'd been training had disobeyed him. Almost always, she said, it would prove in the end to be a good working dog, obedient to every command. He took comfort from that. Ruth advised him to see how Brett reacted when he took out her evening meal. Couldn't he judge from the way she behaves then, what was the best way to continue the training? She was glad to learn, she told him, that never once had he mentioned the idea of giving up training Brett altogether, cut his losses, you might say.

Seth shook his head. No, he wasn't going to give up as easily as that. He'd find a way to get back on good terms again with Brett, make no doubt about it. He was going to build up the relationship between them, so that it was stronger even than it had been before this afternoon.

He took in Meg's meal. She was at the other end of the stables, and greeted him with plenty of tail-wagging before setting about her food with usual relish. Then he took Brett's food-dish along to where she lay, stretched out, her jaw on her front paws. She looked up at him, without raising her head, and remained where she was. He put the food-bowl in front of her, but she didn't eat. He patted her head, and fussed over her, but she didn't respond.

He reflected on the wisdom, after all, of beginning to train her at such a relatively early age, perhaps he should have given her a month or two more before starting with her. But she was such a forward youngster, he hadn't felt it was too soon, especially as she was not only very intelligent for her age but was physically strong as well. He couldn't believe that his early start with her really had anything to do with what had happened that afternoon. In any case, he couldn't stop her training at this stage, and then hope to start again later, that was no way to handle her – he might as well give up the whole idea now.

What had worried him, which he hadn't mentioned to Ruth, was what had been Brett's innermost motives in disobeying him and attempting to mix it with the sheep? Like any other border collie, she was as much a hunter deep down inside her as any wolf, and no man could ever claim to have eradicated totally the sheep-dog's instinct from the days when it ran wild in a pack. The fear that a border collie who had been a great worker and had always given his best could suddenly and for no apparent reason turn into a killer, still nagged at the back of Seth's mind. Might not Brett, had she been given the chance that afternoon, have torn wool from a sheep's throat and with it blood?

Looking at her now, Seth's face clouded over. Brett had hardly stirred from her position. Then he recalled what Ruth had said, that the sort of behaviour Brett had demonstrated had also been shown by other dogs he had been training. He was simply over-reacting to what had happened. He was so inspired by the potential he had seen in Brett that he had taken her first sign of misbehaviour too much to heart. Seth thought of what the deaf girl had said about when you meet a deaf child – smile. He relaxed and smiled at Brett. The smile broadened into a warmly affectionate grin. He couldn't be certain of it, but he thought he saw a twitch of her tail.

He stood up, still smiling at her. Her eyes had never left his face. He turned and walked to the stable-door. He looked back. She had started eating.

Buried Bones

HELEN CRESSWELL

Zero is Jack's hopeless but lovable mongrel dog. In a lively, talented but difficult to live with family, Jack and Zero tend to rely on each other for support. The Bagthorpe household has been reduced to more than usual chaos as a result of having three-year-old Daisy to stay, and from reaping the fruits of a great deal of indiscriminate competition entering. Among other things the Bagthorpe family have been named 'the Happiest Family in England' by Borderland Television. Now Zero's moment of glory is at hand: Rosie Bagthorpe has won a competition with her photographs of Jack training Zero to beg. (Jack had found that the only way to make Zero understand what was required of him was actually to get down and go through the motions of begging himself.)

It was lucky for Mr Bagthorpe that he had left for Tallbuoys Health Farm just before the men came with the news about Zero. He believed, as he said later, that had he been present he would certainly have had a seizure or become demented.

'My hold on sanity is already fragile,' he said, 'and would have snapped.'

The rest of the Bagthorpes, who *were* present, were at first incredulous and then, inevitably, consumed with envy.

Rosie herself was delighted to begin with, especially as the men from BURIED BONES dogfood had brought with them her prize. Mrs Bagthorpe was full of praise.

'Though I hope, Rosie,' she said, 'that you will not allow your interest in photography to take precedence over your Portraits. Your Portraits are truly creative and quite unique.'

'And anyone can take a photo,' added Tess.

It emerged, however, that the BURIED BONES men were interested not primarily in Rosie, but in her subject.

'Show us the dog,' they begged, once the congratulations were over. 'Is he real? Does he exist?'

'Fetch him, Jack,' said Mrs Bagthorpe resignedly.

Jack was pleased to escape. He had cringed when the BURIED BONES men first fetched out huge blow-ups of Rosie's winning photographs. Tess and William had guffawed mercilessly, and the former shrieked:

'Wait till Father sees them! Look at Uncle P holding up that biscuit – are you going to *publish* them? You're *not*!'

Jack went slowly upstairs, wondering how this was going to affect Zero's confidence. He could already feel it affecting his own.

'It was a rotten thing to do to you, Zero old chap,' he thought miserably. 'You'll be the laughing stock of England. And it's my fault, mainly.'

Zero was guarding Jack's comics in his room. He had gone on guarding them long after the necessity to do so had expired. He seemed to have got it into his head that they were valuable, and Jack could not convince him otherwise. In any case, he thought, it was probably a good thing for Zero to *think* he had an important responsibility, even if he had not.

Jack sat on the edge of the bed and gave Zero a lot of patting and praising before he broke the news about the photographs.

'I didn't know Rosie was there, honestly,' he told him. 'It was a mean thing for her to do. But I'm in it as much as you are.

We'll just have to stick together. Don't let it get your ears down.'

At last, reluctantly, he descended, Zero trailing behind.

Their reception was stunning. Instead of the derisory laughter and cutting personal remarks he had expected, Jack found that the BURIED BONES men were almost beside themselves with enthusiasm.

'It's unbelievable!' yelled one.

'Get him outside – let me take some shots!' shouted the other.

A dazed Jack finally came to grasp that he had in Zero something that the world had been waiting for a long time.

'He's a gold mine, I tell you!' cried one.

'You're sure he's a mongrel?' inquired the other anxiously. 'He is unique?'

'He's that all right,' said William. 'Mutton-brained pudding-footed hound.' (He evidently felt entitled to use Mr Bagthorpe's lines in his absence.)

Nobody could quite take in what was happening, least of all Zero himself. He kept edging up to Jack, practically sitting on his feet and giving him little nervous licks.

Mrs Fosdyke, disgusted, told the men, 'you wouldn't believe the wiping up I do after that animal, feet that size!' but they were not sympathetic. They gave her to understand that before long the world would be queueing up for the privilege of wiping Zero's footprints up. What finally convinced the Bagthorpes of the seriousness of the BURIED BONES' intentions was when one of them suddenly clapped a hand to his head and yelled:

'My God! Insurance! Is he insured?'

'Is he *what*?' said William. 'I doubt if he's even got a licence.'

'Quick, Bill,' urged the man with the camera. 'Get on to Head Office. Can we use the 'phone?'

The Bagthorpes listened unashamedly while Bill got on to Head Office and gave orders for Zero's immediate Insurance. What really created a silence was the sum he put on Zero's head. Zero, apparently, was worth one hundred thousand pounds.

Mrs Fosdyke, who was listening along with everyone else, told her cronies later in The Fiddler's Arms, and it was evident from their reactions that they were not representative of the Great British Public confidently expected to become instant fanatical Zero Worshippers.

'Great ugly thing he is!' exclaimed Mrs Bates, 'and footmarks all over everywhere.'

'I should think they'll find their mistake soon enough,' predicted Mrs Pye sagely. 'Dogs in commercials is supposed to do what they're supposed to do, and that one never will.'

'I daresay,' said Mrs Fosdyke, unsoothed, 'but what about the taxpayers' money? A hundred thousand pounds! That's ten times my late hubby, and at least he was *human*!'

While Bill was discussing the finer points of the Insurance (ten thousand for loss of limb, fifty thousand for an eye, and so on) Grandma descended into the hall. Hearing large sums of money being thus bandied about, she leapt to the conclusion that somebody was making wills. As Bill was winding up the conversation she moved to the telephone and whisked it from him.

'Just one moment,' she said, 'I wish to alter *my* will. Are you there? Are you there?'

There followed much confusion. In the end Grandma slammed down the 'phone, exclaiming, 'I shall not consult *that* solicitor again!' and went muttering into the kitchen in search of coffee.

'What are all these men doing here!' she asked, indicating the two BURIED BONES. 'I must have my hair reset before there are any more photographs. Where is Daisy? What have we won this time?'

When she was eventually apprised of the situation she tried at first to capitalize on it.

'The situation is becoming ludicrous,' she said. 'Too many Competitions have been won. Daisy and I are becoming tired of the constant invasions of our privacy. We could, however, if you wished, offer your pet food to the dog. That way, the dog would not be too much in evidence. He is, after all, a mongrel.'

'He's worth a hundred thousand pounds,' Jack told her

immediately, fortified by the knowledge that he at last now had something concrete to put forward in Zero's favour. 'He's just been insured for that.'

Grandma turned to Mrs Bagthorpe.

'How much am I insured for?' she demanded. 'Not that I could be replaced.'

Mrs Bagthorpe was saved from replying by the advent of the Happy Family people, whose visit was expected but had been forgotten in the general turmoil. They could hardly have arrived at a less auspicious moment, the only wholeheartedly happy people present being Jack and the BURIED BONES men, and the latter did not count. Borderland Television was interested only in Happy Bagthorpes.

Fortunately the BURIED BONES and the BTV pair got on very well to begin with, and there was much mutual congratulation between them on their fortunate discovery of the Bagthorpes. The whole family, in fact, overhearing themselves being discussed in this way, began to feel rather like newly upturned buried bones themselves. They began to wonder whether they had ever existed in their own right.

'They are exactly the kind of close-knit nuclear family we were hoping for,' enthused Sue.

'That dog,' said BURIED BONES Man One solemnly, 'could only have been found in a family like this. We shall corner the market within weeks. Have you insured them?'

'Insured whom?' The Borderland Television pair looked blank.

When the BURIED BONES explained, Sue and Jeremy immediately looked apprehensive. The seeds of doubt and fear had been sown.

'What if . . .' BURIED BONES Two lowered his voice, '. . . something were to happen half-way through filming?' He lowered his voice further, 'There's been a spot of Fire and Flood about lately, if you look around. If people are accident prone, they're always having Fires and Floods. I think these people *are* accident prone.'

Grandma overheard most of this by dint of moving right in on the group.

'In my opinion,' she told Borderland Television, 'you should insure the entire family. I think a quarter of a million pounds would be a suitable sum.'

'Oh Mother!' exclaimed Mrs Bagthorpe. 'Don't be absurd!'

'It is a question of self-respect,' said Grandma obstinately, 'and a sense of dignity and worth. If I felt myself to be worthless, I doubt if I could bring myself to look happy and contented for any film.'

There followed a series of telephone calls to and from Borderland Television, and the Bagthorpe family were duly insured.

The week that followed was outstandingly awful despite the absence of Mr Bagthorpe. At times there were as many as forty people in the house, all ruthlessly pursuing their own business and all, quite frequently, at cross purposes. There were carpenters, plasterers and decorators, all of whom wanted to get finished and have their bills paid before Christmas.

There was a production team of twenty from Borderland Television who were themselves inexorably committed to producing a finished film for Christmas Day. And there was a team from BURIED BONES who were hell bent on a commercial out in time for the big Christmas-viewing audiences. None of these people cared who got trodden down in the process, or whether the Bagthorpes themselves were left limp and drained, shadows of their former selves.

The man who turned up to direct THE HAPPIEST FAMILY IN ENGLAND was called P.J. by the crew, and the Bagthorpes hated him on sight. The feeling appeared to be mutual. He had hardly been in the house half an hour before he lighted on the plain truth that the Bagthorpes were *not* the Happiest Family in England.

'Though you had better try and look it,' he told them. 'There is such a thing as breach of contract.'

By the end of the first day's filming the younger Bagthorpes were all for breaching the contract and taking the consequences, but their mother pleaded with them to go on, for all their sakes.

'If we make the effort, and act happy,' she said, 'we may well come to *be* happy. It is a known psychological fact. And besides, we want people to *think* we are happy, don't we? And besides, we *are* happy, really.'

Grandma was adamant that Daisy should figure in the film and the Parkers came over each day. This had a bad effect on Mrs Fosdyke who was now irremediably nervous in the vicinity of Daisy.

She was forced to act happy herself, on occasions. P.J. decided that the Tin Shaking should be shown, as an example of the zany, high-spirited larking the Bagthorpes went in for. On the day scheduled for the filming of this sequence Mrs Fosdyke arrived with her hair newly and drastically permed by Mrs Pye and prepared for the worst.

She went obediently through the routine of asking William, whose turn it was according to the Rota, to open a tin of apricots for dessert. The family, already seated at the table with spoons at the ready, waited for the inevitable minced beef or mushy peas to appear.

William, who considered that he had not so far figured sufficiently prominently in the film, made great play with the tin opener. He finally lifted the lid of the tin with something like reverence to reveal (his first-ever bull's eye) – apricots. The Bagthorpes, as one, broke into hysterical laughter and Mrs Fosdyke herself burst into tears. P.J. fumed and swore and said it was a conspiracy and the whole sequence had to be filmed again, this time with Mrs Fosdyke sniffing and dabbing at her nose throughout.

It was this kind of thing that led to a kind of creeping madness in the Bagthorpe household. Each of its members, as the days went by, began to behave in an increasingly pronounced manner – to become, as it were, twice their usual selves. William, for instance, when not actually needed for filming, would go up to his room and beat out tattoos of hitherto unequalled frenzy and duration. Rosie took to doing unflattering but recognizable Portraits of P.J. and leaving them scattered around everywhere, and Tess quoted from Voltaire in every third sentence and kept using words like 'incontrovertible' and 'charismatic'.

P.J. tried to persuade Mrs Bagthorpe to get her husband back from the Health Farm, but this she steadfastly refused to do. She would not even divulge the name of the place where he was staying. This had been agreed before Mr Bagthorpe had left.

'I don't mind looking happy just once,' he said, 'if I can remember how. I'm used to sacrifices. I'll do my bit at the end.'

During the rest of the film Mr Bagthorpe was to appear only, as it were, by suggestion. The rest of the family, for instance, were made to tiptoe smilingly past his study door, with the implication that they recognized and understood that a creative writer was in there, creating. Even Mrs Fosdyke was made to do this, although her usual practice was to make as much rattling and banging as possible within earshot of the study as retaliation for the looks Mr Bagthorpe sometimes gave her.

P.J. also did a close-up of the notice Mr Bagthorpe had pinned on the study door and read LITTLE CHILDREN WHO COME UNTO ME SUFFER as evidence of his delightful and whimsical humour.

Mrs Bagthorpe had rung her husband on his first evening and told him how well the Happy Family project was going. She did not, however, tell him about Zero.

There was no way, she thought, that any Health Farm would be able to help Mr Bagthorpe if he heard about Zero and the one hundred thousand pounds. She did not believe anybody would be able to help him.

On this occasion, he had begged her not to 'phone during the rest of his stay.

'Don't write, either,' he had said. 'I need silence. I need to feel my way back into being human again.'

Mrs Bagthorpe had thought this sounded hopeful, and was determined to cooperate. She resisted all attempts to invade his privacy, and looked forward to the end of the week when her husband would return to his family a changed man.

'Miracles,' she repeated to herself firmly and often, '*do happen*!'

Zero's hour was now at hand. Jack exulted in the certainty. His dog was now, at least, to have his day.

'His ears will never droop again,' he thought. 'I shall let him watch the commercial every time it comes up. He can take a just pride in his own achievements just like everybody else.'

Making the commercial (which turned out to be only the first of many) was an achievement anyone could have taken a just pride in. Rosie, taking photographs with her new equipment of the BURIED BONES people trying to get Zero to act the way they wanted, realized that she could easily win a Competition with these pictures, too.

Jack was given an outline script to study, and asked to train Zero up to playing his part as much as he could. He only had two days to do this, because BURIED BONES were in such a rush to launch their campaign.

The idea was that Jack and Zero were to be filmed walking along together in an idyllic setting, while an unseen voice said 'Zero goes for a walk every day. He just loves it.' Then Zero, without Jack seeming to notice, was to stop suddenly, and sniff hard. He was then to start digging furiously, and turn up a packet of BURIED BONES dog-biscuits. Jack, meanwhile, was to saunter off into the distance oblivious of the fact that he was no longer accompanied, while the voice said, 'Zero likes walks, all right – but he likes BURIED BONES better. Ask any dog.'

None of this was easy. The walking part was straightforward enough, but when Zero was supposed to stop dead in his tracks and sniff, complications set in. For one thing, Zero had been made nervous lately by the house being always full of noisy strangers, and stayed glued to Jack even more than usual. He did not want to stand there by himself sniffing while Jack walked off and left him alone with a lot of eccentric people with cameras. He did not even want to sniff if Jack stayed with him. He just edged up and sat on Jack's feet and looked dolefully around.

'I don't think he's a very good actor,' Jack told the film people

'Sniff, Zero! Good old boy, Sniff!'

apologetically. 'I don't think he's going to be able to act sniffing.'

It was then suggested that a technique similar to the one Jack had employed for training Zero to Fetch and Beg should be used. This entailed everyone present getting down on all fours and sniffing and snuffing around, while Jack urge 'Sniff, Zero! Good old boy, Sniff!'

Zero was completely thrown by this incomprehensible behaviour and went and hunched right up next to Jack and squeaked a little and kept wetting his lips.

The whole morning was spent like this. After lunch the director asked:

'Is there anything that really excites that dog? Does he ever get eager?'

'He does in the woods, sometimes,' Jack told him. 'He gets eager when he sees squirrels.'

The unit trekked on foot, carrying all their equipment, to the woods. There, indeed, Zero did become excited. He seemed to forget what he was there for, and bounded off and started barking non-stop at the squirrels, as he always did. Jack was pleased.

'He *can* get excited, you see,' he told them.

'The only trouble is,' said the director wearily, 'that he's looking up in the air. I can't see any way he's going to turn up BURIED BONES in the air.'

Someone had brought along two large mutton bones.

'If we can cover them up with soil, and get him sniffing after them, we'll be half-way there,' said the director.

Unfortunately this did not work. It was hard to tell *why* Zero did not want to sniff these bones out. He might just not have been very hungry, or he might have been over-excited by the squirrels. Whatever the reason, he did not sniff.

The film unit all sat down and had a think.

'We've got to think this thing through,' the director told them. 'We must have that dog. We could get a trained alsatian to make this film in ten minutes flat. But we must have that dog.'

He sat a long time thoughtfully watching Zero as he made his futile lunges after squirrels running a full thirty feet above him.

'What we've been doing,' he finally announced, 'has been all wrong.'

No one contradicted what seemed a self-evident truth.

'I'm going to turn the whole idea upside down on its head.'

A respectful silence ensued.

'I am deliberately trying to keep my voice calm and controlled,' he went on, 'because I have just come up with the most stupefying and sensational idea that I believe has ever been used in advertising. And I am dazed and shattered by the pure and immaculate simplicity of it.'

They all sat and waited. In the distance Zero barked on a high monotonous note.

'What would your reaction be,' went on the director, 'if I told you that we are going to film the truth?'

He held up a hand.

'No. Don't answer right away. Take your time. Think about it. Just take in the sheer enormity of the concept. We are going to make a true commercial.'

Jack took a quick look around. Everyone present was looking very concentrated and wise, and he made an effort to assume a similar expression himself.

'That dog,' went on the director discerningly, 'is not clever. He's a numskull. He's a great, clumsy, stupid, lovable numskull. You get the key word? *Lovable*. Now there is nothing lovable about being clever. Even if we did spend six months getting that dog to sniff and turn up BURIED BONES, nobody would love him for it. He'd just be another ordinary, smart dog on a commercial. No. What we do, we ditch the whole script, and we capitalize on his assets.'

This is what happened. The BURIED BONES people went away and came back the following day with not one but two film units. Then the second unit filmed the first one trying to get Zero to sniff. Everyone went down on their hands and knees again and sniffed and snuffed, and Zero just looked hopeless and was the only one *not* sniffing.

The director had written a new commentary. This time, the voice said:

'We wanted to show Zero digging up a packet of BURIED BONES. But Zero is never going to play Hamlet. He can't act. We can't even get him to understand what we want him to do. Sniff! Come on, boy, sniff! You see? Hopeless. But there's one thing Zero doesn't have to act. He really *does* like BURIED BONES. Here Zero – good boy!'

At this point Zero never quite managed to capture the look of keen interest one might have expected. He had by this time had enough of filming, and it was beginning to show. He crunched the BURIED BONES biscuit all right, but only in a resigned, world-weary kind of way. He definitely looked as if he were doing it for the fifth time in an hour.

To Jack's surprise, however, the director seemed enchanted by Zero's performance.

'My God!' he exclaimed after the final take. 'Just look at him!' (meaning Zero). 'I've never seen anything so understated in my life. He just threw the whole thing away. Olivier could take lessons from him when it comes to understatement. The whole thing is brilliant.'

He turned out to be right about this. After the first showing of the BURIED BONES commercial the lines of Borderland TV were jammed all night with calls from people who wanted to give Zero a home. He had apparently given the impression of being orphaned and sad, and half of England, it seemed, wanted to make him happy.

After the third or fourth showing the telephone inquiries were mainly about where one could get a dog exactly like Zero. Everywhere little children were sobbing themselves to sleep because they wanted one so badly, and their parents were trying to get hold of one for Christmas.They would pay anything, they said.

Breeders began to ring up, begging for details of Zero's parentage. They came and examined him and tried to work out the various strains that had come together to produce him. There was a fortune awaiting the man who could breed Zeros. No one seemed very hopeful about this.

'My guess,' said one of them gloomily, 'is that it's taken centuries of unbridled cross-breeding to produce that. This is the biggest single blow ever struck at the Kennel Club. It could even be mortal. No one wants our dogs any more.'

BURIED BONES had posters made of Zero at his most bewildered-looking, and gave one away for every ten packets of their product bought. People with five children thus had to purchase fifty packets at one go, and the sight of people trundling through supermarkets with trolleys piled high with BURIED BONES became a familiar one.

Owing to popular demand a Zero Fan Club was founded, called *Zero Worshippers*, and people got their photographs autographed with a large paw-mark, and badges saying 'I am a Zero Worshipper' or 'Absolute Zero' or 'Zero is the Most'.

None of this had any real effect on Zero. If anything, he became more dislocated than ever because of the habit people now had of suddenly diving at him in the street or in shops, and shouting, and causing crowds to form. These were friendly crowds, but could not have seemed so to him. Jack tried to fend them off by denying Zero's identity, but no one ever believed him. Sometimes Zero would be patted for half an hour on end. It was lucky, as Mr Bagthorpe pointed out, that whatever Zero's other shortcomings, he was not the sort that bit.

'If he was,' he said, 'then this country would be clean out of tetanus shots.'

His own attitude towards Zero did not change much. If anything, it was the same attitude as before, but now tinged with professional jealousy. Most weeks Zero commanded more viewing space than Mr Bagthorpe, and he was certainly better known. No crowds formed when Mr Bagthorpe went into town.

Grandma and Daisy got recognized, though, particularly when the former wore the outfit she had used for her BLUE LAGOON and GENERATION GAP advertisements. Once she persuaded Daisy to wear her outfit as well, and the pair of them signed hundreds of autographs and a policeman had to come and control the crowd. Grandma talked about this a lot when she wanted to goad Mr Bagthorpe into a really first-class row.

'What a pity you are not photogenic, Henry,' she would say, or:

'To advertise toothpaste, one has to show one's teeth, of course. People who never smile cannot expect much interest to be shown in them.'

At this Mr Bagthorpe would almost invariably bare his teeth.

'You and Daisy,' he would say, 'are novices. Within three months people will be sick of the sight of you. Have you not heard of over-exposure? Why do you think I curb myself as I do? I could have a script on every night of the week, if I wanted.'

'People will never get tired of Daisy and me,' Grandma replied. 'We are originals.'

(The man from GENERATION GAP had told her this, though at the time, of course, he did not know about the near-identical BLUE-LAGOON campaign.)

'Amen to that,' said Mr Bagthorpe grimly, and he left the room abruptly, because Grandma could cap anything – even the last word.

Bingo, the Story of My Dog

ERNEST THOMPSON SETON

Bingo

Ye Franckelyn's dogge leaped over a style,
And yey yclept him lyttel Bingo,
B–I–N–G–O,
And yey yclept him lyttel Bingo.

Ye Franckelyn's wyfe brewed nutte-brown
And he yclept ytte rare goode Stingo,
S–T–I–N–G–O,
And he yclept ytte rare goode Stingo.

Now ys not this a prettye rhyme,
I thynke ytte ys bye Jingo,
J–I–N–G–O,
I thynke ytte ys bye Jingo.

I

It was early in November, 1882, and the Manitoba winter had just set in. I was tilting back in my chair for a few lazy moments after breakfast, idly alternating my gaze from the one windowpane of our shanty, through which was framed a bit of the prairie and the end of our cowshed, to the old rhyme of the 'Franckelyn's dogge' pinned on the logs near by. But the dreamy mixture of rhyme and view was quickly dispelled by the sight of a large grey animal dashing across the prairie into the cowshed, with a smaller black and white animal in hot pursuit.

'A wolf,' I exclaimed, and seizing a rifle dashed out to help the dog. But before I could get there they had left the stable, and after a short run over the snow the wolf again turned at bay, and the dog, our neighbour's collie, circled about, watching his chance to snap.

I fired a couple of long shots, which had the effect only of setting them off again over the prairie. After another run this matchless dog closed and seized the wolf by the haunch, but again retreated to avoid the fierce return chop. Then there was another stand at bay, and again a race over the snow. Every few hundred yards this scene was repeated, the dog managing so that each fresh rush should be toward the settlement, while the wolf vainly tried to break back toward the dark belt of trees in the east. At last after a mile of this fighting and running I overtook them, and the dog, seeing that he now had good backing, closed in for the finish.

After a few seconds the whirl of struggling animals resolved itself into a wolf, on his back, with a bleeding collie gripping his throat, and it was now easy for me to step up and end the fight by putting a ball through the wolf's head.

Then, when this dog of marvellous wind saw that his foe was dead, he gave him no second glance, but set out at a lope for a farm four miles across the snow where he had left his master when first the wolf was started. He was a wonderful dog, and even if I had not come he undoubtedly would have killed the wolf alone, as I learned he had already done with others of the kind, in spite of the fact that the wolf, though of the smaller or prairie race, was much larger than himself.

I was filled with admiration for the dog's prowess and at once sought to buy him at any price. The scornful reply of his owner was, 'Why don't you try to buy one of the children?'

Since Frank was not in the market I was obliged to content myself with the next best thing, one of his alleged progeny. That is, a son of his wife. This probable offspring of an illustrious sire was a roly-poly ball of black fur that looked more like a long-tailed bear-cub than a puppy. But he had some tan markings like those on Frank's coat, that were, I hoped, guarantees of future greatness and also a very characteristic ring of white that he always wore on his muzzle.

Having got possession of his person, the next thing was to find him a name. Surely this puzzle was already solved. The rhyme of the 'Franckelyn's dogge' was inbuilt with the foundation of our acquaintance, so with adequate pomp we 'yclept him little Bingo.'

2

The rest of that winter Bingo spent in our shanty, living the life of a lubberly, fat, well-meaning, ill-doing puppy; gorging himself with food and growing bigger and clumsier each day. Even sad experience failed to teach him that he must keep his nose out of the rat-trap. His most friendly overtures to the cat were wholly misunderstood and resulted only in an armed neutrality that, varied by occasional reigns of terror, continued to the end; which came when Bingo, who early showed a mind of his own, got a notion for sleeping at the barn and avoiding the shanty altogether.

When the spring came I set about his serious education. After much pains on my behalf and many pains on his, he learned to go at the word in quest of our old yellow cow, that pastured at will on the unfenced prairie.

Once he had learned his business, he became very fond of it and nothing pleased him more than an order to go and fetch the cow. Away he would dash, barking with pleasure and leaping high in the air that he might better scan the plain for his victim. In a short time he would return driving her at full gallop before him, and gave her no peace until, puffing and blowing, she was safely driven into the farthest corner of her stable.

Less energy on his part would have been more satisfactory, but we bore with him until he grew so fond of this semi-daily hunt that he began to bring 'old Dunne' without being told. And at length not once or twice but a dozen times a day this energetic cowherd would sally forth on his own responsibility and drive the cow home to the stable.

At last things came to such a pass that whenever he felt like taking a little exercise, or had a few minutes of spare time, or even happened to think of it, Bingo would sally forth at racing speed over the plain and a few minutes later return, driving the unhappy yellow cow at full gallop before him.

At first this did not seem very bad, as it kept the cow from straying too far: but soon it was seen that it hindered her feeding. She became thin and gave less milk; it seemed to weigh on her mind too, as she was always watching nervously for that hateful dog, and in the mornings would hang around the stable as though afraid to venture off and subject herself at once to an onset.

This was going too far. All attempts to make Bingo more moderate in his pleasure were failures, so he was compelled to give it up altogether. After this, though he dared not bring her home, he continued to show his interest by lying at her stable door while she was being milked.

As the summer came on the mosquitoes became a dreadful plague, and the consequent vicious switching of Dunne's tail at milking-time even more annoying than the mosquitoes.

Fred, the brother who did the milking, was of an inventive as well as an impatient turn of mind, and he devised a simple plan to stop the switching. He fastened a brick to the cow's tail, then set blithely about his work, assured of unusual comfort while the rest of us looked on in doubt.

Suddenly through the mist of mosquitoes came a dull whack and an outburst of 'language'. The cow went on placidly chewing till Fred got on his feet and furiously attacked her with the milking-stool. It was bad enough to be whacked on the ear with a brick by a stupid old cow, but the uproarious enjoyment and ridicule of the bystanders made it unendurable.

Bingo, hearing the uproar, and divining that he was needed, rushed in and attacked Dunne on the other side. Before the affair quieted down the milk was spilt, the pail and stool were broken, and the cow and the dog severely beaten.

Poor Bingo could not understand it at all. He had long ago learned to despise that cow, and now in utter disgust he decided to forsake even her stable door, and from that time he attached himself exclusively to the horses and their stable.

The cattle were mine, the horses were my brother's, and in transferring his allegiance from the cow-stable to the horse-stable Bingo seemed to give me up too, and anything like daily companionship ceased, and yet, whenever any emergency arose, Bingo turned to me and I to him, and both seemed to feel that the bond between man and dog is one that lasts as long as life.

The only other occasion on which Bingo acted as cowherd was in the autumn of the same year at the Annual Carberry Fair. Among the dazzling inducements to enter one's stock there was, in addition to prospect of glory, a cash prize of 'two dollars', for the 'best collie in training'.

Misled by a false friend, I entered Bingo, and early on the day fixed, the cow was driven to the prairie just outside the village. When the time came she was pointed out to Bingo and the word given – 'Go fetch the cow.' It was the intention of course, that he should bring her to me at the judge's stand.

But the animals knew better. They hadn't rehearsed all summer for nothing. When Dunne saw Bingo's careering form she knew that her only hope for safety was to get into her stable, and Bingo was equally sure that his sole mission in life was to quicken her pace in that direction. So off they raced over the prairie, like a wolf after a deer, and, heading straight toward their home two miles away, they disappeared from view.

That was the last that judge or jury ever saw of dog or cow. The prize was awarded to the only other entry.

3

Bingo's loyalty to the horses was quite remarkable; by day he trotted beside them, and by night he slept at the stable door. Where the team went Bingo went, and nothing kept him away from them. This interesting assumption of ownership lent the greater significance to the following circumstance.

I was not superstitious, and up to this time had no faith in omens, but was now deeply impressed by a strange occurrence in which Bingo took a leading part. There were but two of us now living on the De Winton Farm. One morning my brother set out for Boggy Creek for a load of hay. It was a long day's journey there and back, and he made an early start. Strange to tell, Bingo for once in his life did not follow the team. My brother called to him, but still he stood at a safe distance, and eyeing the team askance, refused to stir. Suddenly he raised his nose in the air and gave vent to a long melancholy howl. He watched the wagon out of sight, and even followed for a hundred yards or so, raising his voice from time to time in the most doleful howlings. All that day he stayed about the barn, the only time that he was willingly separated from the horses, and at intervals howled a very death dirge. I was alone, and the dog's behaviour inspired me with an awful foreboding of calamity that weighed upon me more and more as the hours passed away.

About six o'clock Bingo's howlings became unbearable, so that for lack of a better thought I threw something at him, and ordered him away. But oh, the feeling of horror that filled me! Why did I let my brother go away alone? Should I ever again see him alive? I might have known from the dog's actions that something dreadful was about to happen.

At length the hour for his return arrived, and there was John on his load. I took charge of the horses, vastly relieved, and with an air of assumed unconcern, asked, 'All right?'

'Right,' was the laconic answer.

Who now can say that there is nothing in omens?

And yet, when long afterward, I told this to one skilled in the occult, he looked grave, and said, 'Bingo always turned to you in a crisis?'

'Yes.'

'Then do not smile. It was you that were in danger that day; he stayed and saved your life, though you never knew from what.'

4

Early in the spring I had begun Bingo's education. Very shortly afterwards he began mine.

Midway on the two-mile stretch of prairie that lay between our shanty and the village of Carberry, was the corner-stake of the farm; it was a stout post in a low mound of earth, and was visible from afar.

I soon noticed that Bingo never passed without minutely examining this mysterious post. Next I learned that it was also visited by the prairie wolves, as well as by all the dogs in the neighbourhood, and at length, with the aid of a telescope, I made a number of observations that helped me to an understanding of the matter and enabled me to enter more fully into Bingo's private life.

The post was by common agreement a registry of the canine tribes. Their exquisite sense of smell enabled each individual to tell at once by the track and trace what other had recently been at the post. When the snow came much more was revealed. I then discovered that his post was but one of a system that covered the country; that in short, the entire region was laid out in signal stations at convenient intervals. These were marked by any conspicuous post, stone, buffalo skull, or other object that chanced to be in the desired locality, and extensive observation showed that it was a very complete system for getting and giving the news.

Each dog or wolf makes a point of calling at those stations that are near his line of travel to learn who has recently been there, just as a man calls at his club on returning to town and looks up the register.

I have seen Bingo approach the post, sniff, examine the ground about, then growl, and with bristling mane and glowing eyes, scratch fiercely and contemptuously with his hind feet, finally walking off very stiffly, glancing back from time to time. All of which, being interpreted, said:

'*Grrrh! woof!* there's that dirty cur of McCarthy's. *Woof!* I'll 'tend to him to-night. *Woof! woof!*' On another occasion, after the preliminaries, he became keenly interested and studied a coyote's track that came and went, saying to himself, as I afterwards learned:

'A coyote track coming from the north, smelling of dead cow. Indeed? Pollworth's old Brindle must be dead at last. This is worth looking into.'

At other times he would wag his tail, trot about the vicinity and come again and again to make his own visit more evident, perhaps for the benefit of his brother Bill just back from Brandon! So that it was not by chance that one night Bill turned up at Bingo's home and was taken to the hills where a delicious dead horse afforded a chance to suitably celebrate the reunion.

At other times he would be suddenly aroused by the news, take up the trail, and race to the next station for later information.

Sometimes his inspection produced only an air of grave attention, as though he said to himself, 'Dear me, who the deuce is this?' or 'I think I met that fellow at the Portage last summer.'

One morning on approaching the post Bingo's every hair stood on end, his tail dropped and quivered, and he gave proof that he was suddenly sick at the stomach, sure signs of terror. He showed no desire to follow up or know more of the matter, but returned to the house, and half an hour afterward his mane was still bristling and his expression one of hate or fear.

I studied the dreaded track and learned that in Bingo's language the half-terrified, deep-gurgled '*grrr-wff*' means '*timber wolf.*'

These were among the things that Bingo taught me. And in the after time when I might chance to see him arouse from his frosty nest by the stable door and after stretching himself and shaking the snow from his shaggy coat, disappear into the gloom at a steady trot trot, trot, I used to think:

'Aha! old dog, I know where you are off to, and why you eschew the shelter of the shanty. Now I know why your nightly trips over the country are so well timed, and how you know just where to go for what you want, and when and how to seek it.'

5

In the autumn of 1884, the shanty of De Winton farm was closed and Bingo changed his home to the establishment, that is, to the stable, not the house, of Gordon Wright, our most intimate neighbour.

Since the winter of his puppyhood he had declined to enter a house at any time excepting during a thunder-storm. Of thunder and guns he had a deep dread – no doubt the fear of the first originated in the second, and that arose from some unpleasant shot-gun experiences, the cause of which will be seen. His nightly couch was outside the stable, even during the coldest weather, and it was easy to see that he enjoyed to the full the complete nocturnal liberty entailed. Bingo's midnight wanderings extended across the plains for miles. There was plenty of proof of this. Some farmers at very remote points sent word to old Gordon that if he did not keep his dog home nights, they would use the shot-gun, and Bingo's terror of firearms would indicate that the threats were not idle. A man living as far away as Petrel, said he saw a large black wolf kill a coyote on the snow one winter evening, but afterward he changed his opinion and 'reckoned it must 'a' been Wright's dog'. Whenever the body of a winter-killed ox or horse was exposed, Bingo was sure to repair to it nightly, and, driving away the prairie wolves, feast to repletion.

Sometimes the object of a night foray was merely to maul some distant neighbour's dog, and notwithstanding vengeful threats, there seemed no reason to fear that the Bingo breed would die out. One man even avowed that he had seen a prairie wolf accompanied by three young ones which resembled the mother, excepting that they were very large and black and had a ring of white around the muzzle.

True or not as that may be, I know that late in March, while we were out in the sleigh with Bingo trotting behind, a prairie wolf was started from a hollow. Away it went with Bingo in full chase, but the wolf did not greatly exert itself to escape, and within a short distance Bingo was close up, yet, strange to tell, there was no grappling, no fight!

Bingo trotted amiably alongside and licked the wolf's nose.

We were astounded, and shouted to urge Bingo on. Our shouting and approach several times started the wolf off at speed and Bingo again pursued until he had overtaken it, but his gentleness was too obvious.

'It is a she-wolf, he won't harm her,' I exclaimed as the truth dawned on me. And Gordon said: 'Well, I be darned.'

So we called our unwilling dog and drove on.

For weeks after this we were annoyed by the depredations of a prairie wolf who killed our chickens, stole pieces of pork from the end of the house, and several times terrified the children by looking into the window of the shanty while the men were away.

Against this animal Bingo seemed to be no safeguard. At length the wolf, a female, was killed, and then Bingo plainly showed his hand by his lasting enmity toward Oliver, the man who did the deed.

6

It is wonderful and beautiful how a man and his dog will stick to one another, through thick and thin. Butler tells of an undivided Indian tribe, in the far north which was all but exterminated by an internecine feud over a dog that belonged to one man and was killed by his neighbour; and among ourselves we have lawsuits, fights, and deadly feuds, all pointing the same old moral, 'Love me, love my dog.'

One of our neighbours had a very fine hound that he thought the best and dearest dog in the world. I loved him, so I loved his dog, and when one day poor Tan crawled home terribly mangled and died by the door, I joined my threats of vengeance with those of his master and thenceforth lost no opportunity of tracing the miscreant, both by offering rewards and by collecting scraps of evidence. At length it was clear that one of three men to the southward had had a hand in the cruel affair. The scent was warming up, and soon we should have been in a position to exact rigorous justice at least, from the wretch who had murdered poor old Tan.

Then something took place which at once changed my mind and led me to believe that the mangling of the old hound was not by any means an unpardonable crime, but indeed on second thoughts was rather commendable than otherwise.

Gordon Wright's farm lay to the south of us, and while there one day, Gordon, Jun., knowing that I was tracking the murderer, took me aside and looking about furtively, he whispered, in tragic tones:

'It was Bing done it.'

And the matter dropped right there. For I confess that from that moment I did all in my power to baffle the justice I had previously striven so hard to further.

I had given Bingo away long before, but the feeling of ownership did not die; and of this indissoluble fellowship of dog and man he was soon to take part in another important illustration.

Old Gordon and Oliver were close neighbours and friends; they joined in a contract to cut wood and worked together harmoniously till late on in winter. Then Oliver's old horse died, and he, determining to profit as far as possible, dragged it out on the plain and laid poison baits for wolves around it. Alas, for poor Bingo! He would lead a wolfish life, though again and again it brought him into wolfish misfortunes.

He was as fond of dead horse as any of his wild kindred. That very night, with Wright's own dog Curley, he visited the carcass.

It seemed as though Bing had busied himself chiefly keeping off the wolves, but Curley feasted immoderately. The tracks in the snow told the story of the banquet; the interruption as the poison began to work, and of the dreadful spasms of pain during the erratic course back home where Curley, falling in convulsions at Gordon's feet, died in the greatest agony.

'Love me, love my dog,' no explanations or apology were acceptable; it was useless to urge that it was accidental, the long-standing feud between Bingo and Oliver was now remembered as an important tide-light. The wood-contract was thrown up, all friendly relations ceased, and to this day there is no county big enough to hold the rival factions which were called at once into existence and to arms by Curley's dying yell.

It was months before Bingo really recovered from the poison. We believed indeed that he never again would be the sturdy old-time Bingo. But when the spring came he began to gain strength, and bettering as the grass grew, he was within a few weeks once more in full health and vigour to be a pride to his friends and a nuisance to his neighbours.

The Case of the Hidden Earring

PARTAP SHARMA

Ranjha, the detective dog and Woof, his master, take on many exciting cases in Bombay, and the hill town where Ranjha's human family spend much of their time. This story is set in the jungle surrounding Mahabaleshwar, where Ranjha has found a mysteriously hidden earring.

The tree in which I found the hidden earring grew in the grounds of the Missionary's Bungalow. I was merely poking about as any tracker dog might when I was struck by the strong smell of soap coming from the knot-hole of a tree. It was a quite ordinary tree but the soapy smell was extraordinary. And it was not the smell of toilet soap either; it was the smell of a washing powder used for cleaning clothes. As I caught the unexpected odour I could almost see the flakes dissolving and foaming in a bucket of water.

I put my nose into the knot-hole and took out the earring. Woof gasped. The three large emeralds glittered on their background of gold.

Woof took the earring from me and said, 'Let's return it.'

As I set off, tracking free, with my nose to the ground, I knew

Woof was thinking, as I was, that it was a funny place in which to find an earring. What was perhaps even funnier was that it wasn't a pair of earrings but just one. How had it come to be there?

The Missionary's Bungalow was a gaunt, deserted house. We had never seen a missionary there yet but then perhaps that was just an old name for the crumbling ruin. Mahabaleshwar is full of such places – solitary, uncared for, almost forgotten. I often heard Woof asking passing villagers about these neglected bungalows scattered like milestones of history amid the jungle, but no one could tell us more than that sometimes their owners would come from the cities on a short holiday and camp in those cold, unfurnished rooms only to return to the city in disgust and there sell the structure to some other person who would rarely come.

For a moment I wondered what we would do if the scent led up to the Missionary's Bungalow for I knew there was no one there now. The trail was two days old.

But we went on past the bungalow and down a path leading to some huts. Had we been moving merely instinctively we might have rushed straight into that cluster of huts and asked about for the owner of the earring. We were, however, following a definite trail and the scent led off to the right. Behind me Woof stopped in puzzlement. I had sniffed my way off the path now and was inching up the hill into the woods.

I could understand Woof's puzzlement. After all, there was a road going round the woods. Why hadn't the person we were following taken the open road? Even the little paths that criss-crossed the jungle had been avoided. It was almost as if the earring had been deposited there in stealth; the person had been to the tree and then slipped away through the jungle like a thief.

It is difficult for me to stop and think once I am set on the trail of something or someone. I gave my short, impatient call which is half howl, half moan. Woof saw that my tail was curving up and my hair bristling in excitement; he understood that I was on the track. Human beings sometimes need to be reassured that you are not misleading them. With a shrug and a shake of his head, Woof followed.

We made our way through bramble and fern and past bushes of the yellow wildflower known in these parts as *dingler*. Every now and again, Woof called out to me to wait for him. Tracking free, without the restraint of a harness, I was moving fast and well ahead. The scent was strong and getting stronger for here, in the woods, the wind had not blown it away and the sun had not been able to reach in and destroy it. There was a stale, rotting touch to it, of course; to me it was as clear as the odour of a bad egg in a windless room.

Then we were out in a clearing and going down a slight incline and crossing a road. The road, the incline, the clearing – all seemed familiar to me and yet, for the moment, I couldn't place them. I tried not to think of where we were, my job was to concentrate on the tracking. Now the smell had developed a fresher, sweet overtone. I recognized it as an attar, a kind of cloying perfume. This particular attar was obviously an extract of roses. It was heady and overpowering. It flowed up my nose and blossomed like roses in my nostrils. I sneezed, shook my head clear and rubbed at my muzzle with a paw. Woof began to wonder if I was getting a cold!

Under the smell of roses lay the smell of soap and body odour. And covering it all like a wrapper over a toffee was the smell of wood-smoke. So it was clear that the person I was tracking used perfume, washed clothes and cooked over a wood-fire. And considering that I had taken the scent from an earring, it was fairly obvious that I was trailing a woman. The body odour, too, confirmed this, for men and women smell different from each other. But, of course, Woof had no way yet of knowing all this.

We were now crossing an unkempt, untidy grass verge and heading towards a hut. I looked up now and saw that we were in the large compound of a bungalow. The hut stood at the end of the compound.

It was unnecessary now to keep my nose to the ground-scent, for the body-scent was like a canal of honey in the air. I kept my head up and into it, pulled along like a paper boat by a current.

Tracking can be so enjoyable that a dog loses himself in the delicious symphony of smells as they grow clearer and engulf him in a cloud of ecstasy. That is what happened to me. Foolish as it may seem, I rushed on in my enthusiasm past the woman who had stepped out of the hut and was now hanging clothes out to dry on a line.

Suddenly I realized I had overshot the source of the scent. I turned round, feeling quite silly. I went up to the thin, tired-looking, sari-clad woman and gently held her wrist in my mouth. Then I stepped back a pace and barked. Woof came up to the woman and held out the earring to her.

Instead of being delighted and thankful, she gasped and went white as a sheet.

Woof smiled and took another step forward but she withdrew, trembling, and dropped the clothes she was holding. One of her hands went to her mouth and it seemed as though she was trying to stop herself from screaming. In a second she was perspiring and there was a terrible smell of fear in the air.

Woof mistook her reaction for surprise. He said kindly, 'We found it in a tree by the Missionary's Bungalow.'

'No, no, no!' she cried, 'I didn't put it there. I don't know anything about it!'

Woof was taken aback. He looked at me. I barked at the woman. I knew for certain that it was she who had hidden the earring there. But I could see that Woof was more inclined to believe a human being than a dog. He seemed disappointed in me as if I had made some mistake!

At this point a tall villager dressed in a Gandhi cap and clean white clothes appeared at the door of the hut. The woman ran to him breathlessly and said, pointing at Woof, 'Look! He's got that lady's earring. He says I hid it in some tree. He's accusing me!'

The man took a couple of steps towards Woof and looked down at him with his head cocked slightly to one side. He spoke in a nasty tone.

'Who're you?' he asked.

Woof had by now sensed that something was wrong. He realized that the earring in his hand was a stolen one. The woman recognized it but wished to deny all knowledge of how it came to be in the knot-hole of a tree.

Woof said, 'Never mind who I am. Take me to the owner of this earring.'

The tall man looked at the woman. Then he looked at me. Turning to Woof, he asked, 'Is that a police dog?'

'No,' Woof said, 'but he's trained like one. He tracked this woman here. She stole the earring, I think, and hid it in the tree.'

'Look mister,' the man said, 'you are not a policeman to be going around accusing people. I happen to be the *patil*, the headman, of Mangli village down in the valley. I am appointed by the police. I know the law and I know who is a thief and who is not. This woman is my wife. Your dog has no business to go about chasing innocent people. Such a dog is a danger and a nuisance. He should be shot. Now give me the earring and I shall return it to its owner.'

'No,' said Woof, 'I'll take it back to the owner myself.'

'I am not a man to be trifled with,' the tall fellow said, removing his cap and dusting it forcefully against one hand.

The slapping sound irritated me. It was a threat of violence. He was that kind of man. I growled.

The *patil* put the cap back on his head, turned on his heel and went into the hut.

Woof sighed and motioning me to his side began to walk away.

The woman called something to the man and now he came back to the door of his hut. In his hand was a double-barrelled gun.

'Hey you!' the man shouted. 'Where're you going?'

Woof turned round.

'To the police,' he said.

'No,' said the man, 'you are not. I say you are not.'

I could see that the sight of the gun had not only shocked and frightened Woof, it had also made him angry.

'Surely,' Woof said in an incredulous voice, 'you don't intend to use that silly thing simply because I am going to the police with a stolen earring!'

'This silly thing,' the *patil* said sarcastically, 'is a loaded twelve-bore. It helps me keep peace in the village. It also enables me to hunt rabbits. But today I could use it to destroy a dangerous dog and recover a stolen earring from his master.'

Woof gave a little laugh.

'No one will believe you,' he said.

'You won't be around to worry about that,' the man replied, 'and I have ways of making people believe me. You know what I think? I think you are trying to frame my wife. I think you are accusing her falsely in order to ruin my family name. This is a trick of my enemies. They have got you to do this for them. Perhaps you are innocent of mischief, I grant that. Perhaps you have been misled. You don't look the kind of person to get involved in the politics of a little local village. But who knows? The world is full of strange people. You may be a member of some political party that's trying to gain control of the area. You may be helping some people to dislodge me from my position as *patil* of the village.'

Woof was aghast. 'You must be crazy!' he said.

The man nodded. 'Maybe I am. Maybe I'm clever. Maybe I'm anything. Just give me the earring and get out of here. You're a young man. Don't mess up your life by poking your nose into other people's business.'

'Be reasonable,' Woof said with an attempt at a smile. 'The dog and I happened to find a piece of jewellery and we want only to do the right thing by returning it to the owner.'

The man cocked both barrels of his gun and muttered, 'I've told you – just give it to me and get out.'

His eyes had gone red and he was again looking at us sideways across his hawklike nose. The woman clung to one of his arms but he now shrugged her aside and raised the gun. It pointed at me.

'All right,' Woof said. 'Here you are, take the earring.'

But the man was no fool. He jerked his head and said, 'Throw it at my feet.'

Woof hesitated. Then he said, 'No, one of the emeralds is loose. It'll fall out.'

'Never mind,' said the man. 'If the stone falls out, we'll find it.'

'As you wish,' Woof said and threw the earring at his feet. The man did not even look down.

'Now, I want you to –' he began but before he could say more Woof pointed to a spot near his feet.

'By the way,' Woof said, 'is that a snake crawling into your hut?'

There *are* snakes in Mahabaleshwar but the poisonous kinds are rare. Nevertheless, people have to be careful, especially in the rainy season and soon after. And snakes sometimes do crawl into huts.

The man shifted on his feet and quickly looked down.

'Ranjha, disarm!' Woof shouted and rushed forward.

A dog is always faster than a man. I had leapt past Woof and straight at the *patil* before he could look up. As I threw him to the ground and took the cold steel of the gun in my jaws, a thunderous explosion shook the barrel. I had half wrenched the gun out of the man's hand but now it went flying with the force of the bang. I was also flung aside. I had been trained not to be afraid of gunfire or crackers but I had never known the roar and power of a gun going off while I was holding it. The terrible noise and the effect of it was so awesome that for a moment I thought I was dying. As I got up, dazed and deafened, I saw that the man was getting up too. The woman was screaming. Woof was moaning on the ground.

I went straight to Woof and sniffed at him and licked his face. I forgot everything else. I was terrified that Woof was hurt. Perhaps it was a mistake to worry just then about Woof but I couldn't help it. I didn't mind being shot and killed but I had to see to Woof. The gun was lying by Woof's head. It looked as if he had been struck by a wooden butt.

'Ranjha, disarm!' Woof shouted and rushed forward

The woman was shouting and screaming. She had picked up a thick chunk of firewood and was coming towards me. Her husband was now picking up the gun.

Woof said weakly, 'Attack.' And then he closed his eyes and slumped. I sniffed at him. He was breathing all right. He was just unconscious. He had asked me to attack. That was the ultimate command I could be given. That meant Woof was in grave danger. I had to do everything I could to save him. I had to prevent them from injuring Woof. It took me less than a second to act on Woof's command.

But worried as I was, I was too late.

The woman hit me with the chunk of wood. She must have been quite unnerved by events or perhaps she was frightened of me. She missed my head and the blow caught me on the back. I snarled and jumped. I had her by the arm and hung on. She shrieked and tried to pry me loose but I had been trained to hang on even if I was lifted off the ground and whirled in a circle. The man had the gun now and was shouting to her but he couldn't fire because he was afraid of hitting her. Then I became aware of people running towards us from the big house and some were running along the road.

The woman fainted and fell down. I released her. As I turned, I saw that Woof was trying to sit up and the man was about to shoot at me.

Woof gasped, 'Ranjha, down!'

There was such urgency in his voice though it was low that I immediately flopped down. Just then there was another deafening explosion and something whistled over my head.

The man clicked open the barrel and threw down two smoking cartridge cases, then he ran towards the hut. He was going for more ammunition but by now four or five people had arrived on the scene. He seemed undecided whether to stay or run. Then, amazingly, he sat down on a step and putting the gun aside took his head in his hands. People were gathering round now and asking what was happening. He said nothing.

They helped Woof to get up and they threw cold water on the

woman's face and revived her.

They looked at me, still in the down position, and wondered whether I was to blame for the trouble. Some said aloud that I had probably been raiding the man's chickens, others said that I had most likely attacked the woman for no reason.

'What a lovely dog!' a child's voice said quite inappropriately at that moment. I looked and saw that three well-dressed children had come along with their parents from the house at the farther end of the compound.

While the father of the children stepped into the centre of the growing circle and asked, 'What's going on here?', one of the children made friendly noises in my direction. Even in the down position, I couldn't help wagging my tail. It thumped the ground. That made the children laugh. I began to feel more relaxed. They came up and began to pet me. I felt better. At least someone in the crowd seemed to be on my side.

Woof was explaining what had happened. The father of the children listened and then said, 'I must thank you for what you've done. I've never really trusted this fellow or his wife. He's supposed to be the gardener of this bungalow but he spends all his time being the terror of his village in the valley. His wife does the washing for the house. We've been losing odd bits of jewellery ever since we bought this place and started coming up for the school holidays. Somehow we could never work up the courage to sack this couple. This fellow is such a bully around here that I was . . . well, in a way, frightened of accusing them on mere suspicion. By the way, allow me to introduce myself. My name is Desai. My wife. My children.'

Mrs Desai joined her palms and greeted Woof and thanked him.

Mr Desai said that on hearing the first gunshot he had phoned the police. He said he was going to hand the gardener and his wife over to the police.

Now the gardener stood up and looked down at everyone across the bridge of his nose.

'What a lot of rubbish is being talked!' he said. 'What

accusations are being flung! What threats of action against a poor, innocent man and his wife! If Mr Desai wants me to leave his employ, I will. My wife and I will go away this very minute. But I will not have my good name tarnished. The police know me to be an honest man. The name of my family is being threatened for other reasons. This is a frame-up. Mr Desai is against me for certain deep reasons which I shall explain later. I know things about him. That is why he wants to ruin my good name. No jewellery was ever lost as far as I know. This is the first I'm hearing of it. For that matter, where *is* this precious earring that is supposed to have been brought back by this young man?'

The police had arrived in the middle of this speech and now an Inspector came forward and took charge of the situation.

The crowd had grown and was murmuring.

Mrs Desai was exclaiming at the amazing audacity of the gardener in trying to lie his way out of the whole thing. Mr Desai was spluttering and fuming.

Woof made a full statement of what had happened. The Inspector listened to all that was being said. When Woof gave his name, the Inspector said, 'Ah yes, I've heard of you and your dog. I wasn't on duty the night of the riot in the bazaar but my colleagues have told me how you helped. Now, the first thing, of course, is – where is the earring which you say you found?'

Everyone began to scan the ground for the earring.

The gardener said, 'There's no point looking for the ornament. It doesn't exist. It's all a lot of lies to put me in a bad light with my people.'

The Inspector called out to everybody to stay where they were. Then he began to look around by the hut for the earring. The gardener laughed sarcastically.

After a couple of minutes he said, 'I know you would like to believe this young man but it's just not true. He never threw any earring or whatever on the ground."

Now one of the children said, 'He's a liar. We know that Mummy's lost a lot of things. She lost an earring two days ago.'

'Ah ha,' said the gardener, 'she may have lost these things. I'm not denying that. She may have lost them through carelessness while walking in the bazaar or during a walk. I have never seen this famous earring nor has my wife.'

The children too began to cast their eyes over the ground. In the grass and the soft earth, it was difficult to see any trace of an earring.

'Excuse me, Inspector,' Woof said. 'May I suggest that we ask the dog to search for it?'

'The dog!' the Inspector exclaimed. 'How would he find it?'

'There is a way,' said Woof.

'Don't tell me he knows the meaning of the word *earring*!'

'No, Inspector, he doesn't. He places as much value on an earring as on a piece of wood or a bit of stone. But I've just thought of a way by which he can find it.'

'Hm. All right. No harm in trying. And if there is such an earring about, at least he won't be tempted to pocket it!'

'Ranjha, come,' Woof called.

I went up to him. He cupped his hands over my nose, giving me his own scent; then he asked me to seek and fetch. I began to sniff the ground in the direction in which he pointed.

'I see,' said the Inspector. 'Very clever. Quite sensible. Since you threw the earring and since you carried it all the way here, it'll still have your scent on it.'

'Right,' said Woof and I imagine he must have smiled but I didn't look at him to find out; I was busy with the task I had been set.

I sniffed over the patch of ground and in a few seconds I located the spot where the object had lain. But it had been moved – perhaps by the scrambling about during the struggle, or perhaps because someone had picked it up. Close by was the step on which the gardener had sat with his head in his hands. The smell of the gardener's footwear was mingled with Woof's scent on the spot where the earring had been. That meant the gardener had placed his feet close to or over the earring. However, my job was just to sniff; the conclusions were to be left to Woof. So I continued to sniff about in widening circles. I was sniffing various shoes and sandals and feet now. Woof assured people that there was no risk to them. They stood still. But as I approached the shoes of the gardener, he began to move and complain against me.

'This dog is dangerous, I tell you. He attacked me and then he attacked my wife. He ... he ... he ... don't let him come near me!'

He was moving about, taking short steps. It annoyed me. I knew now that the earring was tucked between his left foot and the *mojri* he was wearing. It must have hurt the sole of his foot. I suppose he'd picked up the earring with his bare foot, taking it up between his toes, while he sat there on the step. Now I made a determined grab for his *mojri*. It came off and out tumbled the earring. I carried it to Woof.

The children burst into spontaneous applause. My tail couldn't help wagging. Everyone else joined in with the children and clapped. It was like being at some kind of public demonstration.

'I hope the applause doesn't go to his head!' Woof said, laughing.

People were chuckling and murmuring, but all this while, the gardener had been sidling away. No one expected him to make a run for it. After all, his wife was still there standing in the veranda of their quarters. But perhaps some kind of panic seized him; perhaps he had decided to abandon his wife to her fate. If they had stolen many things over the years, they must have a tidy sum hidden away somewhere. Perhaps his intention was to escape out of the district entirely.

Anyway, he didn't get far, not even as far as the clearing beyond the road. Everyone took off after him but being a tall man with a big stride he easily outpaced them. Then Woof said, quite casually now, 'Ranjha, arrest!' and waved me in the fleeing gardener's direction.

As I said before, a dog is much faster than human beings.

I must admit that the applause this time did go a little to my head. I leapt all over the children and adults as they petted me.

Later, when Wuff heard about it all she gave me a special reward for having stood by Woof. The snack she served me in my bowl is the one I consider the most delicious treat – chicken livers on toast. That's my very favourite.

Getting into Show Business

BARBARA WOODHOUSE

People have often said to me 'How did you start getting your Juno known and into films and television?' This is a long story. The first thing I did was of course to obedience train her. She was one of the first Danes to take part in public obedience competitions, and she always attracted a lot of attention, especially as we also had Chica the tiny little Black and Tan terrier, as the breed was then known, with Juno. This tiny mite would sit between Juno's paws and of course that was just what made a picture for the Press. Without the Press, practically nothing can be achieved. I was lucky enough to meet dozens of charming people from the Press in conjunction with my next book *Talking to Animals* when I appeared many times on television with Juno, spoke on the radio and was happy to get a lot of Press publicity. It was always Juno who posed for the pictures that were original and were well received by the national newspapers, so the photographers were delighted and used to ring me up and ask me to do some sessions at my home for the magazines and papers. I have literally hundreds and hundreds of photos of my dogs doing just everything. I have ten huge volumes of Press cuttings so I shall never really be without my dogs. I only have to open these books and be lost in the world of my Danes.

The next thing I did was road safety. I trained Juno to look both ways before crossing the road and not cross if there was anything coming. I taught her never to fetch a ball if it ran into the road. I taught her to drop into the down on signal at a great distance to prevent her ever running into the road by mistake even if she was in the country, although I do not advocate any dog being off the lead where there is traffic, however well trained it is. I think only conceited people do this in an effort to show what good trainers they are. Then I started approaching the Road Safety officers in districts within reasonable distance of me, and offered to give road safety training demonstrations for dogs, and talks if they would organize the hall. I borrowed a film on dogs and road safety from the Royal Society for the Prevention of Accidents, and at the end of the talk invited anyone with a dog to let me show them how easy it was to teach it to behave. Slowly I graduated to doing Saturday morning children's cinema matinee performances. In the interval I would take my dogs and draw a white line on the stage and ask the children to shout whether there was a car coming or not. If they yelled 'yes' Juno would not go across the line. If they said 'no' she crossed. The same when we threw an object, if the children said traffic was coming Juno never retrieved it. If the road was clear she would go across and fetch it on command, never without command. The children loved the dogs Juno and Chica and the requests for these demonstrations and talks grew and grew. More press write-ups came our way. Then I decided to start a dog-training class at Croxley Green. I put an advertisement in the local paper asking people to contact me if they would like a dog-training club to be set up with me as trainer. Six people answered and the Croxley Canine Training Club came into being. The only hut we could get on a Sunday morning was the Territorial building at Croxley where the guns were stored, but it was dry and we could do heelwork in the rather confined area around the guns. Juno always demonstrated the correct obedience, and I taught these six people. Soon we were overflowing with requests for training and to cut a long story short I was soon running six clubs in different districts. Every night I ran one within a radius of about ten miles and on Sunday I ran one at my home. Sometimes there were as many as sixty dogs in a class. I used to charge a shilling a lesson to pay for the halls I had to hire in other districts. But mothers and fathers got cunning and I discovered children were borrowing neighbour's dogs and being sent up to me on a Sunday afternoon so that Mum and Dad could put their feet up and let me cope with the children! This was not a good thing as the dogs they borrowed neither loved them nor obeyed them at all and I put a stop to it. Over 7,000 dogs passed through my hands running dog clubs, and Juno was always the dog that showed people how to train their dogs if a demonstration was needed. This led to her being asked to appear at fêtes and give a show of her tricks etc.; I was delighted to do this. Later Junia even surpassed Juno's efforts at fêtes as she learnt to roll the tombola with her paws and bark as I declared the fête open. She would even pick out the winning raffle ticket because I would have shut my eyes and put my hand in the hat and she of course picked the ticket that bore my scent, but everyone thought it was just clever Junia. I went to Chatsworth and gave a dog-training demonstration with Juno for charity; more Press publicity.

Perhaps one of the most amusing things I organized for Juno's publicity to help the Guide Dogs for the Blind was to ask permission to collect at the Championship Cat Show at Olympia one year. Some of the cat owners weren't all that pleased at a dog being at the show, but most of them knowing how gentle Juno was were delighted at the television and national newspaper publicity. Juno was put into a cage of baby kittens and adored them. She always had a very motherly attitude to other animals, and when the champion cat was chosen for the supreme prize it lay between Juno's great paws for innumerable photographs to be taken by the Press. We raised quite a considerable amount in Juno's boxes for the Guide Dogs for the Blind. Neither Juno nor Junia ever chased cats, I think they understood that here in our home anything like that was just not on, as did our cat understand that to kill a bird was a crime in our eyes. Birds built their nests at our front door and baby birds flopped about all over the place but neither cat nor Dane would injure them in any way. Words were enough to teach the two dogs what I wanted, but one good smack taught the cat the only time she caught a bird. I never had to smack my dogs, although I am not one of those sentimental people who say a dog should never be smacked. If I thought a dog warranted that sort of punishment I would do it without regret of any sort. It often shortens the time spent in training when the dog is really doing wrong and not listening to words of reprimand. This doesn't happen if the dog is trained from its earliest days.

I once had to take Juno for an episode of 'The Larkins' for television where there were six cats in the same scene. All the cats were in the kitchen, Juno was to rush in and all the cats were supposed to jump up into different places. This seemed impossible; however in the end I practised each cat separately and it was achieved, but cats are not easy to work like dogs; food is the best way to get them to do things. The cats didn't belong to me either.

I always remember Juno collecting for the Blind at the United Charities Bazaar in the Watford Town Hall. She was a dog who would wag her tail at everyone in the hope they would put money in her boxes. She knew as well as I did that this was something she was supposed to do. One man came up to her and spoke to her and she lifted her upper lip in a warning growl, something I had never seen her do in her life. I told the man to leave her alone and went to the policeman at the Town Hall entrance and asked him to keep an eye on this man. A short time after the man was arrested for shop-lifting. How can a dog sum up character like this and warn me of danger ahead?

I remember one experience with Juno which had extraordinary results. I had left my car in Piccadilly before the age of traffic wardens and on returning to it, some 200 yards away I saw a man with a key trying to open the door. Juno was police-work trained, I let her off the lead and gave her the command to 'get him' which she swiftly did. I arrested the man and handed him to a Police Officer but, and this is the queer story, I got a letter from Scotland Yard telling me they would overlook this instance but I must not put my dog on one of Her Majesty's subjects or I would be liable to prosecution, not being a member of the Police Force. (Although I had trained one of the first Alsatians ever to be accepted by the police in the 1920s and later trained the demonstration Alsatian team belonging to the Thames Valley Police.) After this I saw a bank raid at the White City and had Juno with me, I could easily have freed her and possibly have caught one of the thieves but this time I just watched the escape. What a silly law if you are to let your property be stolen and own a dog who could stop it.

Juno and Junia were trained never to bite. The chases they have done in films were always done with actors without padding, for I had trained my Danes only to slip their teeth on to the clothing of the arm, not the flesh. In one film Junia had to catch someone and swing him around her into a hedge which she did to perfection. In the Montreux Festival winning television entry for the Rose of Montreux, 'Frost Over England' Junia had to chase and catch John Cleese. He was not padded, but the chase certainly looked frightening and I am sure he said a prayer before he started running, not previously having worked with Junia.

This is how I think dogs should be trained to guard the home. Bark and cease barking on command, attack if given the command, and sit instantly the attacked person stands still without threatening anyone. At the slightest move hold him until he stands still again, have no fear of gun fire, and remain a friendly dog to all until told not to be friendly. The ordinary owner would need years of experience to teach a Dane all this, but it is fun trying.

If film and television people know of a well-trained dog and the property master of the big companies is informed, there may one day be a chance for your Dane to appear on 'the box' or the cinema. You will never be told what to do until they want to film you, you will be treated like the 'property' you are, the hours will be long, the nervous tension killing, but the pleasure of watching your dog will compensate for all this. Occasionally you watch and your dog doesn't appear, you have told all your friends to watch, you've spent a fortune on phoning all and sundry to watch or go to the cinema and your dog is not seen. The cruelty of the scissors on the cutting room floor is quite unbelievable, it's happened to all of us, but carry on, one day your dog may be a star like mine were. Even though I have no Dane now, my cheque book still carries the words 'Barbara Woodhouse and Junia' as a reminder of what she and Juno did for our family.

Originally I did the first BBC Pet magazine programme 'The Smokey Club' which was made in Scotland and I used to go up to Scotland each month on the train with Juno to do it. Juno could not be sneaked into the sleeper as some tiny dogs can be, so we used to find an empty carriage and she would spread out on her travelling rug on the whole length of the carriage seat which just fitted her, and I would stretch out on the other side and we would both sleep the long night journey away and be fit and full of pep for the programme next day. After that I did a training series for commercial television using Juno and Chica as demonstrators.

The next big event was with my baby bull calf 'Conquest'. He was not a pedigree but came from one of my best cows and I couldn't bear for him to be slaughtered as was the usual end of a non-pedigree bull calf, so I phoned Richard Dimbleby of 'Panorama' fame and asked if I could bring Conquest, and Juno with him for company, on 'Panorama' and ask for a good home for him with some farmer. This I did. The sight of Juno lying cosily amongst the straw with baby bull Conquest curled up with her head on his shoulder was the most wonderful sight. Six thousand people jammed the BBC's telephones and also my home phone, which number had been given at the end of the programme, for about five hours. Besides this I had 300 letters and dozens of telegrams all wanting Conquest. The silly thing was that quite unsuitable people asked for him. One was a child who wanted him as a pet in the potting shed at the bottom of the garden, one a business man with a flat in London. One application came from a Nunnery. One telegram offered me three peacocks in exchange for him. No one seemed to realize that Conquest would one day be a huge bull weighing nearly a ton. Luckily there were some sensible requests and Conquest was given a wonderful home by a Sussex farmer and I hope his progeny improved the herd. Juno really got known after this public appearance on television and her life as a star of stage, screen and television had really started.

People always ask how dog food commercials are done and whether the dog always eats the food or likes the food it advertises, and I always quote what happened with a famous actor doing a beer commercial in which I was involved. He was a teetotaller and nothing would make him drink beer, so Coca Cola was drunk instead. My dog was supposed to drink a glass of beer too: even if I had allowed such a thing, I am sure she wouldn't have liked beer. I certainly would not have any dog of mine doing such an unnatural thing, so she had red gravy to drink.

Once again for this commercial I was called in to do it at the last moment by a desperate producer who rang me and asked me to get in my car and rush up to London instantly, as they'd been trying for over two hours to get the shot, and the Afghan chosen to do the commercial wouldn't do a thing. I rushed up and Juno was bundled out of the car, rushed into the pub where the action was to take place, shown what the action was to be, which was to jump with her forefeet on to the counter and be given half a pint of 'beer' and drink it with the actor drinking his pint at the same time. She did it immediately and I noticed the sweat running off everyone's brow, and I wondered why they were all so het up. I wasn't worried at all. After being paid a miserable £6 for Juno's efforts, someone said to me, 'You silly fool you should have charged them £50. The actor was getting £1,000, and another £1,000 if the performance wasn't completed by twelve o'clock midday.' It was 11.55 when Juno completed the scene.

Dog food commercials are sometimes a hazard when the camera or actors or clients have difficulties, for no dog can go on eating and eating and eating food however much they like it. On the outside of most tins it gives the right amount for a dog of a certain size for a day. If this is exceeded the dog may get a digestive upset, as anyone might who over-eats. The food in front of the dish has to be made easier to film by being occasionally coloured and sometimes have glycerine over it to make it shine. This is ordinary advertising technique, so the dog mostly eats from the back of the dish if this is done. If the food had to be eaten more times than is good for the dog, due to technical hitches, one of course has to use something else which would not upset the dog by having too much. There is a limit to any dog's appetite so it is usual to take more than one dog of the same breed to the studio. With my Danes this was impossible – everyone knew them from their films and television appearances so I always nagged the production manager to get the camera crew right on their toes and make certain their side of the work didn't let my dog down. In most cases although my dog and I were booked for a day's work it was finished in about two hours. Being Danes they could eat quite a lot anyway!

Moufflou

OUIDA

Moufflou's masters were some boys and girls. They were very poor, but they were very merry. They lived in an old dark, tumbled-down place, and their father had been dead five years; their mother's care was all they knew; and Tasso was the eldest of them all, a lad of nearly twenty, and he was so kind, so good, so laborious, so cheerful, and so gentle, that the children all younger than he adored him. Tasso was a gardener. Tasso, however, though the eldest and mainly the bread-winner, was not so much Moufflou's master as was little Romolo, who was only ten, and a cripple. Romolo, called generally Lolo, had taught Moufflou all he knew; and that all was a very great deal, for nothing cleverer than was Moufflou had ever walked upon four legs.

Why Moufflou?

Well, when the poodle had been given to them by a soldier who was going back to his home in Piedmont, he had been a white woolly creature of a year old, and the children's mother, who was a Corsican by birth, had said that he was just like a Moufflon, as they call sheep in Corsica. White and woolly this dog remained, and he became the handsomest and biggest poodle in all the city, and the corruption of Moufflou from Moufflon remained the name by which he was known; it was silly perhaps, but it suited him and the children, and Moufflou he was.

They lived in an old quarter of Florence, in that picturesque zigzag which goes round the grand church of Or San Michele, and which is almost more Venetian than Tuscan in its mingling of colour, charm, stateliness, popular confusion, and architectural majesty. The tall old houses are weather-beaten into the most delicious hues; the pavement is enchantingly encumbered with pedlars and stalls and all kinds of trades going on in the open air, in that bright, merry, beautiful Italian custom which, alas, alas! is being driven away by new-fangled laws which deem it better for the people to be stuffed up in close, stewing rooms, without air, and would fain do away with all the good-tempered politics and the sensible philosophies and the wholesome chatter which the open-street trades and street gossipry encourage, for it is good for the populace to *sfogare*, and in no other way can it do so one half so innocently. Drive it back into musty shops, and it is driven at once to mutter sedition.... But you want to hear about Moufflou.

Well, Moufflou lived here in that high house with the sign of the lamb in wrought iron, which shows it was once a warehouse of the old guild of the Arte della Lana. They are all old houses here, drawn round about that grand church which I called once, and will call again, like a mighty casket of oxidized silver. A mighty casket indeed, holding the Holy Spirit within it; and with the vermilion and the blue and the orange glowing in its niches and its lunettes like enamels, and its statues of the Apostles strong and noble, like the times in which they were created – St Peter with his keys and St Mark with his open book, and St George leaning on his sword, and others also, solemn and austere as they, austere though benign, for do they not guard the White Tabernacle of Orcagna within?

The church stands firm as a rock, square as a fortress of stone, and the winds and the waters of the skies may beat about it as they will, they have no power to disturb its sublime repose. Sometimes I think of all the noble things in all our Italy Or San

Michele is the noblest, standing there in its stern magnificence, amidst the people's hurrying feet and noisy laughter, memory of God.

The little masters of Moufflou lived right in its shadow, where the bridge of stone spans the space between the houses and the church high in mid-air; and little Lolo loved the church with a great love. He loved it in the morning time, when the sunbeams turned it into dusky gold and jasper; he loved it in the evening time, when the lights of its altars glimmered in the dark, and the scent of its incense came out into the street; he loved it in the great feasts, when the huge clusters of lilies were borne inside it; he loved it in the solemn nights of winter; the flickering gleam of the dull lamps shone on the robes of an apostle, or the sculpture of a shield, or the glow of a casement moulding in majolica. He loved it always and without knowing why he called it *la mia chiesa*.

Lolo, being lame and of delicate health, was not enabled to go to school or to work, though he wove the straw covering of wine-flasks and plaited the cane matting with busy fingers. But for the most part he did as he liked, and spent most of his time sitting on the parapet of Or San Michele, watching the vendors of earthenware at their trucks, or trotting with his crutch (and he could trot a good many miles when he chose) out with Moufflou down a bit of the Stockingmakers' Street, along under the arcades of the Uffizi, and so over the Jewellers' Bridge and out by byways that he knew into the fields on the hillside upon the other bank of Arno. Moufflou and he would spend half the day – all the day – out there in daffodil time; and Lolo would come home with great bundles and sheaves of golden flowers, and he and Moufflou were happy.

His mother never liked to say a harsh word to Lolo, for he was lame through her fault: she had let him fall in his babyhood, and the mischief had been done to his hip never again to be undone. So she never raised her voice to him, though she did often to the others: to curly-pated Cecco, and pretty black-eyed Dina, and saucy Bice, and sturdy Beppo, and even to the good, manly, hardworking Tasso. Tasso was the mainstay of the whole, though he was but a gardener's lad, working in the green Cascine at small wages. But all he earned he brought home to his mother; and he alone kept in order the lazy, high-tempered Sandro, and he alone kept in check Bice's love of finery, and he alone could with shrewdness and care make both ends meet and put *minestra* always in the pot and bread always in the cupboard.

When his mother thought, as she thought indeed almost ceaselessly, that with a few months he would be of the age to draw his number, and might draw a high one and be taken from her for three years, the poor soul believed her very heart would burst and break; and many a day at twilight she would start out unperceived and creep into the great church and pour her soul forth in supplication before the White Tabernacle.

Yet pray as she would, no miracle could happen to make Tasso free of military service; if he drew a fatal number go he must, even though he take all the lives of them to their ruin with him.

One morning Lolo sat as usual on the parapet of the church, Moufflou beside him. It was a brilliant morning in September; the men at the handbarrows and at the stalls were selling the crockery, the silk handkerchiefs, and the straw hats which form the staple of the commerce that goes on round about Or San Michele; very blithe, good-natured, gay commerce, for the most part not got through, however, of course, without bawling and screaming, and shouting and gesticulating, as if the sale of a penny pipkin or a twopenny piepan were the occasion for the exchange of many thousands of pounds sterling, and cause for the whole world's commotion. It was about eleven o'clock; the poor petitioners were going in for alms to the house of the fraternity of S. Giovanni Baptista; the barber at the corner was shaving a big man with a cloth tucked about his chin, and his chair set well out on the pavement; the sellers of the pipkins and piepans were screaming till they were hoarse '*Un soldo l'uno, due soldi tre!*' big bronze bells were booming till they seemed to clang right up to the deep blue sky; some brethren of the Misericordia went by bearing a black bier; a large sheaf of glowing flowers –

dahlias, zinnias, asters, and daturas – were borne through the huge arched door of the church near St Mark and his open book. Lolo looked on at it all, and so did Moufflou, and a stranger looked at them as he left the church.

'You have a handsome poodle there, my little man,' he said to Lolo, in a foreigner's too distinct and careful Italian.

'Moufflou is beautiful,' said Lolo, with pride; 'you should see him when he is just washed, but we can only wash him on Sundays because then Tasso is at home.'

'How old is your dog?'

'Three years old.'

'Does he do any tricks?'

'Does he!' said Lolo, with a very derisive laugh; 'why, Moufflou can do anything! He can walk on two legs ever so long; make ready, present, and fire; die; waltz; beg, of course; shut a door; make a wheelbarrow of himself; there is nothing he will not do. Would you like to see him do something?'

'Very much,' said the foreigner.

To Moufflou and to Lolo the street was the same thing as home; this cheery *piazzetta* by the church, so utterly empty sometimes, and sometimes so noisy and crowded, was but the wider threshold of their home to both the poodle and the child.

So there, under the lofty and stately walls of the old church, Lolo put Moufflou through his exercises. They were second nature to Moufflou, as to most poodles. He had inherited his address at them from clever parents, and as he had never been frightened or coerced, all his lessons and acquirements were but play to him. He acquitted himself admirably, and the crockery vendors came and looked on, and a sacristan came out of the church and smiled, and the barber left his customer's chin all in a lather while he laughed, for the good folk of the quarter were all proud of Moufflou and never tired of him, and the pleasant, easy-going, good-humoured disposition of the Tuscan populace is so far removed from the stupid buckram and whalebone in which the new-fangled democracy wants to imprison it.

The stranger also was much diverted by Moufflou's talents,

and said, half aloud, 'How this clever dog would amuse poor Victor! Would you bring your poodle to please a sick child I have at home?' he said quite aloud to Lolo, who smiled and answered that he would. Where was the sick child?

'At the Gran Bretagna; not far off,' said the gentleman. 'Come this afternoon, and ask for me by this name.'

He dropped his card and a couple of francs into Lolo's hand, and went his way. Lolo, with Moufflou scampering after him, dashed into his own house, and stumped up the stairs, his crutch making a terrible noise on the stone.

'Mother, mother! see what I have got because Moufflou did his tricks,' he shouted. 'And now you can buy those shoes you want so much, and the coffee that you miss so of a morning, and the new linen for Tasso, and the shirts for Sandro.'

For to the mind of Lolo two francs was as two millions; source unfathomable of riches inexhaustible!

With the afternoon he and Moufflou trotted down the arcades of the Uffizi and down the Lung' Arno to the hotel of the stranger, and showing the stranger's card, which Lolo could not read, was shown at once into a great chamber, all gilding and fresco and velvet furniture.

But Lolo, being a little Florentine, was never troubled by externals, or daunted by mere sofas and chairs: he stood and looked around him with perfect composure, and Moufflou, whose attitude, when he was not romping, was always one of magisterial gravity, sat on his haunches and did the same.

Soon the foreigner he had seen in the forenoon entered and spoke to him, and led him into another chamber, where stretched on a couch was a little wan-faced boy of about seven years old; a pretty boy, but so pallid, so wasted, so helpless. This poor little boy was heir to a great name and a great fortune, but all the science in the world could not make him strong enough to run about amongst the daisies, or able to draw a single breath without pain. A feeble smile lit up his face as he saw Moufflou and Lolo; then a shadow chased it away.

'Little boy is lame like me,' he said in a tongue Lolo did not understand.

'Yes, but he is a strong little boy, and can move about, as perhaps the suns of his country will make you do,' said the gentleman, who was the poor little boy's father. 'He has brought you his poodle to amuse you. What a handsome dog! is it not?'

'Oh *bufflins*!' said the poor little fellow, stretching out his wasted hands to Moufflou, who submitted his leonine crest to the caress.

Then Lolo went through the performance, and Moufflou acquitted himself ably as ever; and the little invalid laughed and shouted with his tiny thin voice, and enjoyed it all immensely, and rained cakes and biscuits on both the poodle and its master. Lolo crumpled the pastries with willing white teeth, and Moufflou did no less. Then they got up to go, and the sick child on the couch burst into fretful lamentations and outcries.

'I want the dog! I will have the dog!' was all he kept repeating.

But Lolo did not know what he said, and was only sorry to see him so unhappy.

'You shall have the dog to-morrow,' said the gentleman, to pacify his little son; and he hurried Lolo and Moufflou out of the room, and consigned them to a servant, having given Lolo five francs this time.

'Why, Moufflou,' said Lolo, with a chuckle of delight, 'if we could find a foreigner every day, we could eat meat at supper, Moufflou, and go to the theatre every evening!'

And he and his crutch clattered home with great eagerness and excitement, and Moufflou trotted on his four frilled feet, the blue bow with which Bice had tied up his curls on the top of his head, fluttering in the wind. But, alas! even his five francs could bring no comfort at home. He found his whole family wailing and mourning in utterly inconsolable distress.

Tasso had drawn his number that morning, and the number was seven, and he must go and be a conscript for three years.

The poor young man stood in the midst of his weeping brothers and sisters, with his mother leaning against his shoulder, and down his brown cheeks the tears were falling. He must go, and lose his place in the public gardens, and leave his people to starve as they might, and be put in a tomfool's jacket, and drafted off amongst cursing and swearing and strange faces, friendless, homeless, miserable! And the mother, what would become of the mother?

Tasso was the best of lads and the mildest. He was quite happy sweeping up the leaves in the long alleys of the Cascine, or mowing the green lawns under the ilex avenues, and coming home at supper-time amongst the merry little people and the good woman that he loved. He was quite contented; he wanted nothing, only to be let alone, and they would not let him alone. They would haul him away to put a heavy musket in his hand and a heavy knapsack on his back, and drill him, and curse him, and make him into a human target, a live popinjay.

No one had any heed for Lolo and his five francs, and Moufflou, understanding that some great sorrow had fallen on his friends, sat down and lifted up his voice and howled.

Tasso must go away! – that was all they understood. For three long years they must go without the sight of his face, the aid of his strength, the pleasure of his smile: Tasso must go! When Lolo understood the calamity that had befallen them, he gathered Moufflou up against his breast, and sat down too on the floor beside him and cried as if he would never stop crying.

There was no help for it: it was one of those misfortunes which are, as we say in Italian, like a tile tumbled on the head. The tile drops from a height, and the poor head bows under the unseen blow. That is all.

'What is the use of that?' said the mother passionately when Lolo showed her his five francs. 'It will not buy Tasso's discharge.'

Lolo felt that his mother was cruel and unjust, and crept to bed with Moufflou. Moufflou always slept on Lolo's feet.

The next morning Lolo got up before sunrise, and he and Moufflou accompanied Tasso to his work in the Cascine.

Lolo loved his brother, and clung to every moment whilst they could still be together.

'Can nothing keep you, Tasso?' he said despairingly as they went down the leafy aisles, whilst the Arno water was growing golden as the sun rose.

Tasso sighed.

'Nothing, dear. Unless Gesù would send me a thousand francs to buy a substitute.'

And he knew he might as well have said, 'If one could coin gold ducats out of the sunbeams on Arno water.'

Lolo was very sorrowful as he lay on the grass in the meadow where Tasso was at work, and the poodle lay stretched beside him.

When Lolo went home to dinner (Tasso took his wrapped in a handkerchief) he found his mother very agitated and excited. She was laughing one moment, crying the next. She was passionate and peevish, tender and jocose by turns: there was something forced and feverish about her which the children felt but did not comprehend. She was a woman of not very much intelligence, and she had a secret, and she carried it ill, and knew not what to do with it; but they could not tell that. They only felt a vague sense of disturbance and timidity at her unwonted manner.

The meal over (it was only bean-soup, and that is soon eaten), the mother said sharply to Lolo, 'Your Aunt Anita wants you this afternoon. She has to go out, and you are needed to stay with the children; be off with you.'

Lolo was an obedient child; he took his hat and jumped up as quickly as his halting hip would let him. He called Moufflou, who was asleep.

'Leave the dog,' said his mother sharply. ''Nita will not have him messing and carrying mud about her nice clean rooms. She told me so. Leave him, I say.'

'Leave Moufflou!' echoed Lolo, for never in all Moufflou's life had Lolo parted from him. Leave Moufflou! He stared open-eyed and open-mouthed at his mother. What could have come to her?

'Leave him, I say,' she repeated more sharply than ever 'Must

I speak twice to my own children? Be off with you and leave the dog, I say.'

And she clutched Moufflou by his long silky mane and dragged him backwards, whilst with the other hand she thrust out of the door Lolo and Bice.

Lolo began to hammer with his crutch at the door thus closed on him: but Bice coaxed and entreated him.

'Poor mother has been so worried about Tasso,' she pleaded. 'And what harm can come to Moufflou? And I do think he was tired, Lolo; the Cascine is a long way; and it is quite true that Aunt 'Nita never liked him.'

So by one means and another she coaxed her brother away; and they went almost in silence to where their Aunt Anita dwelt, which was across the river, near the dark-red bell-shaped dome of Santa Spirito.

It was true that her aunt had wanted them to mind her room and her babies whilst she was away carrying home some lace to a villa outside the Roman gate, for she was a lace-washer and clear-starcher by trade. There they had to stay in the little dark room with two babies, with nothing to amuse the time except the clang of the bells of the church of the Holy Spirit, and the voices of the lemonade-sellers shouting in the street below. Aunt Anita did not get back till it was more than dusk, and the two children trotted homeward hand-in-hand, Lolo's leg dragging itself painfully along, for without Moufflou's white figure dancing on before him he felt very tired indeed. It was pitch dark when they got to Or San Michele, and the lamps burned dully.

Lolo stumped up the stairs wearily, with a vague, dull fear at his small heart.

'Moufflou, Moufflou!' he called. Where was Moufflou? Always at the first sound of his crutch the poodle came flying towards him. 'Moufflou, Moufflou!' he called all the way up the long, dark, twisting stone stair. He pushed open the door, and he called again, 'Moufflou, Moufflou!'

But no dog answered to his call.

'Mother, where is Moufflou?' he asked, staring with blinking, dazzled eyes into the oil-lit room where his mother sat knitting. Tasso was not then home from work. His mother went on with her knitting; there was an uneasy look on her face.

'Mother, what have you done with Moufflou, *my* Moufflou?' said Lolo, with a look that was almost stern on his ten-year-old face.

Then his mother, without looking up and moving her knitting-needles, very rapidly said:

'Moufflou is sold!'

And little Dina, who was a quick, pert child, cried with a shrill voice:

'Mother has sold him for a thousand francs to the foreign gentleman.'

'Sold him!'

Lolo grew white and grew cold as ice; he stammered, threw up his hands over his head, gasped a little for breath, then fell down in a dead swoon, his poor useless limb doubled under him.

When Tasso came home that sad night and found his little brother shivering, moaning, and half-delirious, and when he heard what had been done, he was sorely grieved.

'Oh, mother, how could you do it?' he cried. 'Poor, poor Moufflou! and Lolo loves him so!'

'I have got the money,' said his mother feverishly, 'and you will not need to go for a soldier, we can buy your substitute. What is a poodle that you mourn about it? We can get another poodle for Lolo.'

'Another will not be Moufflou,' said Tasso, and yet was seized with such a frantic happiness himself at the knowledge that he would not need go to the army, that he too felt as if he were drunk on new wine, and had not the heart to rebuke his mother.

'A thousand francs!' he muttered, 'a thousand francs! *Dio mio!* Who could ever have fancied anybody would have given such a price for a common white poodle? One would think the gentleman had bought the church and the tabernacle!'

'Fools and their money are soon parted,' said his mother with cross contempt.

It was true; she had sold Moufflou.

The English gentleman had called on her while Lolo and the dog had been in the Cascine, and had said that he was desirous of buying the poodle, which had so diverted his sick child that the little invalid would not be comforted unless he possessed it. Now, at any other time the good woman would have sturdily refused any idea of selling Moufflou; but that morning the thousand francs which would buy Tasso's substitute were for ever in her mind and before her eyes. When she heard the foreigner her heart gave a great leap and her head swam giddily, and she thought, in a spasm of longing – if she could get those thousand francs! But though she was so dizzy and so upset she retained her grip on her native Florentine shrewdness. She said nothing of her need of the money; not a syllable of her sore distress. On the contrary, she was coy and wary, affected great reluctance to part with her pet, invented a great offer made for him by a director of a circus, and finally let fall a hint that less than a thousand francs she could never take for poor Moufflou.

The gentleman assented with so much willingness to the price that she instantly regretted not having asked double. He told her that if she would take the poodle that afternoon to his hotel the money should be paid to her; so she dispatched her children after their noon-day meal in various directions, and herself took Moufflou to his doom. She could not believe her senses when ten hundred-franc notes were put into her hand. She scrawled her signature, Rosina Calabucci, to a formal receipt and went away, leaving Moufflou in his new owner's rooms, and hearing his howls and moans pursue her all the way down the staircase and out into the air.

She was not easy at what she had done.

'It seemed,' she said to herself, 'like selling a Christian.'

But then to keep her eldest son at home – what a joy that was! On the whole, she cried so and laughed so as she went down the Lung' Arno that once or twice people looked at her, thinking her out of her senses, and a guard spoke to her angrily.

Meanwhile, Lolo was sick and delirious with grief. Twenty

times he got out of his bed and screamed to be allowed to go with Moufflou, and twenty times his mother and his brothers put him back again and held him down and tried in vain to quiet him.

The child was beside himself with misery. 'Moufflou, Moufflou!' he sobbed at every moment; and by night he was in a raging fever, and when his mother, frightened, ran in and called in the doctor of the quarter, that worthy shook his head and said something as to a shock of the nervous system and muttered a long word, 'meningitis.'

Lolo took a hatred to the sight of Tasso, and thrust him away, and his mother too.

'It is for you Moufflou is sold,' he said, with his little teeth and hands tight clenched.

After a day or two Tasso felt as if he could not bear his life, and went down to the hotel to see if the foreign gentleman would allow him to have Moufflou back for half an hour to quiet his little brother by a sight of him. But at the hotel he was told that the *Milord Inglese* who had bought the dog of Rosina Calabucci had gone that same night of the purchase to Rome, to Naples, to Palermo, *chi sa*?

'And Moufflou with him?' asked Tasso.

'The *barbone* he had bought went with him,' said the porter of the hotel. 'Such a beast! Howling, shrieking, raging all the day and all the paint scratched off the *salon* door.'

Poor Moufflou! Tasso's heart was heavy as he heard of that sad helpless misery of their bartered favourite and friend.

'What matter?' said his mother fiercely, when he told her. 'A dog is a dog. They will feed him better than we could. In a week he will have forgotten – *chè*!'

But Tasso feared that Moufflou would not forget. Lolo certainly would not. The doctor came to the bedside twice a day, and ice and water were kept on the aching hot little head that had got the malady with the long name, and for the chief part of the time Lolo lay quiet, dull, and stupid, breathing heavily, and then at intervals cried and sobbed and shrieked hysterically for Moufflou.

'Can you not get what he calls for to quiet him with a sight of it?' said the doctor. But that was not possible, and poor Rosina covered her head with her apron and felt a guilty creature.

'Still you will not go to the army,' she said to Tasso, clinging to that immense joy for her consolation. 'Only think! we can pay Guido Squarcione to go for you. He always said he would go if anybody would pay him. Oh, my Tasso, surely to keep you is worth a dog's life!'

'And Lolo's?' said Tasso gloomily. 'Nay, mother, it works ill to meddle too much with fate. I drew my number; I was bound to go. Heaven would have made it up to you somehow.'

'Heaven sent me the foreigner; the Madonna's own self sent him to ease a mother's pain,' said Rosina rapidly and angrily. 'There are the thousand francs safe to hand in the *cassone*, and what, pray, is it we miss? Only a dog like a sheep, that brought gallons of mud in with him every time it rained, and ate as much as any one of you.'

'But Lolo?' said Tasso under his breath.

His mother was so irritated and so tormented by her own conscience that she upset all the cabbage broth into the burning charcoal.

'Lolo was always a little fool, thinking of nothing but the church and the dog and nasty field-flowers,' she said angrily. 'I humoured him ever too much because of the hurt to his hip, and so – and so —'

Then the poor soul made matters worse by dropping her tears into the saucepan, and fanning the charcoal so furiously that the flame caught her fan of cane-leaves, and would have burned her arm had not Tasso been there.

'You are my prop and safety always. Who would not have done what I did? Not St Felicita herself,' she said with a great sob.

But all this did not cure poor Lolo.

The days and the weeks of the golden autumn weather passed away, and he was always in danger, and the small close room where he slept with Sandro and Beppo and Tasso was not one to cure such an illness as had now beset him. Tasso went to his work with a sick heart in the Cascine, where the colchicum was all lilac amongst the meadow grass, and the ashes and elms were taking their first flush of the coming autumnal change. He did not think Lolo would ever get well, and the good lad felt as if he had been the murderer of his little brother.

True, he had had no hand or voice in the sale of Moufflou, but Moufflou had been sold for his sake. It made him feel half guilty, very unhappy, quite unworthy all the sacrifice that had been made for him. 'Nobody should meddle with fate,' thought Tasso, who knew his grandfather had died in S. Bonifazio because he had driven himself mad over the dreambook trying to get lucky numbers for the lottery, and become a rich man at a stroke.

It was rapture, indeed, to know that he was free of the army for a time at least, that he might go on undisturbed at his healthful labour, and get a rise in wages as time went on, and dwell in peace with his family, and perhaps – perhaps in time earn enough to marry pretty flaxen-haired Biondina, the daughter of the barber in the piazzetta. It was rapture indeed; but then poor Moufflou! – and poor, poor Lolo! Tasso felt as if he had bought his own exemption by seeing his little brother and the good dog torn in pieces and buried alive for his service.

And where was poor Moufflou?

Gone far away somewhere south in the hurrying, screeching, vomiting, braying train that it made Tasso giddy only to look at as it rushed by the green meadows beyond the Cascine on its way to the sea.

'If he could see the dog he cries so for, it might save him,' said the doctor, who stood with a grave face watching Lolo.

But that was beyond anyone's power. No one could tell where Moufflou was. He might be carried away to England, to France, to Russia, to America, who could say? They did not know where his purchaser had gone. Moufflou even might be dead.

The poor mother, when the doctor said that, went and looked at the ten hundred-franc notes that were once like angels' faces to her, and said to them.

'Oh, you children of Satan, why did you tempt me? I sold the poor, innocent, trustful beast to get you, and now my child is dying!'

Her eldest son would stay at home, indeed; but if this little lame one died! Rosina Calabucci would have given up the notes and consented never to own five francs in her life if only she could have gone back over the time and kept Moufflou, and seen his little master running out with him into the sunshine.

More than a month went by and Lolo lay in the same state; his yellow hair shorn, his eyes dilated and yet stupid, life kept in him by a spoonful of milk, a lump of ice, a drink of lemon-water; always muttering, when he spoke at all, 'Moufflou, Moufflou, *dov' è* Moufflou?' and lying for days together in somnolence and unconsciousness, with the fire eating at his brain and the weight lying on it like a stone.

The neighbours were kind, and brought fruit and the like, and sat up with him, and chattered so all at once in one continuous brawl, that they were enough in themselves to kill him, for such is ever the Italian fashion of sympathy in all illness.

But Lolo did not get well, did not even seem to see the light at all, or distinguish any sounds around him; and the doctor in plain words told Rosina Calabucci that her little boy must die. Die, and the church so near? She could not believe it. Could St Mark, and St George, and the rest that he had loved so do nothing for him? No, said the doctor, they could do nothing; the dog might do something, since the brain had so fastened on that one idea; but then they had sold the dog.

'Yes; I sold him!' said the poor mother breaking into floods of remorseful tears.

So at last the end drew so nigh that one twilight time the priest came out of the great arched door that is next St Mark, with the Host uplifted, and a little acolyte ringing the bell before it, and passed across the piazzetta, and went up the dark staircase of Rosina's dwelling, and passed through the weeping, terrified children, and went to the bedside of Lolo.

Moufflou dashed through the room and leaped upon the bed

Lolo was unconscious, but the holy man touched his little body and limbs with the sacred oil, and prayed over him, and then stood sorrowful with bowed head.

Lolo had had his first communion in the summer, and in his preparation for it had shown an intelligence and devoutness that had won the priest's gentle heart.

Standing there, the holy man commended the innocent soul to God. It was the last service to be rendered to him save that very last of all when the funeral office should be read above his little grave amongst the millions of nameless dead at the sepulchres of the poor at Trebbiano.

All was still as the priest's voice ceased; only the sobs of the mother and of the children broke the stillness as they kneeled; the hand of Biondina had stolen into Tasso's.

Suddenly, there was a loud scuffling noise; hurrying feet came patter, patter, patter up the stairs, a ball of mud and dust flew over the heads of the kneeling figures, fleet as the wind Moufflou dashed through the room and leaped upon the bed.

Lolo opened his heavy eyes, and a sudden light of consciousness gleamed in them like a sunbeam. 'Moufflou!' he murmured in his little thin faint voice. The dog pressed close to his breast and kissed his wasted face.

Moufflou was come home!

And Lolo came home too, for death let go its hold upon him. Little by little, very faintly and flickeringly and very uncertainly at the first, life returned to the poor little body, and reason to the tormented, heated little brain. Moufflou was his physician; Moufflou, who, himself a skeleton under his matted curls, would not stir from his side and looked at him all day long with two beaming brown eyes full of unutterable love.

Lolo was happy; he asked no questions; was too weak, indeed, even to wonder. He had Moufflou; that was enough.

Alas! though they dared not say so in his hearing, it was not enough for his elders. His mother and Tasso knew that the poodle had been sold and paid for; that they could lay no claim to keep him; and that almost certainly his purchaser would seek him out, and assert his indisputable right to him. And then how would Lolo ever bear that second parting? – Lolo, so weak that he weighed no more than if he had been a little bird.

Moufflou had, no doubt, travelled a long distance and suffered much. He was but skin and bone; he bore the marks of blows and kicks; his once silken hair was all discoloured and matted; he had, no doubt, travelled far. But then his purchaser would be sure to ask for him, soon or late, at his old home; and then? Well, then if they did not give him up themselves, the law would make them.

Rosina Calabucci and Tasso, though they dared say nothing before any of the children, felt their hearts in their mouths at every step on the stair, and the first interrogation of Tasso every evening when he came from his work was, 'Has anyone come for Moufflou?' For ten days no one came, and their first terrors lulled a little.

On the eleventh morning, a feast day, on which Tasso was not going to his labours in the Cascine, there came a person, with a foreign look, who said the words they so much dreaded to hear, 'Has the poodle that you sold to an English gentleman come back to you?'

Yes: his English master claimed him!

The servant said that they had missed the dog in Rome a few days after buying him and taking him there; that he had been searched for in vain, and that his master had thought it possible the animal might have found his way back to his old home: there had been stories of such wonderful sagacity in dogs: anyhow he had sent for him on the chance; he was himself back on the Lung' Arno. The servant pulled from his pocket a chain, and said his orders were to take the poodle away at once: the little sick gentleman had fretted very much about his loss.

Tasso heard in a very agony of despair. To take Moufflou away now would be to kill Lolo – Lolo so feeble still, so unable to understand, so passionately alive to every sight and sound of Moufflou, lying for hours together motionless with his hand buried in the poodle's curls, saying nothing, only smiling now and then, and murmuring a word or two in Moufflou's ear.

'The dog did come home,' said Tasso at length, in a low voice; 'angels must have shown him the road, poor beast! From Rome! Only to think of it, from Rome! And he a dumb thing! I tell you he is here, honestly, so will you not trust me just so far as this? Will you let me go with you and speak to the English lord before you take the dog away? I have a little brother sorely ill —'

He could not speak more for tears that choked his voice.

At last the messenger agreed so far as this. Tasso might go first and see the master, but he would stay here and have a care they did not spirit the dog away – 'for a thousand francs were paid for him,' added the man, 'and a dog that can come all the way from Rome by itself must be an uncanny creature.'

Tasso thanked him; went upstairs; was thankful that his mother was at mass and could not dispute with him; took the ten hundred-franc notes from the old oak *cassone*, and with them in his breast-pocket walked out into the air. He was but a poor working lad, but he had made up his mind to do an heroic deed, for self-sacrifice is always heroic. He went straightway to the hotel where the English *milord* was, and when he had got there remembered that still he did not know the name of Moufflou's owner; but the people of the hotel knew him as Rosina Calabucci's son, and guessed what he wanted, and said the gentleman who had lost the poodle was within upstairs and they would tell him.

Tasso waited some half-hour with his heart beating sorely against the packet of hundred-franc notes. At last he was beckoned upstairs, and there he saw a foreigner with a mild fair face, and a very lovely lady, and a delicate child who was lying on a couch. 'Moufflou! Where is Moufflou?' cried the little child impatiently, as he saw the youth enter.

Tasso took his hat off, and stood in the doorway, an embrowned, healthy, not ungraceful figure, in his working clothes of rough blue stuff.

'If you please, most illustrious,' he stammered, 'poor Moufflou has come home.'

The child gave a cry of delight; the gentleman and lady one of wonder. Come home! All the way from Rome!

'Yes, he has, most illustrious,' said Tasso, gaining courage and eloquence, 'and now I want to beg something of you. We are poor, and I drew a bad number, and it was for that my mother sold Moufflou. For myself, I did not know anything of it; but she thought she would buy my substitute, and of course she could; but Moufflou is come home, and my little brother Lolo, the little boy your most illustrious first saw playing with the poodle, fell ill of the grief of losing Moufflou, and for a month has lain saying nothing sensible, but only calling for the dog, and my old grandfather died worrying himself mad over the lottery numbers, and Lolo was so near dying that the Blessed Host had been brought, and the holy oil had been put on him, when all at once there rushes in Moufflou, skin and bone, and covered with mud, and at the sight of him Lolo comes back to his senses, and that is now ten days ago, and though Lolo is still as weak as a new-born thing, he is always sensible, and takes what we give him to eat, and lies always looking at Moufflou, and smiling and saying "Moufflou! Moufflou!" and, most illustrious, I know well you have bought the dog, and the law is with you, and by the law you claim it; but I thought perhaps, as Lolo loves him so, you would let us keep the dog and would take back the thousand francs, and myself I will go and be a soldier, and heaven will take care of them all somehow.'

Then Tasso, having said all this in one breathless, monotonous recitative, took the thousand francs out of his breast-pocket and held them out timidly towards the foreign gentleman, who motioned them aside and stood silent.

'Did you understand, Victor?' he said, at last, to his little son.

The child hid his face in his cushions.

'Yes, I did understand something; let Lolo keep him; Moufflou was not happy with me.'

But he burst out crying as he said it.

Moufflou had run away from him.

Moufflou had never loved him, for all his sweet cakes and fond caresses, and platesful of delicate savoury meats. Moufflou had run away and found his own road over two hundred miles and more to go back to some little hungry children, who never had enough to eat themselves, and so, certainly, could never give enough to eat to the dog. Poor little boy! He was so rich and so pampered and so powerful, and yet he could never make Moufflou love him!

Tasso, who understood nothing that was said, laid the ten hundred-franc notes down on a table near him.

'If you would take them, most illustrious, and give me back what my mother wrote when she sold Moufflou,' he said, timidly, 'I would pray for you night and day, and Lolo would too; and as for the dog, we will get a puppy and train him for your little *signorino*; they can all do tricks, more or less, it comes by nature; and as for me I will go to the army willingly; it is not right to interfere with fate; my old grandfather died mad because he would try to be a rich man, by dreaming about it and pulling destiny by the ears, as if she were a kicking mule; only, I do pray of you, do not take away Moufflou. And to think he trotted all those miles and miles, and you carried him by train too, and he never could have seen the road, and he has no power of speech to ask —'

Tasso broke down again in his eloquence, and drew the back of his hand across his wet eyelashes.

The English gentleman was not altogether unmoved.

'Poor faithful dog!' he said, with a sigh. 'I am afraid we were very cruel to him, meaning to be kind. No; we will not claim him, and I do not think you should go for a soldier; you seem so good a lad, and your mother must need you. Keep the money, my boy, and in payment you shall train up the puppy you talk of, and bring him to my little boy. I will come and see your mother and Lolo to-morrow. All the way from Rome! What wonderful sagacity; what matchless fidelity!'

You can imagine, without any telling of mine, the joy that reigned in Moufflou's home when Tasso returned thither with the money and the good tidings both. His substitute was bought without a day's delay, and Lolo rapidly recovered. As for Moufflou, he could never tell them his troubles, his wanderings, his difficulties, his perils; he could never tell them by what miraculous knowledge he had found his way across Italy, from the gates of Rome to the gates of Florence. But he soon grew plump again, and merry, and his love for Lolo was yet greater than before.

By the winter all the family went to live on an estate near Spezia that the English gentleman had purchased, and there Moufflou was happier than ever. The little English boy is gaining strength in the soft air, and he and Lolo are great friends, and play with Moufflou and the poodle puppy half the day upon the sunny terraces and under the green orange boughs. Tasso is one of the gardeners there; he will have to serve as a soldier probably in some category or another, but he is safe for the time, and is happy. Lolo, whose lameness will always exempt him from military service, when he grows to be a man means to be a florist, and a great one. He has learned to read as the first step on the road of his ambition.

'But oh, Moufflou, how *did* you find your way home?' he asks the dog a hundred times a week.

How indeed!

No one ever knew how Moufflou had made that long journey on foot, so many weary miles; but beyond a doubt he had done it alone and unaided, for if anyone had helped him they would have come home with him to claim the reward.

Humblepuppy

JOAN AIKEN

Our house was furnished mainly from auction sales. When you buy furniture that way you get a lot of extra things besides the particular piece that you were after, since the stuff is sold in Lots: Lot 13, two Persian rugs, a set of golf-clubs, a sewing-machine, a walnut radio-cabinet, and a plinth.

It was in this way that I acquired a tin deedbox, which came with two coal-scuttles and a broom cupboard. The deedbox is solid metal, painted black, big as a medium-sized suitcase. When I first brought it home I put it in my study, planning to use it as a kind of filing-cabinet for old typescripts. I had gone into the kitchen, and was busy arranging the brooms in their new home, when I heard a loud thumping coming from the direction of the study.

I went back, thinking that a bird must have flown through the window; no bird, but the banging seemed to be inside the deedbox. I had already opened it as soon as it was in my possession, to see if there were any diamonds or bearer bonds worth thousands of pounds inside (there weren't), but I opened it again. The key was attached to the handle by a thin chain. There was nothing inside. I shut it. The banging started again. I opened it.

Still nothing inside.

Well, this was broad daylight, two o'clock on Thursday afternoon, people going past in the road outside and a radio schools programme chatting away to itself in the next room. It was not a ghostly kind of time, so I put my hand into the empty box and moved it about.

Something shrank away from my hand. I heard a faint, scared whimper. It could almost have been my own, but wasn't. Knowing that someone – something? – else was afraid too put heart into me. Exploring carefully and gently around the interior of the box I felt the contour of a small, bony, warm, trembling body with big awkward feet, and silky dangling ears, and a cold nose that, when I found it, nudged for a moment anxiously but trustingly into the palm of my hand. So I knelt down, put the other hand into the box as well, cupped them under a thin little ribby chest, and lifted out Humblepuppy.

He was quite light.

I couldn't see him, but I could hear his faint inquiring whimper, and I could hear his toenails scratch on the floor-boards.

Just at that moment the cat, Taffy, came in.

Taffy has a lot of character. Every cat has a lot of character, but Taffy has more than most, all of it inconvenient. For instance, although he is very sociable, and longs for company, he just despises company in the form of dogs. The mere sound of a dog barking two streets away is enough to make his fur stand up like a porcupine's quills and his tail swell like a mushroom cloud.

Which it did the instant he saw Humblepuppy.

Now here is the interesting thing. I could feel and hear Humblepuppy, but couldn't see him; Taffy, apparently, could see and smell him, but couldn't feel him. We soon discovered this. For Taffy, sinking into a low, gladiator's crouch, letting out all the time a fearsome throaty wauling like a bagpipe revving up its drone, inched his way along to where Humblepuppy huddled trembling by my left foot, and then dealt him what ought to have been a swinging right-handed clip on the ear. 'Get out of my house, you filthy little canine scum!' was what he was plainly intending to convey.

But the swipe failed to connect; instead it landed on my shin.

I've never seen a cat so astonished. It was like watching a kitten meet itself for the first time in a looking-glass. Taffy ran round to the back of where Humblepuppy was sitting; felt; smelt; poked gingerly with a paw; leapt back nervously; crept forward again. All the time Humblepuppy just sat, trembling a little, giving out this faint beseeching sound that meant: 'I'm only a poor little mongrel without a smidgeon of harm in me. *Please* don't do anything nasty! I don't even know how I came here.'

It certainly was a puzzle how he had come. I rang the auctioneers (after shutting Taffy *out* and Humblepuppy *in* to the study with a bowl of water and a handful of Boniebisk, Taffy's favourite breakfast food).

The auctioneers told me that Lot 12, Deedbox, coal-scuttles and broom cupboard, had come from Riverland Rectory, where Mr Smythe, the old rector, had lately died aged ninety. Had he ever possessed a dog, or a puppy? They couldn't say; they had merely received instructions from a firm of lawyers to sell the furniture.

I never did discover how poor little Humblepuppy's ghost got into that deedbox. Maybe he was shut in by mistake, long ago, and suffocated; maybe some callous Victorian gardener dropped him, box and all, into a river, and the box was later found and fished out.

Anyway, and whatever had happened in the past, now that Humblepuppy had come out of his box, he was very pleased with the turn his affairs had taken, ready to be grateful and affectionate. As I sat typing I'd often hear a patter-patter, and feel his small chin fit itself comfortably over my foot, ears dangling. Goodness knows what kind of a mixture he was; something between a spaniel and a terrier, I'd guess. In the evening, watching television or sitting by the fire, one would suddenly find his warm weight leaning against one's leg. (He didn't put on a lot of weight while he was with us, but his bony little ribs filled out a bit.)

For the first few weeks we had a lot of trouble with Taffy, who was very surly over the whole business and blamed me bitterly for not getting rid of this low-class intruder. But Humblepuppy was extremely placating, got back into his deedbox whenever the atmosphere became too volcanic, and did his very best not to be a nuisance.

By and by Taffy thawed. As I've said, he is really a very sociable cat. Although quite old, seventy cat years, he dearly likes cheerful company, and generally has some young cat friend who comes to play with him, either in the house or the garden. In the last few years we've had Whisky, the black-and-white pub cat, who used to sit washing the smell of fish-and-chips off his fur under the dripping tap in our kitchen sink; Tetanus, the hairdresser's thick-set black, who took a fancy to sleep on top of our china-cupboard every night all one winter, and used to startle me very much by jumping down heavily on to my shoulder as I made the breakfast coffee; Sweet Charity, a little grey Persian who came to a sad end under the wheels of a police-car; Charity's grey-and-white stripey cousin Fred, whose owners presently moved from next door to another part of the town.

It was soon after Fred's departure that Humblepuppy arrived, and from my point of view he couldn't have been more welcome. Taffy missed Fred badly, and expected *me* to play with him instead; it was sad to see this large elderly tabby rushing hopefully up and down the stairs after breakfast, or hiding behind the armchair and jumping out on to nobody; or howling, howling, howling at me until I escorted him out into the garden, where he'd rush to the lavender-bush which had been the traditional hiding-place of Whisky, Tetanus, Charity, and Fred in succession. Cats have their habits and histories, just the same as humans.

So sometimes, on a working morning, I'd be at my wits' end, almost on the point of going across the town to our ex-neighbours, ringing their bell, and saying, 'Please can Fred come and play?' Specially on a rainy, uninviting day when Taffy was pacing gloomily about the house with drooping head and switching tail, grumbling about the weather and the lack of company, and blaming me for both.

Humblepuppy's arrival changed all that.

At first Taffy considered it necessary to police him, and that kept him fully occupied for hours. He'd sit on guard by the deedbox till Humblepuppy woke up in the morning, and then he'd follow officiously all over the house, wherever the visitor went. Humblepuppy was slow and cautious in his explorations, but by degrees he picked up courage and found his way into every corner. He never once made a puddle; he learned to use Taffy's cat-flap and go out into the garden, though he was always more timid outside and would scamper for home at any loud noise. Planes and cars terrified him, he never became used to them; which made me still more certain that he had been in that deedbox for a long, long time, since before such things were invented.

Presently he learned, or Taffy taught him, to hide in the lavender-bush like Whisky, Charity, Tetanus, and Fred; and the two of them use to play their own ghostly version of touch-last for hours on end while I got on with my typing.

When visitors came, Humblepuppy always retired to his deedbox; he was decidedly scared of strangers; which made his behaviour with Mr Manningham, the new rector of Riverland, all the more surprising.

I was dying to learn anything I could of the old rectory's history, so I'd invited Mr Manningham to tea.

He was a thin, gentle, quiet man, who had done missionary work in the Far East and fell ill and had to come back to England. He seemed a little sad and lonely; said he still missed his Far East friends and work. I liked him. He told me that for a large part of the nineteenth century the Riverland living had belonged to a parson called Swannett, the Reverend Timothy Swannett, who lived to a great age and had ten children.

'He was a great-uncle of mine, as a matter of fact. But why do you want to know all this?' Mr Manningham asked. His long thin arm hung over the side of his chair; absently he moved his hand sideways and remarked, 'I didn't notice that you had a puppy.' Then he looked down and said, 'Oh!'

'He's never come out for a stranger before,' I said.

Taffy, who maintains a civil reserve with visitors, sat motionless on the nightstore heater, eyes slitted, sphinxlike.

Humblepuppy climbed invisibly on to Mr Manningham's lap.

We agreed that the new rector probably carried a familiar smell of his rectory with him; or possibly he reminded Humblepuppy of his great-uncle, the Rev. Swannett.

Anyway, after that, Humblepuppy always came scampering joyfully out if Mr Manningham dropped in to tea, so of course I thought of the rector when summer holiday time came round.

During the summer holidays we lend our house and cat to a lady publisher and her mother who are devoted to cats and think it a privilege to look after Taffy and spoil him. He is always amazingly overweight when we get back. But the old lady has an allergy to dogs, and is frightened of them too; it was plainly out of the question that she should be expected to share her summer holiday with the ghost of a puppy.

So I asked Mr Manningham if he'd be prepared to take Humblepuppy as a boarder, since it didn't seem a case for the usual kind of boarding-kennels; he said he'd be delighted.

I drove Humblepuppy out to Riverland in his deedbox; he was rather miserable on the drive, but luckily it is not far. Mr Manningham came out into the garden to meet us. We put the box down on the lawn and opened it.

I've never heard a puppy so wildly excited. Often I'd been sorry that I couldn't see Humblepuppy, but I was never sorrier than on that afternoon, as we heard him rushing from tree to familiar tree, barking joyously, dashing through the orchard grass – you could see it divide as he whizzed along – coming back to bounce up against us, all damp and earthy and smelling of leaves.

'He's going to be happy with you, all right,' I said, and Mr Manningham's grey, lined face crinkled into its thoughtful smile as he said, 'It's the place more than me, I think.'

Well, it was both of them, really.

After the holiday, I went to collect Humblepuppy, leaving Taffy haughty and standoffish, sniffing our cases. It always takes him a long time to forgive us for going away.

Mr Manningham had a bit of a cold and was sitting by the fire in his study, wrapped in a shetland rug. Humblepuppy was on his knee. I could hear the little dog's tail thump against the arm of the chair when I walked in, but he didn't get down to greet me. He stayed in Mr Manningham's lap.

'So you've come to take back my boarder,' Mr Manningham said.

There was nothing in the least strained about his voice or smile but – I just hadn't the heart to take back Humblepuppy. I put my hand down, found his soft wrinkly forehead, rumpled it a bit, and said,

'Well – I was sort of wondering: our spoilt old cat seems to have got used to being on his own again; I was wondering whether – by any chance – you'd feel like keeping him?'

Mr Manningham's face lit up. He didn't speak for a minute; then he put a gentle hand down to find the small head, and rubbed a finger along Humblepuppy's chin.

'Well,' he said. He cleared his throat. 'Of course, if you're *quite* sure –'

'Quite sure.' My throat needed clearing too.

'I hope you won't catch my cold,' Mr Manningham said. I shook my head and said, 'I'll drop in to see if you're better in a day or two,' and went off and left them together.

Poor Taffy was pretty glum over the loss of his playmate for several weeks; we had two hours' purgatory every morning after breakfast while he hunted for Humblepuppy high and low. But gradually the memory faded and, thank goodness, now he has found a new friend, Little Grey Furry, a nephew, cousin or other relative of Charity and Fred. Little Grey Furry has learned to play hide-and-seek in the lavender-bush, and to use our cat-flap, and clean up whatever's in Taffy's food bowl, so all is well in that department.

But I still miss Humblepuppy. I miss his cold nose exploring the palm of my hand, as I sit thinking, in the middle of a page, and his warm weight leaning against my knee as he watches the commercials. And the scritch-scratch of his toenails on the dining-room floor and the flump, flump, as he comes downstairs, and the small hollow in a cushion as he settles down with a sigh.

Oh well. I'll get over it, just as Taffy has. But I was wondering about putting an ad. into *Our Dogs* or *Pets' Monthly*: Wanted, ghost of mongrel puppy. Warm welcome, loving home. Any reasonable price paid.

It might be worth a try.

'No Dogs Permitted'

ELEANOR ATKINSON

This is the true story of a small terrier's amazing loyalty to the memory of his master, an old shepherd, who died in Edinburgh. After Auld Jock's death Bobby was taken back to the farm he had grown up at, to be a pet for the farmer's daughter. Shut in a cow byre for the night, he is determined to escape and return to Edinburgh and Auld Jock.

The byre was no sooner locked than Bobby began, in the pitch darkness, to explore the walls. The single promise of escape that was offered was an inch-wide crack under the door, where the flooring stopped short and exposed a strip of earth. That would have appalled any but a desperate little dog. The crack was so small as to admit but one paw, at first, and the earth was packed as hard as wood by generations of trampling cattle.

There he began to dig. He came of a breed of dogs used by farmers and hunters to dig small, burrowing animals out of holes, a breed whose courage and persistence know no limit. He dug patiently, steadily, hour after hour, enlarging the hole by inches. Now and then he had to stop to rest. When he was able to use both forepaws he made encouraging progress; but when he had to reach under the door, quite the length of his stretched legs, and drag every bit of earth back into the byre, the task must have been impossible to any little creature not urged by utter misery. But Skye terriers have been known to labour with such fury that they have perished of their own exertions. Bobby's nose sniffed liberty long before he could squeeze his weasel-like body through the tunnel. His back bruised and strained by the struggle through a hole too small, he stood, trembling with exhaustion, in the windy dawn.

An opening door, a barking sheep-dog, the shuffle of the moving flock were signs that the farm day was beginning, although all the stars had not faded out of the sky. A little flying shadow, Bobby slipped out of the cow-yard, past the farm-house, and literally tumbled down the brae. From one level to another he dropped, several hundred feet in a very few minutes, and from the clear air of the breezy hilltop to a nether world that was buried fathoms deep in a sea-fog as white as milk.

Hidden in a deep fold of the spreading skirts of the range, and some distance from the road, lay a pool, made by damming a burn, and used in the shearing season, for washing sheep. Surrounded by brushy woods, and very damp and dark, at other seasons it was deserted. Bobby found this secluded place with his nose, curled up under a hazel thicket, and fell sound asleep. And while he slept, a nipping wind from the far northern Highlands swooped down on the mist and sent it flying away. The Lowlands cleared like magic. From the high point where Bobby lay the road could be seen to fall, by short rises and long descents, all the way to Edinburgh. From its crested ridge and flanking hills the city trailed a dusky banner of smoke out over the fishing fleet in the Firth.

A little dog cannot see such distant views. Bobby could only read and follow the guide-posts of odours along the way. He had begun the ascent to the toll-bar when he heard the clatter of a cart and the pounding of hoofs behind him. He did not wait to learn if this was the Cauldbrae farmer in pursuit. Certain knowledge on that point was only to be gained at his peril. He sprang into the shelter of a stone wall, scrambled over it, worked his way along it a short distance, and disappeared into a brambly path that skirted a burn in a woody dell.

Immediately the little dog was lost in an unexplored country. The narrow glen was musical with springs, and the low growth was undercut with a maze of rabbit runs, very distracting to a dog of a hunting breed. Bobby knew, by much journeying with Auld Jock, that running water is a natural highway. Sheep drift along the lowest level until they find an outlet down some declivity, or up some foaming steep, to new pastures.

But never before had Bobby found, above such a rustic brook, a many-chimneyed and gabled house of stone, set in a walled garden and swathed in trees. It was only a farm-house, fallen from a more romantic history, and it had no attraction for Bobby. He merely sniffed at dead vines of clematis, sleeping briar bushes, and very live, bright hedges of holly, rounded a corner of its wall, and ran into a group of lusty children romping on the brae, below the very prettiest, thatch-roofed and hill-sheltered hamlet within many a mile of Edinburgh town. The bairns were lunching from grimy, mittened hands, gypsy fashion, life being far too short and playtime too brief for formal meals. Seeing them eating, Bobby suddenly discovered that he was hungry. He rose before a well-provided laddie and politely begged for a share of his meal.

Such an excited shouting of admiration and calling on mithers to come and see the bonny wee dog was never before heard on Swanston village green. Doors flew open and bare-headed women ran out. Then the babies had to be brought, and the old grandfaithers and grandmithers. Everybody oh-ed and ah-ed and clapped hands, and doubled up with laughter, for, a tempting bit held playfully just out of reach, Bobby rose, again and again, jumped for it, and chased a teasing laddie. Then he bethought him to roll over and over, and to go through other winsome little tricks, as Auld Jock had taught him to do, to win the reward. All this had one quite unexpected result. A shrewd-eyed woman pounced upon Bobby and captured him.

'He's no' an ordinar' dog. Some leddy has lost her pet. I'll juist shut 'im up, an' syne she'll pay a shullin' or twa to get 'im again.'

With a twist and a leap Bobby was gone. He scrambled straight up the steep, thorn-clad wall of the glen, where no laddie could follow, and was over the crest. It was a narrow escape, made by terrific effort. His little heart pounding with exhaustion and alarm, he hid under a whin bush to get his breath and strength. The sheltered dell was windless, but here a stiff breeze blew. Suddenly shifting a point, the wind brought to the little dog's nose a whiff of the acrid coal smoke of Edinburgh three miles away.

Straight as an arrow he ran across country, over roadway and wall, ploughed fields and rippling burns. He scrambled under hedges and dashed across farmsteads and cottage gardens. As he neared the city the hour bells aided him, for the Skye terrier is keen of hearing. It was growing dark when he climbed up the last bank and gained Lauriston Place. There he picked up the odours of milk and wool, and the damp smell of the kirkyard.

Now for something comforting to put into his famished little body. A night and a day of exhausting work, of anxiety and grief, had used up the last ounce of fuel. Bobby raced down Forrest Road and turned the slight angle into Greyfriars Place. The lamplighter's progress towards the bridge was marked by the double row of lamps that bloomed, one after the one, on the dusk. The little dog had come to the steps of Mr Traill's place, and lifted himself to scratch on the door, when the bugle began to blow. He dropped with the first note and dashed to the kirkyard gate.

None too soon! Mr Brown was setting the little wicket gate inside, against the wall. In the instant his back was turned, Bobby slipped through. After nightfall, when the caretaker had made his rounds, he came out from under the fallen table-tomb of Mistress Jean Grant.

Lights appeared at the rear windows of the tenements, and families sat at supper. It was snell[1] weather again, the sky dark with threat of snow, and the windows were all closed. But with a

[1]Fresh.

sharp bark beneath the lowest of them Bobby could have made his presence and his wants known. He watched the people eating, sitting wistfully about on his haunches here and there, but remaining silent. By and by there were sounds of crying babies, of crockery being washed, and the ringing of church bells far and near. Then the lights were extinguished, and huge bulks of shadow, of tenements and kirk, engulfed the kirkyard.

When Bobby lay down on Auld Jock's grave, pellets of frozen snow were falling and the air had hardened toward frost.

Sleep alone goes far to revive a little dog, and fasting sharpens the wits. Bobby was so tired that he slept soundly, but so hungry that he woke early, and instantly alert to his situation. It was so very early of a dark winter morning that not even the sparrows were out foraging in the kirkyard for dry seeds. The drum and bugle had not been sounded from the Castle when the milk and dustmen's carts began to clatter over the frozen streets. With the first hint of dawn, stout fishwives, who had tramped all the way in from the piers of Newhaven with heavily laden creels on their heads, were lustily crying their 'caller herrin''.[1] Soon fagot men began to call up the courts of tenements, where fuel was bought by the scant bundle: 'Are ye cauld?'

Many a human waif in the tall buildings about the lower end of Greyfriars kirkyard was cold, even in bed, but, in his thick underjacket of fleece, Bobby was as warm as a plate of breakfast toast. With a vigorous shaking he broke and scattered the crust of snow that burdened his shaggy thatch. Then he lay down on the grave again, with his nose on his paws. Urgent matters occupied the little dog's mind. To deal with these affairs he had the long head of the canniest Scot, wide and high between the ears, and a muzzle as determined as a little steel trap. Small and forlorn as he was, courage, resource, and purpose marked him.

As soon as the door of the caretaker's lodge opened he would have to creep under the fallen slab again. To lie in such a cramped position, hour after hour, day after day, was enough to

[1]What the Edinburgh fishwives who sell herrings cry.

break the spirit of any warm-blooded creature that lives. It was an exquisite form of torture not long to be endured. And to get his single meal a day at Mr Traill's place Bobby had to watch for the chance opening of the wicket to slip in and out like a thief. The furtive life is not only perilous, it outrages every feeling of an honest dog. It is hard for him to live at all without the approval and the cordial consent of men. The human order hostile, he quickly loses his self-respect and drops to the Pariah class. Already wee Bobby had the look of the neglected. His pretty coat was dirty and unkempt. In his run across country, leaves, twigs, and burrs had become entangled in his long hair, and his legs and underparts were caked with mire.

Instinctively any dog struggles to escape the fate of the outcast. By every art he possesses he ingratiates himself with men. One that has his usefulness in the human scheme of things often is able to make his own terms with life, to win the niche of his choice. Bobby's one talent that was of practical value to society was his hunting instinct for every small animal that burrows and prowls and takes toll of men's labour. In Greyfriars kirkyard was work to be done that he could do. For quite three centuries rats and mice had multiplied in this old sanctuary garden from which cats were chased and dogs excluded. Every breeze that blew carried challenges to Bobby's offended nose. Now, in the crisp grey dawn, a big rat came out into the open and darted here and there over the powdering of dry snow that frosted the kirkyard.

A leap, as if released from a spring, and Bobby captured it. A snap of his long muzzle, a jerk of his stoutly set head, and the victim hung limp from his grip. And he followed another deeply seated instinct when he carried the slain to Auld Jock's grave. Trophies of the chase were always to be laid at the feet of the master.

'Gude dog! eh, but ye're a bonny wee fechter!' Auld Jock had always said after such an exploit; and Bobby had been petted and praised until he nearly wagged his crested tail off with happiness and pride. Then he had been given some choice titbit of food as a reward for his prowess. The farmer of Cauldbrae had on such occasions admitted that Bobby might be of use about barn and dairy, and Mr Traill had commended his capture of prowlers in the dining-room. But Bobby was 'ower young' and had not been 'put to the vermin' as a definite business in life. He caught a rat, now and then, as he chased rabbits, merely as a diversion. When he had caught this one he lay down again. But after a time he got up deliberately and trotted down to the encircling line of old courtyarded tombs. There were nooks and crannies between and behind these along the wall into which the caretaker could not penetrate with sickle, rake, and spade, that formed sheltered runways for rodents.

A long, low, weasel-like dog that could flatten himself on the ground, Bobby squeezed between railings and pedestals, scrambled over fallen fragments of sculptured urns, trumpets, angels' wings, altars, skull and crossbones, and Latin-inscribed scrolls. He went on his stomach under holly and laurel shrubs, burdocks, thistles, and tangled dead vines. Here and there he lay in such rubbish as motionless as the effigies carven on marble biers. With the growing light grew the heap of the slain on Auld Jock's grave.

Having done his best, Bobby lay down again, worse in appearance than before, but with a stouter heart. He did not stir, although the shadows fled, the sepulchres stood up around the field of snow, and slabs and shafts camped in ranks on the slope. Smoke began to curl up from high, clustered chimney-pots; shutters were opened, and scantily clad women had hurried errands on decaying gallery and reeling stairway. Suddenly the Castle turrets were gilded with pale sunshine, and all the little cells in the tall, old houses hummed and buzzed and clacked with life. The University bell called scattered students to morning prayers. Pinched and elfish faces of children appeared at the windows overlooking the kirkyard. The sparrows had instant news of that, and the little winged beggars fluttered up to the lintels of certain deep-set casements, where ill-fed bairns scattered breakfasts of crumbs.

Bobby watched all this without a movement. He shivered when the lodge door was heard to open and shut and heavy footsteps crunched on the gravel and snow around the church. 'Juist fair silly' on his quaking legs he stood up, head and tail drooped. But he held his ground bravely, and when the caretaker sighted him he trotted to meet the man, lifted himself on his hind legs, his short, shagged forepaws on his breast, begging attention and indulgence. Then he sprawled across the great boots, asking pardon for the liberty he was taking. At last, all in a flash he darted back to the grave, sniffed at it, and stood again, head up, plumy tail crested, all excitement, as much as to say:

'Come awa' ower, man, an' leuk at the braw sicht.'

If he could have barked, his meaning would have carried more convincingly, but he 'hauded 'is gab' loyally. And, alas, the caretaker was not to be beguiled. Mr Traill had told him Bobby had been sent back to the hill farm, but here he was, 'perseestent' little rascal, and making some sort of bid for the man's favour. Mr Brown took his pipe out of his mouth in surprised exasperation, and glowered at the dog.

'Gang awa' oot wi' ye!'

But Bobby was back again coaxing undauntedly, abasing himself before the angry man, insisting that he had something of interest to show. The caretaker was literally badgered and cajoled into following him. One glance at the formidable heap of the slain, and Mr Brown dropped to a seat on the slab.

'Preserve us a'!'

He stared from the little dog to his victims, turned them over with his stout stick and counted them, and stared again. Bobby fixed his pleading eyes on the man and stood at strained attention while fate hung in the balance.

'Gude wark! Gude wark! A braw doggie, an' an unco' fechter. Losh! but ye're deil o' a bit dog!'

All this was said in a tone of astonished comment, so non-committal of feeling that Bobby's tail began to twitch in the stress of his anxiety. When the caretaker spoke again, after a long, puzzled frowning, it was to express a very human bewilderment and irritation.

'Noo, what am I gangin' to do wi' ye?'

Ah, that was encouraging! A moment before he had ordered Bobby out in no uncertain tone. After another moment he referred the question to a higher court.

'Jeanie, woman, come awa' oot a meenit, wull ye?'

A hasty pattering of carpet-slippered feet on the creaking snow, around the kirk, and there was the neatest little apple-cheeked peasant woman in Scotland, snod[1] from her smooth, frosted hair, spotless linen mutch, and lawn kerchief, to her white, lamb's-wool stockings.

'Here's the bit dog I was tellin' ye aboot; an' see for yersel' what he's done noo.'

'The wee beastie couldna do a' that! It's as muckle as his ain wecht in fou' vermin!'[2] she cried.

'Ay, he did. Thae terriers are sperity, by the ordinar'. Ane o' them, let into the Corn Exchange a murky nicht, killed saxty in ten meenits, an' had to be dragged awa' by the tail. Noo, what I am gangin' to do wi' the takin' bit I dinna ken.'

It is very certain that simple Mistress Jean Brown had never heard of Mr Dick's advice to Miss Betsy Trotwood on the occasion when young David Copperfield presented himself, travel-stained and weary, before his good aunt. But out of her experience of wholesome living she brought forth the same wise opinion.

'I'd gie him a gude washin' first of a' Jamie. He leuks like some puir, gaen-aboot dog.' And she drew her short, blue-stuff gown back from Bobby's grateful attentions.

Mr Brown slapped his corduroy-breeked knee and nodded his grizzled head. 'Richt ye are. It's maist michty, noo, I wadna think o' that. When I was leevin' as an under-gairdener wi' a laird i' Argyllshire I was aye aboot the kennels wi' the gillies. That was lang syne. The sma' terrier dogs were aye washed i' claes[3] tubs wi' warm water an' soap. Come awa', Bobby.'

[1]Neat, tidy.

[2]As much as his own weight in foul vermin.

[3]Clothes.

The caretaker got up stiffly, for such snell weather was apt to give him twinges in his joints. In him a youthful enthusiasm for dogs had suddenly revived. Besides, although he would have denied it, he was relieved at having the main issue, as to what was to be done with this four-footed trespasser, side-tracked for a time. Bobby followed him to the lodge at an eager trot, and he dutifully hopped into the bath that was set on the rear doorstep. Mr Brown scrubbed him vigorously, and Bobby splashed and swam and churned the soapy water to foam. He scrambled out at once, when told to do so, and submitted to being dried with a big, tow-linen towel. This was all a delightful novelty to Bobby. Heretofore he had gone into any convenient tarn or burn to swim, and then dried himself by rolling on the heather and running before the wind. Now he was bundled up ignominiously in an old flannel petticoat, carried across a sanded kitchen floor, and laid on a warm hearth.

'Doon wi' ye!' was the gruff order. Bobby turned around and around on the hearth, like some little wild dog making a bed in the jungle, before he obeyed. He kept very still during the reading of a chapter and the singing of a Psalm, as he had been taught to do at the farm by many a reminder from Auld Jock's boot. And he kept away from the breakfast-table, although the walls of his stomach were collapsed as flat as the sides of an empty pocket.

It was such a clean, shining little kitchen, with the scoured deal table, chairs, and cupboard, and the firelight from the grate winked so on pewter mugs, copper kettle, willow-patterned plates, and diamond panes, that Bobby blinked too. Flowers bloomed in pots on the casement sills, and a little brown skylark sang, fluttering as it it would soar, in a gilded cage. Afer the morning meal Mr Brown lighted his pipe and put on his bonnet to go out again, when he bethought him that Bobby might be needing something to eat.

'What'll ye gie 'im, Jeanie? At the laird's, noo, the terriers were aye fed wi' bits o' livers an' cheese an' moor-fowls' eggs, an' sic-like, fried.'

'Havers, Jamie, it's no' releegious to feed a dog better than puir bairns. He'll do fair weel wi' table scraps.'

She set down a plate with a spoonful of porridge on it, a cold potato, some bread crusts, and the leavings of a broiled caller herrin'. It was a generous breakfast for so small a dog, but Bobby had been without food for quite forty hours, and had done an amazing amount of work in the meantime. When he had eaten all of it he was still hungry. As a polite hint, he polished the empty plate with his pink tongue and looked up expectantly; but the best-intentioned people, if they have had little to do with dogs, cannot read such signs.

'Ye needna lick the posies aff,' the wifie said, good-humouredly, as she picked the plate up to wash it. She thought to put down a tin basin of water. Bobby lapped it so eagerly, yet so daintily, that she added: 'He's a weel-broucht-up tyke, Jamie.'

'He is so. Noo, we'll see hoo weel he can leuk.' In a shamefaced way he fetched from a tool-box a long-forgotten, strong little curry-comb, such as is used on shaggy Shetland ponies. With that he proceeded to give Bobby such a grooming as he had never had before. It was a painful operation, for his thatch was a stubborn mat of crisp waves and knotty tangles to his plumy tail and down to his feathered paws. He braced himself and took the punishment without a whimper, and when it was done he stood cascaded with dark-silver ripples to the floor.

'The bonny wee!' cried Mistress Jeanie. 'I canna tak' ma twa een aff o' 'im.'

'Ay, he's bonny by the ordinar'. It wad be grand, noo, gin the meenister'd fancy 'im an tak' 'im into the manse.'

The wifie considered this ruefully. 'Jamie, I was wishin' ye didna hae to –'

But what she wished he did not have to do, Mr Brown did not stop to hear. He suddenly clapped his bonnet on his head and went out. He had an urgent errand on High Street, to buy grass and flower seeds and tools that would certainly be needed in April. It took him an hour or more of shrewd looking about for the best bargains, in a swarm of little barnacle and cellar shops, to spend a few of the kirk's shillings. When he found himself, to his disgust, looking at a nail-studded collar for a little dog he called himself a 'doited auld fule',[1] and tramped back across the bridge.

At the kirkyard gate he stopped and read the notice through twice: 'No dogs permitted'. That was as plain as 'Thou shalt not'. To the pious caretaker and trained servant it was the eleventh commandment. He shook his head, sighed, and went in to dinner. Bobby was not in the house, and the master of it avoided inquiring for him. He also avoided the wifie's wistful eye, and he busied himself inside the two kirks all the afternoon.

Because he was in the kirks, and the beautiful memorial windows of stained glass were not for the purpose of looking out, he did not see a dramatic incident that occurred in the kirkyard after three o'clock in the afternoon. The prelude to it really began with the report of the time-gun at one. Bobby had insisted upon being let out of the lodge kitchen, and had spent the morning near Auld Jock's grave and in nosing about neighbouring slabs and thorn bushes. When the time-gun boomed he trotted to the gate quite openly and waited there inside the wicket.

In such nipping weather there were no visitors to the kirkyard and the gate was not opened. The music bells ran the gamut of old Scotch airs and ceased, while he sat there and waited patiently. Once a man stopped to look at the little dog, and Bobby promptly jumped on the wicket, plainly begging to have it unlatched. But the passer-by decided that some lady had left her pet behind, and would return for him. So he patted the attractive little Highlander on the head and went on about his business.

Discouraged by the unpromising outlook for dinner that day, Bobby went slowly back to the grave. Twice afterward he made hopeful pilgrimages to the gate. For diversion he fell noiselessly upon a prowling cat and chased it out of the kirkyard. At last he

[1]Senile old fool.

sat upon the table-tomb. He had escaped notice from the tenements all the morning because the view from most of the windows was blocked by washings, hung out and dripping, then freezing and clapping against the old tombs. It was half past three o'clock when a tiny, wizened face popped out of one of the rude little windows in the decayed Cunzie Neuk at the bottom of Candlemaker Row. Crippled Tammy Barr called out in shrill excitement:

'Ailie! O-o-oh, Ailie Lindsey, there's the wee doggie!'

'Whaur?' The lassie's elfin face looked out from a low, rear window of the Candlemakers' Guildhall at the top of the Row.

'On the stane[1] by the kirk wa'.'

'I see 'im noo. Isna he bonny? I wish Bobby could bide i' the kirkyaird, but they wadna let 'im. Tammy, gin ye tak' 'im up to Maister Traill, he'll gie ye the shullin'!'

'I couldna tak' 'im by ma lane,' was the pathetic confession. 'Wad ye gang wi' me, Ailie? Ye could drap ower an' catch 'im, an' I could come by the gate. Faither made me some grand crutches frae an' auld chair back.'

Tears suddenly drowned the lassie's blue eyes and ran down her pinched little cheeks. 'Nae I couldna gang. I haena ony shoon to ma feet.'

'It's no' so cauld. Gin I had twa gude feet I could gang the bit way wi'oot shoon.'

'I ken it isna so cauld,' Ailie admitted, 'but for a lassie it's no' respectable to gang to a grand place bare-feeted.'

That was undeniable, and the eager children fell silent and tearful. But oh, necessity is the mother of makeshifts among the poor! Suddenly Ailie cried: 'Bide a meenit, Tammy,' and vanished. Presently she was back, with the difficulty overcome. 'Grannie says I can wear her shoon. She doesna wear 'em i' the hoose, ava.'

'I'll gie ye a saxpence, Ailie,' offered Tammy.

The sordid bargain shocked no feeling of these tenement bairns nor marred their pleasure in the adventure. Presently

[1]Stone.

there was a tap-tap-tapping of crutches on the heavy gallery that fronted the Cunzie Neuk, and on the stairs that descended from it to the steep and curving Row. The lassie draped a fragment of an old plaid deftly over her thinly clad shoulders, climbed through the window, to the pediment of the classic tomb that blocked it, and dropped into the kirkyard. To her surprise Bobby was there at her feet, frantically wagging his tail, and he raced her to the gate. She caught him on the steps of the dining-room, and held his wriggling body fast until Tammy came up.

It was a tumultuous little group that burst in upon the astonished landlord: barking fluff of an excited dog, flying lassies in clattering big shoes, and wee, tapping Tammy. They literally fell upon him when he was engaged in counting out his money.

'Whaur did you find him?' asked Mr Traill in bewilderment.

Six-year-old Ailie slipped a shy finger into her mouth, and looked to the very much more mature five-year-old crippled laddie to answer:

'He was i' the kirkyaird.'

'Sittin' upon a stane by 'is ainsel',' added Ailie.

'An' no' hidin', ava. It was juist like he was leevin' there.'

'An' syne, when I drapped oot o' the window he louped at me so bonny, and I couldna keep up wi' 'im to the gate.'

Wonder of wonders! It was plain that Bobby had made his way back from the hill farm and, from his appearance and manner, as well as from this account, it was equally clear that some happy change in his fortunes had taken place. He sat up on his haunches listening with interest and lolling his tongue! And that was a thing the bereft little dog had not done since his master died. In the first pause in the talk he rose and begged for his dinner.

'Noo, what am I to pay? It took ane, twa, three o' ye to fetch ane sma' dog. A saxpence for the laddie, a saxpence for the lassie, an' a bit meal for Bobby.'

While he was putting the plate down under the settle Mr Traill heard an amazed whisper: 'He's gien the doggie a chuckie[1] bane!'

[1]Chicken.

'He's gien the doggie a chuckie bane!'

The landlord switched the plate from under Bobby's protesting little muzzle and turned to catch the hungry look on the faces of the children. Chicken, indeed, for a little dog, before these ill-fed bairns! Mr Traill had a brilliant thought.

'Preserve me! I didna think to eat ma ain dinner. I hae so muckle to eat I canna eat it by ma lane.'

The idea of having too much to eat was so preposterously funny that Tammy doubled up with laughter and nearly tumbled over his crutches. Mr Traill set him upright again.

'Did ye ever gang on a picnic, bairnies?' And what was a picnic? Tammy ventured the opinion that it might be some kind of a cart for lame laddies to ride in.

'A picnic is when ye gang gypsying in the summer,' Mr Traill explained. 'Ye walk to a bonny green brae, an' sit doon under a hawthorn tree a' covered wi' posies, by a babblin' burn, an ye eat oot o' yer ain hands. An' syne ye hear a throstle or a redbreast sing an' a saucy blackbird whustle.'

'Could ye tak' a dog?' asked Tammy.

'Ye could that, mannie. It's no' a picnic wi'oot a sonsie doggie to rin on the brae wi' ye.'

'Oh!' Ailie's blue eyes slowly widened in her pallid little face, 'But ye couldna hae a picnic i' the snawy weather.'

'Ay, ye could. It's the bonniest of a' when ye're no' expectin' it. I aye keep a picnic hidden i' the ingleneuk aboon.' He suddenly swung Tammy up on his shoulder, and calling, gaily, 'Come awa',' went out the door, through another beside it, and up a flight of stairs to the dining-room above. A fire burned there in the grate, the tables were covered with linen, and there were blooming flowers in pots in the front windows. Patrons from the University, and the well-to-do streets and squares to the south and east, made of this upper room a sort of club in the evenings. At four o'clock in the afternoon there were no guests.

'Noo,' said Mr Traill, when his overcome little guests were seated at a table in the ingleneuk. 'A picnic is whaur ye hae onything ye fancy to eat; gude things ye wullna be haein' ilka day, ye mind.' He rang a call-bell and a grinning waiter laddie popped up so quickly the lassie caught her breath.

'Eneugh broo for aince,' said Tammy.

'Porridge that isna burned,' suggested Ailie. Such pitiful poverty of the imagination!

'Nae, it's bread an' butter, an' strawberry jam, an' tea wi' cream an' sugar, an' cauld chuckie at a snawy picnic,' announced Mr Traill. And there it was, served very quickly and silently, after some manner of magic. Bobby had to stand on the fourth chair to eat his dinner, and when he had dispatched it he sat up and viewed the little party with the liveliest interest and happiness.

'Tammy,' Ailie said, when her shyness had worn off, 'it's like the grand tales ye mak' up i' yer heid.'

'Preserve me! Does the wee mannie mak' up stories?'

'It's juist fulish things, aboot haein' mair to eat an' a sonsie doggie to play wi' an' twa gude legs to tak' me aboot. I think 'em oot at nicht when I canna sleep.'

'Eh, laddie, do ye noo?' Mr Traill suddenly had a terrible 'cauld in 'is heid', that made his eyes water. 'Hoo auld are ye?'

'Five, gangin' on sax.'

'Losh! I thoucht ye war fifty, gangin' on saxty.' Laughter saved the day from overmoist emotions. And presently Mr Traill was able to say in a businesslike tone:

'We'll hae to tak' ye to the Infirmary. An' if they canna mak' yer legs ower ye'll get a pair o' braw crutches that are the niest thing to gude legs. An' syne we'll see if there's no' a place in Heriot's for a sma' laddie that mak's up bonny tales o' his ain in the murky auld Cunzie Neuk.'

Now the gay little feast was eaten, and early dark was coming on. If Mr Traill had entertained the hope that Bobby had recovered from his grief and might remain with him he was disappointed. The little dog began to be restless. He ran to the door and back; he begged, and he scratched on the panel. And then he yelped! As soon as the door was opened he shot out of it, tumbled down the stairway, and waited at the foot impatiently for the lower door to be unlatched. Ailie's thin, swift legs were left behind when Bobby dashed to the kirkyard.

Tammy followed at a surprising pace on his rude crutches, and Mr Traill brought up the rear. If the children could not smuggle the frantic little dog inside the landlord meant to put him over the wicket and, if necessary, to have it out with the caretaker, and then to go before the kirk minister and officers with his plea. He was still concealed by the buildings, from the alcoved gate, when he heard Mr Brown's gruff voice taking the frightened bairns to task.

'Gie me the dog; an' dinna ye tak' him oot ony mair wi'oot speirin' me.'

The children fled. Peeping around the angle of the Book Hunter's Stall, Mr Traill saw the caretaker lift Bobby over the wicket to his arms, and start with him towards the lodge. He was perishing with curiosity about this astonishing change of front on the part of Mr Brown, but it was a delicate situation in which it seemed best not to meddle. He went slowly back to the restaurant, begrudging Bobby to the luckier caretaker.

His envy was premature. Mr Brown set Bobby inside the lodge kitchen and announced briefly to his wife: 'The bit dog wull sleep i' the hoose the nicht.' And he went about some business at the upper end of the kirkyard. When he came in an hour later Bobby was gone.

'I couldna keep 'im in, Jamie. He didna blatter, but he greeted so sair to be let oot, an syne he scratched a' the paint aff the door.'

Mr Brown glowered at her in exasperation, 'Woman, they'll hae me up afore kirk sessions for brakin' the rules, an' syne they'll turn us a' oot i' the cauld warld togither.'

He slammed the door and stormed angrily around the kirk. It was still light enough to see the little creature on the snowy mound and, indeed, Bobby got up and wagged his tail in friendly greeting. At that all the bluster went out of the man, and he began to argue the matter with the dog.

'Come awa', Bobby. Ye canna be leevin' i' the kirkyaird.'

Bobby was of a different opinion. He turned around and

around, thoughtfully, several times, then sat up on the grave. Entirely willing to spend a social hour with his new friend, he fixed his eyes hospitably upon him. Mr Brown dropped to the slab, lighted his pipe, and smoked for a time, to compose his agitated mind. By and by he got up briskly and stooped to lift the little dog. At that Bobby dug his claws in the clods and resisted with all his muscular body and determined mind. He clung to the grave so desperately, and looked up so piteously, that the caretaker surrendered. And there was snod Mistress Jeanie, forgetting her spotless gown and kneeling in the snow.

'Puir Bobby, puir wee Bobby!' she cried, and her tears fell on the little tousled head. The caretaker strode abruptly away and waited for the wifie in the shadow of the auld kirk. Bobby lifted his muzzle and licked the caressing hand. Then he curled himself up comfortably on the mound and went to sleep.

Garm – a Hostage

RUDYARD KIPLING

One night, a very long time ago, I drove to an Indian military cantonment called Mian Mir to see amateur theatricals. At the back of the Infantry barracks a soldier, his cap over one eye, rushed in front of the horses and shouted that he was a dangerous highway robber. As a matter of fact he was a friend of mine, so I told him to go home before any one caught him; but he fell under the pole, and I heard voices of a military guard in search of someone.

The driver and I coaxed him into the carriage, drove home swiftly, undressed him and put him to bed, where he waked next morning with a sore headache, very much ashamed. When his uniform was cleaned and dried, and he had been shaved and washed and made neat, I drove him back to barracks with his arm in a fine white sling, and reported that I had accidentally run over him. I did not tell this story to my friend's sergeant, who was a hostile and unbelieving person, but to his lieutenant, who did not know us quite so well.

Three days later my friend came to call, and at his heels slobbered and fawned one of the finest bull-terriers – of the old-fashioned breed, two parts bull and one terrier – that I had ever set eyes on. He was pure white, with a fawn-coloured saddle just behind his neck, and a fawn diamond at the root of his thin whippy tail. I had admired him distantly for more than a year; and Vixen, my own fox-terrier, knew him too, but did not approve.

''E's for you', said my friend; but he did not look as though he liked parting with him.

'Nonsense! That dog's worth more than most men, Stanley', I said.

''E's that an' more. 'Tention!'

The dog rose on his hind legs, and stood upright for a full minute.

'Eyes right!'

He sat on his haunches and turned his head sharp to the right. At a sign he rose and barked thrice. Then he shook hands with his right paw and bounded lightly to my shoulder. Here he made himself into a necktie, limp and lifeless, handing down on either side of my neck. I was told to pick him up and throw him in the air. He fell with a howl, and held up one leg.

'Part o' the trick', said his owner. 'You're going to die now. Dig yourself your little grave an' shut your little eye'.

Still limping, the dog hobbled to the garden-edge, dug a hole and lay down in it. When told that he was cured he jumped out, wagging his tail, and whining for applause. He was put through half a dozen other tricks, such as showing how he would hold a man safe (I was that man, and he sat down before me, his teeth bared, ready to spring), and how he would cease eating at the word of command. I had no more than finished praising him when my friend made a gesture that stopped the dog as though he had been shot, took a piece of blue-ruled canteen-paper from his helmet, handed it to me and ran away, while the dog looked after him and howled. I read:

Sir – I give you the dog because of what you got me out of. He is the best I know, for I made him myself, and he is as good as a man. Please do not give him too much to eat, and please do not give him back to me, for I'm not going to take him, if you will keep him. So please do not try to give him back any more. I have kept his name back, so you can call him anything and he will answer, but please do not give him back. He can kill a man as easy as anything, but please do not give him too much meat. He knows more than a man.

Vixen sympathetically joined her shrill little yap to the bull-terrier's despairing cry, and I was annoyed, for I knew that a man who cares for dogs is one thing, but a man who loves one dog is quite another. Dogs are, at the best, no more than verminous vagrants, self-scratchers, foul feeders, and unclean by the law of Moses and Mohammed; but a dog with whom one lives alone for at least six months in the year; a free thing, tied to you so strictly by love that without you he will not stir or exercise; a patient, temperate, humorous, wise soul, who knows your moods before you know them yourself, is not a dog under any ruling.

I had Vixen, who was all my dog to me; and I felt what my friend must have felt, at tearing out his heart in this style and leaving it in my garden. However, the dog understood clearly enough that I was his master, and did not follow the soldier. As soon as he drew breath I made much of him, and Vixen, yelling with jealousy, flew at him. Had she been of his own sex, he might have cheered himself with a fight, but he only looked worriedly when she nipped his deep iron sides, laid his heavy head on my knee, and howled anew. I meant to dine at the Club that night, but as darkness drew in, and the dog snuffed through the empty house like a child trying to recover from a fit of sobbing, I felt that I could not leave him to suffer his first evening alone. So we fed at home, Vixen on one side and the stranger-dog on the other; she watching his every mouthful, and saying explicitly what she thought of his table manners, which were much better than hers.

It was Vixen's custom, till the weather grew hot, to sleep in my bed, her head on the pillow like a Christian; and when morning came I would always find that the little thing had braced her feet against the wall and pushed me to the very edge of the cot. This night she hurried to bed purposefully, every hair up and one eye on the stranger, who had dropped on a mat in a helpless, hopeless sort of way, his four feet spread out, sighing heavily. She settled her head on the pillow several times, to show her little airs and graces, and struck up her usual whiney sing-song before slumber. The stranger-dog softly edged towards me. I put out my hand and he licked it. Instantly my wrist was between Vixen's teeth, and her warning *aaarh*! said as plainly as speech that if I took any further notice of the stranger she would bite.

I caught her behind her fat neck with my left hand, shook her severely, and said:

'Vixen, if you do that again you'll be put into the veranda. Now, remember!'

She understood perfectly, but the minute I released her she mouthed my right wrist once more, and waited with her ears back and all her body flattened, ready to bite. The big dog's tail thumped the floor in a humble and peace-making way.

I grabbed Vixen a second time, lifted her out of bed like a rabbit (she hated that and yelled), and, as I had promised, set her out in the veranda with the bats and the moonlight. At this she howled. Then she used coarse language – not to me, but to the bull-terrier – till she coughed with exhaustion. Then she ran round the house trying every door. Then she went off to the stables and barked as though someone were stealing the horses, which was an old trick of hers. Last she returned, and her snuffing yelp said, 'I'll be good! Let me in and I'll be good!'

She was admitted and flew to her pillow. When she was quieted I whispered to the other dog, 'You can lie on the foot of the bed.' The bull jumped up at once, and though I felt Vixen quiver with rage, she knew better than to protest. So we slept till the morning, and they had early breakfast with me, bite for bite, till the horse came round and we went for a ride. I don't think the bull had ever followed a horse before. He was wild with excitement, and Vixen, as usual, squealed and scuttered and scooted, and took charge of the procession.

There was one corner of a village near by, which we generally passed with caution, because all the yellow pariah-dogs of the place gathered about it. They were half-wild, starving beasts, and though utter cowards, yet where nine or ten of them get together they will mob and kill and eat an English dog. I kept a whip with a long lash for them. That morning they attacked Vixen, who, perhaps of design, had moved from beyond my horse's shadow.

The bull was ploughing along in the dust, fifty yards behind, rolling in his run, and smiling as bull-terriers will. I heard Vixen squeal. Half a dozen of the curs closed in on her; a white streak came up behind me; a cloud of dust rose near Vixen, and, when it cleared, I saw one tall pariah with his back broken, and the bull wrenching another to earth. Vixen retreated to the protection of my whip, and the bull paddled back smiling more than ever, covered with the blood of his enemies. That decided me to call him 'Garm of the Bloody Breast,' who was a great person in his time, or 'Garm' for short; so, leaning forward, I told him what his temporary name would be. He looked up while I repeated it, and then raced away. I shouted 'Garm!' He stopped, raced back, and came up to ask my will.

Then I saw that my soldier-friend was right, and that that dog knew, and was worth, more than a man. At the end of the ride I gave an order which Vixen knew and hated: 'Go away and get washed!' I said. Garm understood some part of it, and Vixen interpreted the rest, and the two trotted off together soberly. When I went to the back veranda Vixen had been washed snowy-white, and was very proud of herself, but the dog-boy would not touch Garm on any account unless I stood by. So I waited while he was being scrubbed, and Garm, with the soap creaming on the top of his broad head, looked at me to make sure that this was what I expected him to endure. He knew perfectly that the dog-boy was only obeying orders.

'Another time,' I said to the dog-boy, 'you will wash the great dog with Vixen when I send them home.'

'Does *he* know?' said the dog-boy, who understood the ways of dogs.

'Garm,' I said, 'another time you will be washed with Vixen.'

I knew that Garm understood. Indeed, next washing-day, when Vixen as usual fled under my bed, Garm stared at the doubtful dog-boy in the veranda, stalked to the place where he had been washed last time, and stood rigid in his tub.

But the long days in my office tried him sorely. We three would drive off in the morning at half past eight and come home at six or later. Vixen, knowing the routine of it, went to sleep under my table; but the confinement ate into Garm's soul. He generally sat on the veranda looking out on the Mall; and well I knew what he expected.

Sometimes a company of soldiers would move along on their way to the Fort, and Garm rolled forth to inspect them; or an officer in uniform entered into the office, and it was pitiful to see poor Garm's welcome to the cloth – not the man. He would leap at him, and sniff and bark joyously, then run to the door and back again. One afternoon I heard him bay with a full throat – a thing he had never done before – and he disappeared. When I drove into my garden at the end of the day a soldier in white uniform scrambled over the wall at the far end, and the Garm that met me was a joyous dog. This happened twice or thrice a week for a month.

I pretended not to notice, but Garm knew and Vixen knew. He would glide homewards from the office about four o'clock, as though he were only going to look at the scenery, and this he did so quietly that but for Vixen I should not have noticed him. The jealous little dog under the table would give a sniff and a snort, just loud enough to call my attention to the flight. Garm might go out forty times in the day and Vixen would never stir, but when he slunk off to see his true master in my garden she told me in her own tongue. That was the one sign she made to show that Garm did not altogether belong to the family. They were the best of friends at all times, *but*, Vixen explained that I was never to forget Garm did not love me as she loved me.

I never expected it. The dog was not my dog – could never be my dog – and I knew he was as miserable as his master who tramped eight miles a day to see him. So it seemed to me that the sooner the two were reunited the better for all. One afternoon I sent Vixen home alone in the dog-cart (Garm had gone before), and rode over to cantonments to find another friend of mine, who was an Irish soldier and a great friend of the dog's master.

I explained the whole case, and wound up with:

'And now Stanley's in my garden crying over his dog. Why doesn't he take him back? They're both unhappy.'

'Unhappy! There's no sense in the little man any more. But 'tis his fit.'

'What *is* his fit? He travels fifty miles a week to see the brute, and he pretends not to notice me when he sees me on the road; and I'm as unhappy as he is. Make him take the dog back.'

'It's his penance he's set himself. I told him by way av a joke, afther you'd run over him so convenient that night, whin he was dhrunk – I said if he was a Catholic he'd do penance. Off he went wid that fit in his little head *an'* a dose av fever, an' nothin' would suit but givin' you the dog as a hostage.'

'Hostage for what? I don't want hostages from Stanley.'

'For his good behaviour. He's keepin' straight now, the way it's no pleasure to associate wid him.'

'Has he taken the pledge?'

'If 'twas only *that* I need not care. Ye can take the pledge for three months on an' off. He sez he'll never see the dog again, an' *so*, mark you, he'll keep straight for evermore. Ye know his fits? Well, this is wan av them. How's the dog takin' it?'

'Like a man. He's the best dog in India. Can't you make Stanley take him back?'

'I can do no more than I have done. But ye know his fits. He's just doin' his penance. What will he do when he goes to the Hills? The docthor's put him on the list.'

It is the custom in India to send a certain number of invalids from each regiment up to stations in the Himalayas for the hot weather; and though the men ought to enjoy the cool and the comfort, they miss the society of the barracks down below, and do their best to come back or to avoid going. I felt that this move would bring matters to a head, so I left Terence hopefully, though he called after me:

'He won't take the dog, sorr. You can lay your month's pay on that. Ye know his fits.'

I never pretended to understand Private Ortheris; and so I did the next best thing – I left him alone.

That summer the invalids of the regiment to which my friend belonged were ordered off to the Hills early, because the doctors thought marching in the cool of the day would do them good. Their route lay south to a place called Umballa, a hundred and twenty miles or more. Then they would turn east and march up into the hills to Kasauli or Dugshai or Subathoo. I dined with the officers the night before they left – they were marching at five in the morning. It was midnight when I drove into my garden and surprised a white figure flying over the wall.

'That man,' said my butler, 'has been here since nine, making talk to that dog. He is quite mad. I did not tell him to go away because he has been here many times before, and because the dog-boy told me that if I told him to go away, that great dog would immediately slay me. He did not wish to speak to the Protector of the Poor, and he did not ask for anything to eat or drink.'

'Kadir Buksh,' said I, 'that was well done, for the dog would surely have killed thee. But I do not think the white soldier will come any more.'

Garm slept ill that night and whimpered in his dreams. Once he sprang up with a clear, ringing bark, and I heard him wag his tail till it waked him and the bark died out in a howl. He had dreamed he was with his master again, and I nearly cried. It was all Stanley's silly fault.

The first halt which the detachment of invalids made was some miles from their barracks, on the Amritzar road, and ten miles distant from my house. By a mere chance one of the officers drove back for another good dinner at the Club (cooking on the line of march is always bad), and there I met him. He was a particular friend of mine, and I knew that he knew how to love a dog properly. His pet was a big fat retriever who was going up to the Hills for his health, and though it was still April, the round brown brute puffed and panted in the Club veranda as though he would burst.

'It's amazing,' said the officer, 'what excuses these invalids of mine make to get back to barracks. There's a man in my company now asked for leave to go back to cantonments to pay a debt he'd forgotten. I was so taken by the idea I let him go, and he jingled off in an *ekka* as pleased as Punch. Ten miles to pay a debt! Wonder what it was really?'

'If you'll drive me home I think I can show you,' I said.

So we went over to my house in his dog-cart with the retriever; and on the way I told him the story of Garm.

'I was wondering where that brute had gone to. He's the best dog in the regiment,' said my friend. 'I offered the little fellow twenty rupees for him a month ago. But he's a hostage, you say, for Stanley's good conduct. Stanley's one of the best men I have – when he chooses.'

'That's the reason why,' I said. 'A second-rate man wouldn't have taken things to heart as he has done.'

We drove in quietly at the far end of the garden, and crept round the house. There was a place close to the wall all grown about with tamarisk trees, where I knew Garm kept his bones. Even Vixen was not allowed to sit near it. In the full Indian moonlight I could see a white uniform bending over the dog.

'Good-bye, old man.' We could not help hearing Stanley's voice. 'For 'Eving's sake don't get bit and go mad by any measly pi-dog. But you can look after yourself, old man. *You* don't get drunk an' run about 'ittin' your friends. You takes your bones an' you eats your biscuit, an' you kills your enemy like a gentleman. I'm goin' away – don't 'owl – I'm goin' off to Kasauli where I won't see you no more.'

I could hear him holding Garm's nose as the dog threw it up to the stars.

'You'll stay here an' be'ave, an' – an' I'll go away an' try to be'ave, an' I don't know 'ow to leave you. I don't know –'

'I think this is damn' silly,' said the officer, patting his foolish fubsy old retriever. He called to the private, who leaped to his feet, marched forward, and saluted.

'You here?' said the officer, turning away his head.

'Yes, sir, but I'm goin' back.'

'I shall be leaving here at eleven in my cart. You come with me. I can't have sick men running about all over the place. Report yourself at eleven, *here*.'

We did not say much when we went indoors, but the officer muttered and pulled his retriever's ears.

He was a disgraceful, overfed door-mat of a dog; and when he waddled off to my cookhouse to be fed, I had a brilliant idea.

At eleven o'clock that officer's dog was nowhere to be found, and you never heard such a fuss as his owner made. He called and shouted and grew angry, and hunted through my garden for half an hour.

Then I said:

'He's sure to turn up in the morning. Send a man in by rail, and I'll find the beast and return him.'

'Beast?' said the officer. 'I value that dog considerably more than I value any man I know. It's all very fine for you to talk. Your dog's here.'

So she was – under my feet – and, had she been missing, food and wages would have stopped in my house till her return. But some people grow fond of dogs not worth a cut of the whip. My friend had to drive away at last with Stanley in the back-seat. And then the dog-boy said to me:

'What kind of animal is Bullen Sahib's dog? Look at him!'

I went to the boy's hut, and the fat old reprobate was lying on a mat carefully chained up. He must have heard his master calling for twenty minutes, but had not even attempted to join him.

'He has no face,' said the dog-boy scornfully. 'He is a *punniar-kooter* [a spaniel]. He never tried to get that cloth off his jaws when his master called. Now Vixen-*baba* would have jumped through the window, and the Great Dog would have slain me with his muzzled mouth. It is true that there are many kinds of dogs.'

Next evening who should turn up but Stanley. The officer had sent him back fourteen miles by rail with a note begging me to return the retriever if I had found him, and, if I had not, to offer huge rewards. The last train to camp left at half past ten, and Stanley stayed till ten talking to Garm. I argued and entreated, and even threatened to shoot the bull-terrier, but the little man was as firm as a rock, though I gave him a good dinner and talked to him most severely. Garm knew as well as I that this was the last time he could hope to see his man, and followed Stanley like a shadow. The retriever said nothing, but licked his lips after his meal and waddled off without so much as saying 'Thank you' to the disgusted dog-boy.

So that last meeting was over and I felt as wretched as Garm, who moaned in his sleep all night. When we went to the office he found a place under the table close to Vixen, and dropped flat till it was time to go home. There was no more running out into the verandas, no slinking away for stolen talks with Stanley. As the weather grew warmer the dogs were forbidden to run beside the cart, but sat at my side on the seat, Vixen with her head under the crook of my left elbow, and Garm hugging the handrail.

Here Vixen was ever in great form. She had to attend to all the moving traffic, such as bullock-carts that blocked the way, and camels, and led ponies; as well as to keep up her dignity when she passed low friends running in the dust. She never yapped for yapping's sake, but her shrill, high bark was known all along the Mall, and other men's terriers ki-yied in reply, and bullock-drivers looked over their shoulders and gave us the road with a grin.

But Garm cared for none of these things. His big eyes were on the horizon and his terrible mouth was shut. There was another dog in the office who belonged to my Chief. We called him 'Bob the Librarian,' because he always imagined vain rats behind the bookshelves, and in hunting for them would drag out half the old newspaper-files. Bob was a well-meaning idiot, but Garm did not encourage him. He would slide his head round the door, panting, 'Rats! Come along, Garm!' and Garm would shift one fore-paw over the other, and curl himself round, leaving Bob to whine at a most uninterested back. The office was nearly as cheerful as a tomb in those days.

Once, and only once, did I see Garm at all contented with his surroundings. He had gone for an unauthorized walk with Vixen early one Sunday morning, and a very young and foolish artilleryman (his battery had just moved to that part of the world) tried to steal them both. Vixen, of course, knew better than to take food from soldiers, and, besides, she had just finished her breakfast. So she trotted back with a large piece of the mutton that they issue to our troops, laid it down on my veranda, and looked up to see what I thought. I asked her where Garm was, and she ran in front of the horse to show me the way.

About a mile up the road we came across our artilleryman sitting very stiffly on the edge of a culvert with a greasy handkerchief on his knees. Garm was in front of him, looking rather pleased. When the man moved leg or hand, Garm bared his teeth in silence. A broken string hung from his collar, and the other half of it lay, all warm, in the artilleryman's still hand. He explained to me, keeping his eyes straight in front of him, that he had met this dog (he called him awful names) walking alone, and was going to take him to the Fort to be killed for a masterless pariah.

I said that Garm did not seem to me much of a pariah, but that he had better take him to the Fort if he thought best. He said he did not care to do so. I told him to go to the Fort alone. He said he did not want to go at that hour, but would follow my advice as soon as I had called off the dog. I instructed Garm to take him to the Fort, and Garm marched him solemnly up to the gate, one mile and a half under a hot sun, and I told the quarter-guard what had happened; but the young artilleryman was more angry than was at all necessary when they began to laugh. Several regiments, he was told, had tried to steal Garm in their time.

That month the hot weather shut down in earnest, and the

About a mile up the road we came across our artilleryman

dogs slept in the bathroom on the cool wet bricks where the bath is placed. Every morning, as soon as the man filled my bath, the two jumped in, and every morning the man filled the bath a second time. I said to him that he might as well fill a small tub specially for the dogs. 'Nay,' said he smiling, 'it is not their custom. They would not understand. Besides, the big bath gives them more space.'

The punkah-coolies who pull the punkahs day and night came to know Garm intimately. He noticed that when the swaying fan stopped I would call out to the coolie and bid him pull with a long stroke. If the man still slept I would wake him up. He discovered, too, that it was a good thing to lie in the wave of air under the punkah. Maybe Stanley had taught him all about this in barracks. At any rate, when the punkah stopped, Garm would first growl and cock his eye at the rope, and if that did not wake the man – it nearly always did – he would tiptoe forth and talk in the sleeper's ear. Vixen was a clever little dog, but she could never connect the punkah and the coolie; so Garm gave me grateful hours of cool sleep. But he was utterly wretched – as miserable as a human being; and in his misery he clung so closely to me that other men noticed it and were envious. If I moved from one room to another Garm followed; if my pen stopped scratching, Garm's head was thrust into my hand; if I turned, half awake, on the pillow, Garm was up and at my side, for he knew that I was his only link with his master, and day and night, and night and day, his eyes asked one question – 'When is this going to end?'

Living with the dog as I did, I never noticed that he was more than ordinarily upset by the hot weather, till one day at the Club a man said: 'That dog of yours will die in a week or two. He's a shadow.' Then I dosed Garm with iron and quinine, which he hated; and I felt very anxious. He lost his appetite, and Vixen was allowed to eat his dinner under his eyes. Even that did not make him swallow, and we held a consultation on him, of the best man-doctor in the place; a lady-doctor, who cured the sick wives of kings; and the Deputy Inspector-General of the veterinary service of all India. They pronounced upon his symptoms, and I told them his story, and Garm lay on a sofa licking my hand.

'He's dying of a broken heart,' said the lady-doctor suddenly.

''Pon my word,' said the Deputy Inspector-General, 'I believe Mrs Macrae is perfectly right – as usual.'

The best man-doctor in the place wrote a prescription, and the veterinary Deputy Inspector-General went over it afterwards to be sure that the drugs were in the proper dog-proportions; and that was the first time in his life that our doctor ever allowed his prescriptions to be edited. It was a strong tonic, and it put the old boy on his feet for a week or two; then he lost flesh again. I asked a man I knew to take him up to the Hills with him when he went, and the man came to the door with his kit packed on the top of the carriage. Garm took in the situation at one red glance. The hair rose along his back; he sat down in front of me and delivered the most awful growl I have ever heard in the jaws of a dog. I shouted to my friend to get away at once, and as soon as the carriage was out of the garden Garm laid his head on my knee and whined. So I knew his answer, and devoted myself to getting Stanley's address in the Hills.

My turn to go to the cool came late in August. We were allowed thirty days' holiday in a year, if no one fell sick, and we took it as we could be spared. My Chief and Bob the Librarian had their holiday first, and when they were gone I made a calendar, as I always did, and hung it up at the head of my cot, tearing off one day at a time till they returned. Vixen had gone up to the Hills with me five times before; and she appreciated the cold and the damp and the beautiful wood fires there as much as I did.

'Garm,' I said, 'we are going back to Stanley at Kasauli. Kasauli – Stanley; Stanley – Kasauli.' And I repeated it twenty times. It was not Kasauli really, but another place. Still I remembered what Stanley had said in my garden on the last night, and I dared not change the name. Then Garm began to tremble; then he barked; and then he leaped up at me, frisking and wagging his tail.

'Not now,' I said, holding my hand. 'When I say "Go," we'll go, Garm.' I pulled out the little blanket coat and spiked collar that Vixen always wore up in the Hills, to protect her against sudden chills and thieving leopards, and I let the two smell them and talk it over. What they said of course I do not know, but it made a new dog of Garm. His eyes were bright; and he barked joyfully when I spoke to him. He ate his food, and he killed rats for the next three weeks, and when he began to whine I had only to say 'Stanley – Kasauli; Kasauli – Stanley,' to wake him up. I wish I had thought of it before.

My Chief came back, all brown with living in the open air, and very angry at finding it so hot in the Plains. That same afternoon we three and Kadir Buksh began to pack for our month's holiday, Vixen rolling in and out of the bullock-trunk twenty times a minute, and Garm grinning all over and thumping on the floor with his tail. Vixen knew the routine of travelling as well as she knew my office-work. She went to the station, singing songs, on the front seat of the carriage, while Garm sat with me. She hurried into the railway carriage, saw Kadir Buksh make up my bed for the night, got her drink of water, and curled up with her black-patch eye on the tumult of the platform. Garm followed her (the crowd gave him a lane all to himself) and sat down on the pillows with his eyes blazing, and his tail a haze behind him.

We came to Umballa in the hot misty dawn, four or five men, who had been working hard for eleven months, shouting for our dâks – the two-horse travelling carriages that were to take us up to Kalka at the foot of the Hills. It was all new to Garm. He did not understand carriages where you lay at full length on your bedding, but Vixen knew and hopped into her place at once; Garm following. The Kalka Road, before the railway was built, about forty-seven miles long, and the horses were changed every eight miles. Most of them jibbed, and kicked, and plunged, but they had to go, and they went rather better than usual for Garm's deep bay in their rear.

There was a river to be forded, and four bullocks pulled the carriage and Vixen stuck her head out of the sliding-door and nearly fell into the water while she gave directions. Garm was silent and curious, and rather needed reassuring about Stanley and Kasauli. So we rolled, barking and yelping, into Kalka for lunch, and Garm ate enough for two.

After Kalka the road wound among the hills, and we took a curricle with half-broken ponies, which were changed every six miles. No one dreamed of a railroad to Simla in those days, for it was seven thousand feet up in the air. The road was more than fifty miles long, and the regulation pace was just as fast as the ponies could go. Here, again, Vixen led Garm from one carriage to the other, jumping into the back seat, and shouted. A cool breath from the snows met us above five miles out of Kalka, and she whined for her coat, wisely fearing a chill on the liver. I had had one made for Garm too, and, as we climbed to the fresh breezes, I put it on, and Garm chewed it uncomprehendingly, but I think he was grateful.

'Hi-yi-yi-yi!' sang Vixen as we shot round the curves; 'Toot-toot-toot!' went the driver's bugle at the dangerous places, and 'Yow! yow! yow!' bayed Garm. Kadir Buksh sat on the front seat and smiled. Even he was glad to get away from the heat of the Plains that stewed in the haze behind us. Now and then we would meet a man we knew going down to his work again, and he would say: 'What's it like below?' and I would shout: 'Hotter than cinders. What's it like up above?' and he would shout back: 'Just perfect!' and away we would go.

Suddenly Kadir Buksh said, over his shoulder: 'Here is Solon'; and Garm snored where he lay with his head on my knee. Solon is an unpleasant little cantonment, but it has the advantage of being cool and healthy. It is all bare and windy, and one generally stops at a rest-house near by for something to eat. I got out and took both dogs with me, while Kadir Buksh made tea. A soldier told us we should find Stanley 'out there', nodding his head towards a bare, bleak hill.

When we climbed to the top we spied that very Stanley, who had given me all this trouble, sitting on a rock with his face in his hands and his overcoat hanging loose about him. I never saw anything so lonely and dejected in my life as this one little man, crumpled up and thinking, on the great grey hillside.

Here Garm left me.

He departed without a word, and, so far as I could see, without moving his legs. He flew through the air bodily, and I heard the whack of him as he flung himself at Stanley, knocking the little man clean over. They rolled on the ground together, shouting, and yelping, and hugging. I could not see which was dog and which was man, till Stanley got up and whimpered.

He told me that he had been suffering from fever at intervals, and was very weak. He looked all he said, but even while I watched, both man and dog plumped out to their natural sizes, precisely as dried apples swell in water. Garm was on his shoulder and his breast and feet all at the the same time, so that Stanley spoke all through a cloud of Garm – gulping, sobbing, slavering Garm. He did not say anything that I could understand, except that he had fancied he was going to die, but that now he was quite well, and that he was not going to give up Garm any more to anybody under the rank of Beelzebub.

Then he said he felt hungry, and thirsty, and happy.

We went down to tea at the rest-house, where Stanley stuffed himself with sardines and raspberry jam, and beer, and cold mutton and pickles, when Garm wasn't climbing over him; and then Vixen and I went on.

Garm saw how it was at once. He said good-bye to me three times, giving me both paws one after another, and leaping on to my shoulder. He further escorted us, singing Hosannas at the top of his voice, a mile down the road. Then he raced back to his own master.

Vixen never opened her mouth, but when the cold twilight came, and we could see the lights of Simla across the hills, she snuffled with her nose at the breast of my ulster. I unbuttoned it, and tucked her inside. Then she gave a contented little sniff, and fell fast asleep, her head on my breast, till we bundled out at Simla, two of the four happiest people in all the world that night.

Journey's End

ERIC KNIGHT

After the hardship of being out of work for some months, Sam Carraclough took the very good offer made him by the Duke of Rudling for his beautiful collie, Lassie, inseparable companion to his son Joe. Endlessly escaping from her new home, Lassie was then dispatched far away to the Duke's Scottish estate. However this did not lessen her determination to return home to Joe.

Sam Carraclough had spoken the truth early that year when he told his son Joe that it was a long way from Greenall Bridge in Yorkshire to the Duke of Rudling's place in Scotland. And it is just as many miles coming the other way, a matter of four hundred miles.

But that would be for a man, travelling straight by road or by train. For an animal how far would it be – an animal that must circle and quest at obstacles, wander and err, backtrack and sidetrack till it found a way?

A thousand miles it would be – a thousand miles through strange terrain it had never crossed before, with nothing but instinct to tell direction.

Yes, a thousand miles of mountain and dale, of highland and

moor, ploughland and path, ravine and river, beck and burn; a thousand miles of tor and brae, of snow and rain and fog and sun; of wire and thistle and thorn and flint and rock to tear the feet – who could expect a dog to win through that?

Yet, if it were almost a miracle, in his heart Joe Carraclough tried to believe in that miracle – that somehow, wonderfully, inexplicably, his dog would be there some day; there, waiting by the school gate. Each day as he came out of school, his eyes would turn to the spot where Lassie had always waited. And each day there was nothing there, and Joe Carraclough would walk home slowly, silently, stolidly as did the people of his country.

Always, when school ended, Joe tried to prepare himself – told himself not to be disappointed, because there could be no dog there. Thus, through the long weeks, Joe began to teach himself not to believe in the impossible. He had hoped against hope so long that hope began to die.

But if hope can die in a human, it does not in an animal. As long as it lives, the hope is there and the faith is there. And so, coming across the schoolyard that day, Joe Carraclough would not believe his eyes. He shook his head and blinked, and rubbed his fists in his eyes, for he thought what he was seeing was a dream. There, walking the last few yards to the school gate was – his dog!

He stood, for the coming of the dog was terrible – her walk was a thing that tore at her breath. Her head and her tail were down almost to the pavement. Each footstep forward seemed a separate effort. It was a crawl rather than a walk. But the steps were made, one by one, and at last the animal dropped in her place by the gate and lay still.

Then Joe roused himself. Even if it were a dream, he must do something. In dreams one must try.

He raced across the yard and fell to his knees, and then, when his hands were touching and feeling fur, he knew it was reality. His dog had come to meet him!

But what a dog this was – no prize collie with fine tricolor coat glowing, with ears lifted gladly over the proud, slim head with its perfect black mask. It was not a dog whose bright eyes were alert, and who jumped up to bark a glad welcome. This was a dog that lay, weakly trying to lift a head that would no longer lift; trying to move a tail that was torn and matted with thorns and burrs, and managing to do nothing very much except to whine in a weak, happy, crying way. For she knew that at last the terrible driving instinct was at peace. She was at the place. She had kept her lifelong rendezvous, and hands were touching her that had not touched her for so long a time.

By the Labour Exchange, Ian Cawper stood with the other out-of-work miners, waiting until it was tea time so that they could all go back to their cottages.

You could have picked out Ian, for he was much the biggest man even among the many big men that Yorkshire grows. In fact, he was reputed to be the biggest and strongest man in all that Riding of Yorkshire. A big man, but gentle and often very slow of thinking and speech.

And so Ian was a few seconds behind the others in realizing that something of urgency was happening in the village. Then he too saw it – a boy struggling, half running, along the main street, his voice lifted in excitement, a great bundle of something in his arms.

The men stirred and moved forward. Then, when the boy was nearer, they heard his cry:

'She's come back! She's come back!'

The men looked at each other and blew out their breath and then stared at the bundle the boy was carrying. It was true. Sam Carraclough's collie had walked back home from Scotland.

'I must get her home, quick!' the boy was saying. He staggered on.

Ian Cawper stepped forward.

'Here,' he said. 'Run on ahead, tell 'em to get ready.'

His great arms cradled the dog – arms that could have carried ten times the weight of this poor, thin animal.

'Oh, hurry, Ian!' the boy cried, dancing in excitement.

'I'm hurrying, lad. Go on ahead.'

So Joe Carraclough raced along the street, turned up the side street, ran down the garden path, and burst into the cottage:

'Mother! Feyther!'

'What is it, lad?'

Joe paused. He could hardly get the words out – the excitement was choking up in his throat, hot and stifling. And then the words were said:

'Lassie! She's come home! Lassie's come home!'

He opened the door, and Ian Cawper, bowing his head to pass under the lintel, carried the dog to the hearth and laid her there.

There were many things that Joe Carraclough was to remember from that evening. He was never to forget the look that passed over his father's face as he first knelt beside the dog that had been his for many years, and let his hands travel over the emaciated frame. He was to remember how his mother moved about the kitchen, not grumbling or scolding now, but silently and with a sort of terrific intensity, poking the fire quickly, stirring the condensed milk into warm water, kneeling to hold the dog's head and lift open the jowl.

Not a word did his parents speak to him. They seemed to have forgotten him altogether. Instead, they both worked over the dog with a concentration that seemed to put them in a separate world.

Joe watched how his father spooned in the warm liquid, he saw how it drooled out again from the unswallowing dog's jowls and dribbled down on to the rug. He saw his mother warm up a blanket and wrap it round the dog. He saw them try again and again to feed her. He saw his father rise at last.

'It's no use, lass,' he said to his mother.

Between his mother and father many questions and answers passed unspoken except through their eyes.

'Pneumonia,' his father said at last. 'She's not strong enough now . . .'

For a while his parents stood, and then it was his mother who seemed to be somehow wonderfully alive and strong.

'I won't be beat!' she said. 'I just *won't* be beat.'

She pursed her lips, and as if this grimace had settled something, she went to the mantelpiece and took down a vase. She turned it over and shook it. The copper pennies came into her hand. She held them out to her husband, not explaining nor needing to explain what was needed. But he stared at the money.

'Go on, lad,' she said. 'I were saving it for insurance, like.'

'But how'll we . . .'

'Hush,' the woman said.

Then her eyes flickered over her son, and Joe knew that they were aware of him again for the first time in an hour. His father looked at him, at the money in the woman's hand, and at last at the dog. Suddenly he took the money. He put on his cap and hurried out into the night. When he came back he was carrying bundles – eggs and a small bottle of brandy – precious and costly things in that home.

Joe watched as they were beaten together, and again and again his father tried to spoon some into the dog's mouth. Then his mother blew in exasperation. Angrily she snatched the spoon. She cradled the dog's head on her lap, she lifted the jowls, and poured and stroked the throat – stroked it and stroked it, until at last the dog swallowed.

'Aaaah!'

It was his father, breathing a long, triumphant exclamation. And the firelight shone gold on his mother's hair as she crouched there, holding the dog's head – stroking its throat, soothing it with soft, loving sounds.

Joe did not clearly remember about it afterwards, only a faint sensation that he was being carried to bed at some strange hour of darkness.

And in the morning when he rose, his father sat in his chair, but his mother was still on the rug, and the fire was still burning warm. The dog, swathed in blankets, lay quiet.

'Is she – dead?' Joe asked.

His mother smiled weakly.

'Shhh,' she said. 'She's just sleeping. And I suppose I ought to get breakfast – but I'm that played out – if I nobbut had a nice strong cup o' tea . . .'

And that morning, strangely enough, it was his father who got the breakfast, boiling the water, brewing the tea, cutting the bread. It was his mother who sat in the rocking chair, waiting until it was ready.

That evening when Joe came home from school, Lassie still lay where he had left her when he went off to school. He wanted to sit and cradle her, but he knew that ill dogs are best left alone. All evening he sat, watching her, stretched out, with the faint breathing the only sign of life. He didn't want to go to bed.

'Now she'll be all right,' his mother cried. 'Go to bed – she'll be all right.'

'Are you sure she'll get better, Mother?'

'Ye can see for yourself, can't you? She doesn't look any worse, does she?'

'But are you sure she's going to be better?'

The woman sighed.

'Of course – I'm sure – now go to bed and sleep.'

And Joe went to bed, confident in his parents.

That was one day. There were others to remember. There was the day when Joe returned and, as he walked to the hearth, there came from the dog lying there a movement that was meant to be a wag of the tail.

There was another day when Joe's mother sighed with pleasure, for as she prepared the bowl of milk, the dog stirred, lifted herself unsteadily, and waited. And when the bowl was set down, she put down her head and lapped, while her pinched flanks quivered.

And finally there was that day when Joe first realized that – even now – his dog was not to be his own again. So again the cottage rang with cries and protests, and again a woman's voice was lifted, tired and shrilling:

'Is there never to be any more peace and quiet in my home?'

And long after Joe had gone to bed, he heard the voices

continuing – his mother's clear and rising and falling; his father's in a steady, reiterative monotone, never changing, always coming to one sentence:

'But even if he would sell her back, where'd Ah get the brass to buy her – where's the money coming fro'? Ye know we can't get it.'

To Joe Carraclough's father, life was laid out in straight rules. When a man could get work, he worked his best and got the best wage he could. If he raised a dog, he raised the best one he could. If he had a wife and children, he took care of them the best he could.

In this out-of-work collier's mind, there were no devious exceptions and evasions concerning life and its codes. Like most simple men, he saw all these things clearly. Lying, cheating, stealing – they were wrong, and you couldn't make them right by twisting them round in your mind.

So it was that, when he was faced with any problem, he so often brought it smack up against elemental truths.

'Honest is honest, and there's no two ways about it,' he would say.

He had a habit of putting it like that. 'Truth is truth.' Or, 'Cheating is cheating.'

And the matter of Lassie came up against this simple, direct code of morals. He had sold the dog and taken the money and spent it. Therefore the dog did not belong to him any more, and no matter how you argued you could not change that.

But a man has to live with his family, too. When a woman starts to argue with a man . . . well . . .

That next morning when Joe came down to breakfast, while his mother served the oatmeal with pursed lips, his father coughed and spoke as if he had rehearsed a set speech over in his mind many times that night:

'Joe, lad. We've decided upon it – that is, thy mother and me – that Lassie can stay here till she's all better.

'That's all reight, because I believe true in ma heart that

nobody could nurse her better and wi' more care nor we're doing. So that's honest. But when she's better, well . . .

'Now ye have her for a little while yet, so be content. And don't plague us, lad. There's enough things to worry us now wi'out more. So don't plague us no more – and try to be a man about it – and be content.'

With the young, 'for a little while' has two shapes. Seen from one end, it is a great, yawning stretch of time extending into the unlimitable future. From the other, it is a ghastly span of days that has been cruelly whisked away before the realization comes.

Joe Carraclough knew that it was the latter that morning when he went to school and heard a mighty, booming voice. As he turned to look, he saw in an automobile a fearsome old man and a girl with her flaxen hair cascading from under a beret. And the old man, with his ferocious white moustaches looking like an animal's misshapen fangs, was waving an ugly blackthorn stick to the danger of the car, the chauffeur, and the world in general, and shouting at him:

'Hi! Hi, there! Yes, I mean you, m'lad! Damme, Jenkins, will you make this smelly contraption stand still a moment? Whoa, there, Jenkins! Whoa! Why we ever stopped using horses is more than any sane man can understand. Country's going to pot, that's what! Here, m'lad! Come here!'

For a moment Joe thought of running – doing anything to get all these things he feared out of his sight, so that they might, miraculously, be out of his mind, too. But a machine can go faster than a boy, and then, too, Joe had in him the blood of men who might think slowly and stick to old ideas and bear trouble patiently – but who do not run away. So he stood sturdily on the pavement and remembered his manners as his mother had taught him, and said:

'Yes, sir?'

'You're What's-his-name's lad, aren't you?'

Joe's eyes had turned to the girl. She was the one he had seen long ago when he was putting Lassie in the Duke's kennels. Her face was not hearty-red like his own. It was blue-white. On the hand that clutched the edge of the car the veins stood out clear-blue. That hand looked thin. He was thinking that, as his mother would say, she could do with some plumduff.

She was looking at him, too. Something made him draw himself up proudly.

'My father is Sam Carraclough,' he said firmly.

'I know, I know,' the old man shouted impatiently. 'I never forget a name. Never! Used to know every last soul in this village. Too many of you growing up now – younger generation. And, by gad, they're all of them not worth one of the old bunch – not the whole kit and caboodle. The modern generation, why . . .'

He halted, for the girl beside him was tugging his sleeve.

'What is it? Eh? Oh, yes. I was just coming to it. Where's your father, m'lad? Is he home?'

'No, sir.'

'Where is he?'

'He's off over Allerby, sir.'

'Allerby, what's he doing there?'

'A mate spoke for him at the pit, I think, and he's gone to see if there's a chance of getting taken on.'

'Oh, yes – yes, of course. When'll he be back?'

'I don't know, sir. I think about tea.'

'Don't mumble! Not till tea. Damme, very inconvenient – very! Well, I'll drop round about five-ish. You tell him to stay home and I want to see him – it's important. Tell him to wait.'

Then the car was gone, and Joe hurried to school. There was never such a long morning as that one. The minutes in the classroom crawled past as the lessons droned on.

Joe had only one desire – to have it become noon. And when at last the leaden moments that were years were gone, he raced home and burst through the door. It was the same cry – for his mother.

'Mother, Mother!'

'Goodness, don't knock the door down. And close it – anyone would think you were brought up in a barn. What's the matter?'

'Mother, he's coming to take Lassie away!'

'Who is?'

'The Duke . . . he's coming . . .'

'The Duke? How in the world does he know that she's . . .'

'I don't know. But he stopped me this morning. He's coming at tea time . . .'

'Coming here? Are you sure?'

'Yes, he said he'd come at tea. Oh, Mother, please . . .'

'Now, Joe. Don't start! Now I warn ye!'

'Mother, you've got to listen. Please, please!'

'You hear me? I said . . .'

'No, Mother. Please help me. Please!'

The woman looked at her son and heaved a sigh of weariness and exasperation. Then she threw up her hands in despair.

'Eigh, dearie me! Is there never to be any more peace in this house? Never?'

She sank into her chair and looked at the floor. The boy went to her and touched her arm.

'Mother – do something,' the boy pleaded. 'Can't we hide her? He'll be here at five. He told me to tell Father he'd be here at five. Oh, Mother . . .'

'Nay, Joe. Thy father won't . . .'

'Won't you beg him? Please, please! Beg Father to . . .'

'Joe!' his mother cried angrily. Then her voice became patient again. 'Now, Joe, it's no use. So stop thy plaguing. It's just that thy father won't lie. That much I'll give him. Come good, come bad, he'll not lie.'

'But just this once, Mother.'

The woman shook her head sadly and sat by the fire, staring into it as if she would find peace there. Her son went to her and touched her bare forearm.

'Please, Mother. Beg him. Just this once. Just one lie wouldn't hurt him. I'll make it up to him, I will. I will, truly!'

The words began to race from his mouth quickly.

'I'll make it up to both of you. When I'm growed up, I'll get a job. I'll earn money. I'll buy him things – I'll buy you things,

'Mother, he's coming to take Lassie away!'

too. I'll buy you both anything you ever want, if you'll only please, please . . .'

And then, for the first time in all his trouble, Joe Carraclough became a child, his sturdiness gone, and the tears choked his voice. His mother could hear his sobs, and she patted his hand, but she would not look at him. From the magic of the fire she seemed to read deep wisdom, and she spoke slowly.

'Tha mustn't Joe,' she said, her words soft. 'Tha mustn't want like that. Tha must learn never to want anything i' life so hard as tha wants Lassie. It doesn't do.'

It was then that she felt her son's hand trembling with impatience, and his voice rising clear.

'Ye don't understand, Mother. Ye don't understand. It ain't me that wants her. It's her that want us – so terrible bad. That's what made her come home all that way. She wants us, so terrible bad.'

It was then that Mrs Carraclough looked at her son at last. She could see his face, contorted, and the tears rolling openly down his cheeks. And yet, in that moment of childishness, it was as if he were suddenly all the more grown up. Mrs Carraclough felt as if time had jumped, and she were seeing this boy, this son of her own, for the first time in many years.

She stared at him and then she clasped her hands together. Her lips pressed together in a straight line and she got up.

'Joe, come and eat, then. And go back to school and be content. I'll talk to thy father.'

She lifted her head, and her voice sounded firm.

'Yes – I'll talk to him, all right. I'll talk to Mr Samuel Carraclough. I will indeed!'

At five that afternoon, the Duke of Rudling, fuming and muttering in his bad-tempered way, got out of a car that had stopped by a cottage gate. And behind the gate was a boy, who stood sturdily, his feet apart, as if to bar the way.

'Well, well, m'lad! Did ye tell him?'

'Go away,' the boy said fiercely. 'Go away! Thy tyke's not here.'

For once in his life the Duke of Rudling stepped backward. He stared at the boy in amazement.

'Well, drat my buttons, Priscilla,' he breathed. 'Th' lad's touched. He is – he's touched!'

'Thy tyke's net here. Away wi' thee,' the boy said stoutly. And it seemed as if in his determination he spoke in the broadest dialect he could command.

'What's he saying?' Priscilla asked.

'He's saying my dog isn't here. Drat my buttons, are you going deaf, Priscilla? I'm supposed to be deaf, and I can hear him all right. Now, ma lad, what tyke o' mine's net here?'

The Duke, when he answered, also turned to the broadest tones of Yorkshire dialect, as he always did to the people of the cottages – a habit which many of the members of the Duke's family deplored deeply.

'Coom, coom, ma lad. Speak up! What tyke's net here?'

As he spoke he waved his cane ferociously and advanced. Joe Carraclough stepped back from the fearful old man, but he still barred the path.

'No tyke o' thine,' he cried stoutly.

But the Duke continued to advance. The words raced from Joe's mouth with a torrent of despair.

'Us hasn't got her. She's not here. She couldn't be here. No tyke could ha' done it. No tyke could come all them miles. It's not Lassie – it's – it's just another one that looks like her. It isn't Lassie.'

'Well, bless my heart and soul,' puffed the Duke. 'Bless my heart and soul. Where's thy father, lad?'

Joe shook his head grimly. But behind him the cottage door opened and his mother's voice spoke.

'If it's Sam Carraclough ye're looking for – he's out in the shed, and been shut up there half the afternoon.'

'What's this lad talking about – a dog o' mine being here?'

'Nay, ye're mistaken,' the woman said stoutly.

'I'm mistaken?' roared the Duke.

'Yes. He didn't say a tyke o' thine was here. He said it wasn't here.'

'Drat my buttons,' the Duke sputtered angrily. 'Don't twist my words up.'

Then his eyes narrowed, and he stepped a pace forward.

'Well, if he said a dog of mine *isn't*, perhaps you'll be good enough to tell me just *which* dog of mine it is that isn't here. Now,' he finished triumphantly. 'Come, come! Answer me!'

Joe, watching his mother, saw her swallow and then look about her as if for help. She pressed her lips together. The Duke stood waiting for his answer, peering out angrily from beneath his jutting eyebrows. Then Mrs Carraclough drew a breath to speak.

But her answer, truth or lie, was never spoken. For they all heard the rattle of a chain being drawn from a door, and then the voice of Sam Carraclough said clearly:

'This, I give ye my word, is th' only tyke us has here. So tell me, does it look like any dog that belongs to thee?'

Joe's mouth was opening for a last cry of protest, but as his eyes fell on the dog by his father, the exclamation died. And he stared in amazement.

There he saw his father, Sam Carraclough, the collie fancier, standing with a dog at his heels the like of which few men had ever seen before, or would wish to see. It was a dog that sat patiently at his left heel, as any well-trained dog should do – just as Lassie used to do. But this dog – it was ridiculous to think of it at the same moment as Lassie.

For where Lassie's skull was aristocratic and slim, this dog's head was clumsy and rough. Where Lassie's ears stood in the grace of twin-lapped symmetry, this dog had one screw ear and the other standing up Alsatian fashion, in a way that would give any collie breeder the cold shivers.

More than that. Where Lassie's coat faded to delicate sable, this curious dog had ugly splashes of black; and where Lassie's apron was a billowing expanse of white, this dog had muddy puddles of off-colour, blue-merle mixture. Lassie had four white paws, and this one had only one white, two dirty-brown, and one almost black. Lassie's tail flowed gracefully behind her, and this dog's tail looked like something added as an afterthought.

And yet, as Joe Carraclough looked at the dog beside his father, he understood. He knew that if a dog coper could treat a dog with cunning so that its bad points came to look like good ones, he could also reverse the process and make all its good ones look like bad ones – especially if that man were his father, one of the most knowing of dog fanciers in all that Riding of Yorkshire.

In that moment, he understood his father's words, too. For in dog-dealing, as in horse-dealing, the spoken word is a binding contract, and once it is given, no real dog-man will attempt to go back on it.

And that was how his father, in his patient, slow way, had tried to escape with honour. He had not lied. He had not denied anything. He had merely asked a question:

'Tell me, does this dog look like any dog that belongs to thee?'

And the Duke had only to say:

'Why, that's not my dog,' and forever after, it would not be his.

So the boy, his mother and his father, gazed steadily at the old man, and waited with held breath as he continued to stare at the dog.

But the Duke of Rudling knew many things too – many, many things. And he was not answering. Instead he was walking forward slowly, the great cane now tapping as he leaned on it. His eyes never left the dog for a second. Slowly, as it he were in a dream, he knelt down, and his hand made one gentle movement. It picked up a forepaw and turned it slightly. So he knelt by the collie, looking with eyes that were as knowing about dogs as any man in Yorkshire. And those eyes did not waste themselves upon twisted ears or blotched markings or rough head. Instead, they stared steadily at the underside of the paw, seeing only the five black pads, crossed and recrossed with half-healed scars where thorns had torn and stones had lacerated.

Then the Duke lifted his head, but for a long time he knelt, gazing into space, while they waited. When he did get up, he spoke, not using Yorkshire dialect any more, but speaking as one gentleman might address another.

'Sam Carraclough,' he said. 'This is no dog of mine. 'Pon my soul and honour, she never belonged to me. No! Not for a single second did she ever belong to me!'

Then he turned and walked down the path, thumping his cane and muttering: 'Bless my soul! I wouldn't ha' believed it! Bless my soul! Four hundred miles! I wouldn't ha' believed it.'

It was at the gate that his granddaughter tugged his sleeve.

'What you came for,' she whispered. 'Remember?'

The Duke seemed to come from his dream, and then he suddenly turned into his old self again.

'Don't whisper! What's that? Oh, yes, of course. You don't need to tell me – I hadn't forgotten!'

He turned and made his voice terrible.

'Carraclough! Carraclough! Drat my buttons, where are ye? What're ye hiding for?'

'I'm still here, sir.'

'Oh, yes. Yes. Of course. There you are. You working?'

'Eigh, now – working,' Joe's father said. That was the best he could manage.

'Yes, working – working! A job! A job! Do you have one?' the Duke fumed.

'Well, now – it's this road . . .' began Carraclough.

As he fumbled his words, Mrs Carraclough came to his rescue, as good housewives will in Yorkshire – and in most other parts of the world.

'My Sam's not exactly working, but he's got three or four things that he's been considering. Sort of investigating, as ye might say. But – he hasn't quite said yes or no to any of them yet.'

'Then he'd better say no, and quickly,' snapped the Duke. 'I need somebody up at my kennels. And I think, Carraclough . . .' His eyes turned to the dog still sitting at the man's heel. '. . . I think you must know – a lot – about dogs. So there. That's settled.'

'Nay, hold on,' Carraclough said. 'Ye see, I wouldn't like to think I got a chap into trouble and then took his job. Ye see, Mr Hynes couldn't help . . .'

'Hynes!' snorted the Duke. 'Hynes? Utter nincompoop. Had to sack him. Didn't know a dog from a ringtailed filly. Should ha' known no Londoner could ever run a kennel for a Yorkshireman's taste. Now, I want you for the job.'

'Nay, there's still summat,' Mrs Carraclough protested.

'What now?'

'Well, how much would this position be paying?'

The Duke puffed his lips.

'How much do you want, Carraclough?'

'Seven pounds a week, and worth every penny,' Mrs Carraclough cut in, before her husband could even get round to drawing a preparatory breath.

But the Duke was a Yorkshireman, too, and that meant he would scorn himself if he missed a chance to be 'practical', as they say, where money is concerned.

'Five,' he roared. 'And not a penny more.'

'Six pounds, ten,' bargained Mrs Carraclough.

'Six even,' offered the Duke cannily.

'Done,' said Mrs Carraclough, as quickly as a hawk's swoop.

They both glowed, self-righteously pleased with themselves. Mrs Carraclough would have been willing to settle for three pounds a week in the first place – and as for the Duke, he felt he was getting a man for his kennels who was beyond price.

'Then it's settled, ' the Duke said.

'Well, almost, ' the woman said. 'I presume, of course . . .' She liked the taste of what she considered a very fine word, so she repeated it. '. . . I presume that means we get the cottage on the estate, too.'

'Ye drive a fierce bargain, ma'am,' said the Duke, scowling. 'But ye get it – on one condition.' He lifted his voice and roared. 'On condition that as long as ye live on my land, you never allow that thick-skulled, screw-lugged, gay-tailed eyesore of an excuse for a collie on my property. Now, what do ye say?'

He waited, rumbling and chuckling happily to himself as Sam Carraclough stooped, perplexed. But it was the boy who answered gladly: 'Oh, no, sir. She'll be down at school waiting for me most o' the time. And, anyway, in a day or so we'll have her fixed up so's ye'd never recognize her.'

'I don't doubt that,' puffed the Duke, as he stumped toward his car. 'I don't doubt ye could do exactly that. Hmm . . . Well, I never . . .'

It was afterwards in the car that the girl edged close to the old man.

'Now don't wriggle,' he protested. 'I can't stand anyone wriggling.'

'Grandfather,' she said. 'You are kind – I mean about their dog.'

The old man coughed and cleared his throat.

'Nonsense,' he growled. 'Nonsense. When you grow up, you'll understand that I'm what people call a hard-hearted Yorkshire realist. For five years I've sworn I'd have that dog. And now I've got her.'

Then he shook his head slowly.

'But I had to buy the man to get her. Ah, well. Perhaps that's not the worst part of the bargain.'

'More Faithful than Favoured'

ANDREW LANG

There never was a more faithful watch-dog than the great big-limbed, heavy-headed mastiff that guarded Sir Harry Lee's Manor-house, Ditchley, in Oxfordshire. The sound of his deep growl was the terror of all the gypsies and vagrants in the county, and there was a superstition among the country people, that he was never known to sleep. Even if he was seen stretched out on the stone steps leading up to the front entrance of the house, with his massive head resting on his great fore-paws, at the sound of a footfall, however distant, his head would be raised, his ears fiercely cocked, and an ominous stiffening of the tail would warn a stranger that his movements were being closely watched, and that on the least suspicion of anything strange or abnormal in his behaviour, he would be called to account by Leo. Strangely enough, the mastiff had never been a favourite of his master's. The fact that dogs of his breed are useless for purposes of sport, owing to their unwieldy size and defective sense of smell, had prevented Sir Harry from taking much notice of him. He looked upon the mastiff merely as a watch-dog. The dog would look after him, longing to be allowed to join him in his walk, or to follow him when he rode out, through the lanes and fields round his house, but poor Leo's affection received little encouragement. So long as he guarded the house faithfully by day and night, that was all that was expected of him: and as in doing this he was only doing his duty, and fulfilling the purpose for which he was there, little notice was taken of him by any of the inmates of the house. His meals were supplied to him with unfailing regularity, for his services as insuring the safety of the house were fully recognized; but as Sir Harry had not shown him any signs of favour, the servants did not think fit to bestow unnecessary attention on him. So he lived his solitary neglected life, in summer and winter, by night and day, zealous in his master's interests, but earning little reward in the way of notice or affection.

One night, however, something occurred that suddenly altered the mastiff's position in the household, and from being a faithful slave, he all at once became the beloved friend and constant companion of Sir Harry Lee. It was in winter, and Sir Harry was going up to his bedroom as usual, about eleven o'clock. Great was his astonishment on opening the library door, to find the mastiff stretched in front of it. At sight of his master Leo rose, and, wagging his tail and rubbing his great head against Sir Harry's hand, he looked up at him as if anxious to attract his attention. With an impatient word Sir Harry turned away, and went up the oak-panelled staircase, Leo following closely behind him. When he reached his bedroom door, the dog tried to follow him into the room, and if Sir Harry had been a more observant man, he must have noticed a curious look of appeal in the dog's eyes, as he slammed the door in his face, ordering him in commanding tones to 'Go away!' an order which Leo did not obey. Curling himself up on the mat outside the door, he lay with his small deep-sunk eyes in eager watchfulness, fixed on the door, while his heavy tail from time to time beat an impatient tattoo upon the stone floor of the passage.

Antonio, the Italian valet, whom Sir Harry had brought home with him from his travels, and whom he trusted absolutely, was waiting for his master, and was engaged in spreading out his things on the toilet table.

'That dog is getting troublesome, Antonio,' said Sir Harry. 'I must speak to the keeper tomorrow, and tell him to chain him up at night outside the hall. I cannot have him disturbing me, prowling about the corridors and passages all night. See that you drive him away, when you go downstairs.'

'Yes, signor,' replied Antonio, and began to help his master to undress. Then, having put fresh logs of wood on the fire, he wished Sir Harry good-night, and left the room. Finding Leo outside the door, the valet whistled and called gently to him to follow him; and, as the dog took no notice, he put out his hand to take hold of him by the collar. But a low growl and a sudden flash of the mastiff's teeth, warned the Italian of the danger of resorting to force. With a muttered curse he turned away, determined to try bribery where threats had failed. He thought that if he could secure a piece of raw meat from the kitchen, he would have no difficulty in inducing the dog to follow him to the lower regions of the house, where he could shut him up, and prevent him from further importuning his master.

Scarcely had Antonio's figure disappeared down the passage, when the mastiff began to whine in an uneasy manner, and to scratch against his master's door. Disturbed by the noise, and astonished that his faithful valet has disregarded his injunctions, Sir Harry got up and opened the door, on which the mastiff pushed past him into the room, with so resolute a movement that his master could not prevent his entrance. The instant he got into the room, the dog's uneasiness seemed to disappear. Ceasing to whine, he made for the corner of the room where the bed stood in a deep alcove, and, crouching down, he sunk beneath it, with an evident determination to pass the night there. Much astonished, Sir Harry was too sleepy to contest the point with the dog, and allowed him to remain under the bed, without making any further attempt to dislodge him from the strange and unfamiliar resting-place he had chosen.

When the valet returned shortly after with the piece of meat with which he hoped to tempt the mastiff downstairs, he found the mat deserted. He assumed that the dog had abandoned his caprice of being outside his master's door, and had betaken himself to his usual haunts in the basement rooms and passages of the house.

Whether from the unaccustomed presence of the dog in his room, or from some other cause, Sir Harry Lee was a long time in going to sleep that night. He heard the different clocks in the house strike midnight, and then one o'clock; and as he lay awake watching the flickering light of the fire playing on the old furniture and on the dark panels of the wainscot, he felt an increasing sense of irritation against the dog, whose low, regular breathing showed that he, at any rate, was sleeping soundly. Towards two in the morning Sir Harry must have fallen into a deep sleep, for he was quite unconscious of the sound of stealthy steps creeping along the stone corridor and pausing a moment on the mat outside his room. Then the handle of the door was softly turned, and the door itself, moving on its well-oiled hinges, was gently pushed inward. In another moment there was a tremendous scuffle beneath the bed, and with a great bound the mastiff flung himself on the intruder, and pinned him to the floor. Startled by the unexpected sounds, and thoroughly aroused, Sir Harry jumped up, and hastily lit a candle. Before him on the floor lay Antonio, with the mastiff standing over him, uttering his fierce growls, and showing his teeth in a dangerous manner. Stealthily the Italian stole out his hand along the floor, to conceal something sharp and gleaming that had fallen from him, on the dog's unexpected onslaught, but a savage snarl from Leo warned him to keep perfectly still. Calling off the mastiff, who instantly obeyed the sound of his master's voice, though with bristling hair and stiffened tail he still kept his eyes fixed on the Italian, Sir Harry demanded from the valet the cause of his unexpected intrusion into his bedroom at that hour, and in that way. There was so much embarrassment and hesitation in Antonio's reply, that Sir Harry's suspicions were aroused. In the meantime the unusual sounds at that hour of the night had awakened the household. Servants came hurrying along the passage to their master's room. Confronted by so many witnesses, the Italian became terrified and abject, and stammered out such contradictory statements, that it was impossible to get at the truth of his story, and Sir Harry saw that the only course open to him was to have the man examined and tried by the magistrate.

At the examination the wretched valet confessed that he had entered his master's room with the intention of murdering and robbing him, and had only been prevented by the unexpected attack of the mastiff.

Among the family pictures in the possession of the family of the Earls of Lichfield, the descendants of Sir Harry Lee, there is a full-length portrait of the knight with his hand on the head of the mastiff, and beneath this legend, 'More faithful than favoured.'

(More about this gentleman and his dog may be read in *Woodstock*, by Sir Walter Scott.)

Acknowledgements

The publishers would like to extend their grateful thanks to the following authors, publishers and others for kindly granting permission to reproduce the extracts and stories included in this anthology.

DODO from *My Family and Other Animals* by Gerald Durrell. Reprinted by permission of the author, Granada Publishing and Curtis Brown Ltd.

HUMAN FRIENDS from *The Incredible Journey* by Sheila Burnford. Reprinted by permission of the author, Hodder & Stoughton Ltd and Michael Joseph Ltd.

MIRACLE NEEDED from *The Hundred and One Dalmations* by Dodie Smith. © 1956 Dodie Smith. Reprinted by permission of the author, William Heinemann Ltd and Viking Penguin Inc.

CLANCY from *All Things Bright and Beautiful* by James Herriot. Reprinted by permission of the author, Michael Joseph Ltd and St Martin's Press, Inc. Copyright © 1973, 1974 by James Herriot.

NATUK by Major George Bruce. Reprinted by permission of William Blackwood & Sons Ltd.

THE PARTNERSHIP BEGINS from *Emma and I* by Sheila Hocken. Reprinted by permission of the author and Victor Gollancz Ltd.

THE DOGSBODIES from *Himself and the Kerry Crusher* by Kenneth Bird. Reprinted by permission of the author, Macdonald & Jane's Ltd and Bolt & Watson Ltd.

REX by D. H. Lawrence from *Phoenix: The Posthumous Papers of D. H. Lawrence*, edited by Edward D. McDonald. Copyright 1936 by Frieda Lawrence. Copyright renewed 1964 by Angelo Ravagli and C. M. Neckley. Reprinted by permission of William Heinemann Ltd, Laurence Pollinger Ltd, the Estate of the late Mrs Frieda Lawrence Ravagli and Viking Penguin Inc.

CHIQUITITO-BROWN from *A Dog So Small* by Philippa Pearce (Longman Young Books, 1962). Copyright © 1962 Philippa Pearce. Reprinted by permission of Penguin Books Ltd.

ALL YOU NEED IS PATIENCE from *Dog of the Storm* by Ernest Dudley. Reprinted by permission of the author and Frederick Muller Ltd.

Acknowledgements

BURIED BONES from *Absolute Zero* by Helen Cresswell. Copyright © Helen Cresswell 1978. Reprinted by permission of Faber & Faber Ltd and Macmillan Publishing Co., Inc.

THE CASE OF THE HIDDEN EARRING from *Dog Detective Ranjha* by Partap Sharma. © 1978 Partap Sharma. Reprinted by permission of Macmillan, London and Basingstoke.

GETTING INTO SHOW BUSINESS from *Almost Human* by Barbara Woodhouse. Copyright © Barbara Woodhouse 1976. Reprinted by permission of Penguin Books Ltd.

HUMBLEPUPPY from *A Harp of Fishbones/Not What You Expected* by Joan Aiken. Copyright © 1974 by Joan Aiken. Reprinted by permission of the author, Jonathan Cape Ltd and Doubleday and Company Inc.

'NO DOGS PERMITTED' from *Greyfriars Bobby* by Eleanor Atkinson. Reprinted by permission of Hamish Hamilton Ltd and Harper & Row, Inc.

GARM – A HOSTAGE from *Actions and Reactions* by Rudyard Kipling. Reprinted by permission of the National Trust and Macmillan London Ltd.

JOURNEY'S END from *Lassie Come-Home* by Eric Knight. Copyright © 1940 by Jere Knight, copyright renewed © 1968 by Jere Knight, Betty Noyes Knight, Winifred Knight Newborn, and Jennie Knight Moore. Reprinted by permission of the author, Cassell Ltd and Curtis Brown, Ltd.

Every effort has been made to clear all copyrights and the publishers trust that their apologies will be accepted for any errors or omissions.